Promoting a Global Community
Through Multicultural Children's Literature

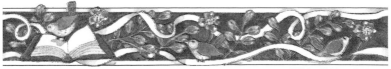

---

# Promoting a Global Community
# Through Multicultural Children's Literature

---

## Stanley F. Steiner

**Illustrations by Peggy Hokom © 2001**
**Foreword by Alma Flor Ada**

**2001**
**Libraries Unlimited, Inc.**
**and Its Division**
**Teacher Ideas Press**
**Englewood, Colorado**

Libraries Unlimited, Inc.
and Its Division
Teacher Ideas Press
P.O. Box 6633
Englewood, CO 80155-6633
1-800-237-6124
www.lu.com

**Library of Congress Cataloging-in-Publication Data**

Steiner, Stanley F.
    Promoting a global community through multicultural children's literature / Stanley F. Steiner ; illustrations by Peggy Hokom ; foreword by Alma Flor Ada.
        p. cm.
    Includes bibliographical references and indexes.
    ISBN 1-56308-705-7 (soft)
        1. International education--Bibliography. 2. Multicultural education--Bibliography. 3. Children's literature--Bibliography. I. Title.

Z5814.I5 S74 2001
[LC1090]
016.8088'99282--dc21
                                                                00-050702

*I dedicate this book to my parents,
John and Anna Marie, who taught us
by example to accept all people regardless
of their heritage or abilities.*

# Contents

# Foreword

## Alma Flor Ada

We live on a planet of diversity. It could even be affirmed that diversity is the only norm in our planet. In nature there is nothing that could be a flower, the flower, but roses and carnations, tulips and jasmine, daffodils and bougainvillea, myriad of forms, colors, and fragrances. There is not a bird, the bird, but creatures as diverse as ostriches and hummingbirds. And what is an insect, a fish, a tree, but beetles and bees, trout and sharks, oaks and palms?

This constant reminder of variety in nature becomes even more poignant when we learn that these diverse species of our planet coexist in close contact with each other. They develop a synergy that allows them not only to share reduced space and resources but to thrive in their contact to the extent of becoming indispensable to the survival of each other.

Human beings have yet to learn this message from nature: We can all grow and bloom in the richness of sharing with others. Unless we learn to respect, appreciate, celebrate, and cherish each other, we will not be able to achieve social justice, peace, and well-being. Unless we learn the lessons of nature, we will continue to bring destruction, pain, and despair as prejudice, discrimination, and multiple wars have done throughout the history of humanity.

Children's literature is a realm of discovery for the young mind and nurturance for the young spirit. By facilitating the "magical encounter" between children and books of diverse human experiences, we foster their contact with a diversity of realities and nurture their appreciation for ways of life different from their own.

Many times, cultural contact begins at a superficial level, the one provided by food and festivals. These colorful and pleasurable experiences may well be a portal to the richness and diversity in the world. It will be necessary, however, to transcend quickly these manifestations, understanding that culture is far deeper, that it goes beyond food, heroes, and holidays.

We need to facilitate the understanding that cultures have equally respectable worldviews or approaches to the human experience. Children and young adults need to understand that communities of people who have joined in common efforts have developed specific ways of interacting among themselves to provide sustenance and support to the members of their group. They not only prefer certain food, and celebrate in particular ways, but they also have ways of communicating, of caring for each other, of responding to grief, to challenges, to joy.

The primary message we wish children would receive from a rich and diverse literature is that their own culture is strong, viable, coherent, consistent. At the same time they need to see their culture as vital and in a state of change. Cultures are not static; they are the product of daily endeavors, constantly in the making.

The next essential message we wish children to discover is that theirs is but one of the many cultures of the world, all of which are equally viable, coherent, consistent, and deserving of respect. As they develop self-affirmation in their own cultural identity, they open generously to all others, both those found in remote areas of the globe and those comprising the multicultural reality of the United States. It is not infrequent that people willing to travel abroad, or to enjoy books or films of distant lands, will have difficulties celebrating people from cultures different from their own even when they all share the same country. The United States as a land of immigrants, where only native people can have the claim of being autochthonous, has become one of the most culturally diverse countries of the Earth. In this cultural diversity lies the country's greatest promise—if only it be recognized as such.

Children's literature reflecting authentic multiethnic cultures can help young minds recognize the diversity of their families and communities. Books that allow children to see themselves, in a positive role particularly when the prevailing vision of their own culture has been ignored, distorted, or hurt by stereotypes, is to give them an opportunity to affirm their identity. Once a child's sense of dignity and belonging is truly affirmed, it will be possible to accept and celebrate the dignity of others, and to develop full understanding of the uniqueness and humanness of others. Children and youth also need books that show the interaction of people of diverse cultures, their ways of encountering and solving conflicts, their ways of developing respect for each other, their ways of creating solidarity.

Stan Steiner, a humanist, filled with respect for the minds of children, knows that they need access to the best that has been written for them. His scholarship and dedication has led to the writing of this generous book. It is a book of service, a valuable tool in the hands of librarians, educators, and parents to facilitate their efforts of enriching young lives and minds with books celebrating the world's diversity and the multicolored mosaic of our own society.

# Acknowledgments

I am very grateful to Judy O'Malley, former editor of *Book Links,* for accepting earlier versions of Parts II, III, and IV to help solidify some of my thinking about social consciousness. To Lane Cobiskey and Joy, my wife, who helped with the earlier versions of this work that appeared in *Book Links.* To Peggy Hokom, teacher, artist, parent, and friend extraordinaire. To my colleague and good friend Robert Bahruth, who continues to be a sounding board and mentor toward social activism. To Gale Sherman, for her constant friendship, words of encouragement, and support toward the completion of this idea. To my friend and heroine Alma Flor Ada, who has made a career of bringing literacy to all the people she meets. To Vincent Muli Kituku, for his friendship and words of wisdom through stories. To Gary Dulabaum, modern-day troubadour and good friend who enlightens thousands through song, poetry, words of encouragement, and his positive outlook on life. To the thousands of teachers, librarians, students, and parents that I have met through my teaching career. Their passion for reading and learning about multicultural children's literature continues to be an inspiration.

To my children, Ben, Lea, and Avi, who are proving to be friends of the Earth and humanity, for their love of story and shared opinions of the thousands of books we read together over the years. May they continue to share their love for reading and social consciousness with the future people they encounter in their lives. And to my best friend and soul mate, Joy. It is through her questions, editing, encouraging words, and love of story and life that this book became a reality.

# Introduction

This book grew out of my research and the continued quest to understand the Earth's rich cultural diversity. I believe that ethnic diversity strengthens our world. Our collective heritage brings both beauty and challenge to our planet, and creating a world that embraces all humanity and its resources is one of the greatest challenges we face in the 21st century. I am not alone in my thinking. As the earliest moments of the new millennium moved from a dark December midnight to the first bright dawn, the Public Broadcasting System recorded the celebrations around the globe in a live television broadcast. Over and over, the hope that each culture expressed was that we unite as one world, as one people living in harmony. From all around the globe, people recognize that our survival depends on our capacity for conservation, interdependence, cooperation, and respect for all humanity among all nations. This challenge is no small task, but it is hoped that this volume will provide a way to work toward it, using literature as a tool.

To achieve a cooperative world, we must increase our understanding of each other. We must get beyond the rhetoric touted on political platforms that results in too little action. It seems evident to me that dialogue at the grassroots level in our own communities has been the most effective means for initiating change. Anthropologist Margaret Mead said, "Never doubt that a small group of thoughtful committed citizens can change the world; indeed, it's the only thing that ever has." It is of utmost importance that we open this dialogue about social issues among our youth, yet these issues often are not covered in the prescribed curricula. This volume presents a list of books that can open dialogue and allow readers to walk in the shoes of another without judgment. It is my hope that such dialogue will move us to make the changes we need to reach sustainability in the new millennium. As world citizens, we must actively challenge illiteracy and the withholding of literacy. We must fight ethnic cleansing, power seekers who cause death or refugee conditions, and crimes of hate and bigotry inflicted upon innocent people because of their ethnic heritage or cultural alignment. We must fight homelessness and substandard living conditions that result from unethical labor practices.

Our society shows evidence of a continued disregard for humanity. I find this trend to be extremely unsettling. A fog of inhumanity has crept slowly but surely into our schools. Teachers can no longer pretend that flippant racist or harassing remarks by students are "part of being a kid." Not too long ago, the *USA Today* weekend edition (March 26–28, 1999) reported finding some 250 hate-group sites on the Internet. Unfortunately, school curricula have not done enough to fight this frightening trend over the years. Class lessons have not provided enough space to talk about social issues until they are in our backyards. Too often there is an aura of complacency in our immediate world, while the greater world has been undergoing rapid and alarming changes. We overlook the fact that all people are connected in this world by the resources needed to sustain life on this planet. Whether we want to admit it or not, all of us on Earth are interdependent. As human beings, we all have the same basic needs—food, shelter, well-being, and education—regardless of who we are and where we live.

Often the dominant sentiment in American society is one of complacency and self-imposed ignorance. Until a problem affects us personally, we do nothing. Perhaps one reason for this inertia is the exclusion of young minds from the discussion. Perhaps as educators, we have not included in our curricula enough literature that raises awareness of the social issues. Good literature builds understanding. A book is different from current events portrayed in the media because it tells the story from inside the culture, sometimes from the perspective of a character very much like ourselves. Likewise, a trade book is different from a textbook because it tells one story at a time capturing the emotions. Today it is more critical than ever before to begin teaching our students about all peoples in this world. We must take the time to evaluate our future through a global lens, rather than the perspective of our own comfort and pleasure.

Humans are not born with a gene for bigotry and hatred; these are learned behaviors. And how does this way of thinking evolve? Surely our environment influences it. This includes the people with whom we interact, the "rules of the hood." It is in the broadcasts we view and hear, and in the print media we read. As a teacher, I believe the printed materials that educators use can have a great impact on social consciousness. Because books have an influence on our thinking, why not ensure that children have access to books that celebrate the beauty of diversity and understanding? Why not introduce children to books that can expose injustice, but also teach them about the wonder of other cultures. Such literature builds critical thinking.

My quest in compiling this volume was twofold. I wanted to find literature that reflected the realities of social issues and that brought people together, across ethnic lines, in realistic and positive ways. When students read about people from diverse backgrounds who act in harmonious ways and work through social issues, it increases the likelihood that they will believe this is the way conscientious people behave. Books become a catalyst to break down the historic enslavement of racism and hate.

In my quest, I pictured myself as a world traveler seeking an understanding of the rich cultures and people that make up this planet. What I found was more than I ever could have imagined. Each book brought me closer to people I have yet to meet. Reading nourished within me a burning desire to interact with all of the rich cultures this world has to offer. This is the kind of interaction Anabel and Barnabas Kindersley must have felt when they wrote *Children Just Like Me* or that Maya Ajmera and John Ivanko experienced while collecting photos and stories to create *To Be a Kid*. The children in these books did not seem to be enemies, but friends separated only by distance.

I discovered a wide range of books that identified and portrayed the challenges of the social issues we face. Many of the books also offered solutions and examples of success in communities around the world. These books gave me great hope for humanity: Opportunities abound for classrooms, families, and communities to make the world a better place. Careful screening of the media reveals evidence of children and adults around the world making a difference for others. Several examples can be found in the book extension sections in this volume.

The landscapes and settlements of the wonderful people I discovered enthralled me. The geography was as varied as their homes and shelters. Environmental conditions often created unique living conditions. The rich colors of foods, clothing styles, and celebrations among the multicolored peoples I encountered were invigorating. I was reminded that all people strive for the same things: food to eat, shelter to protect ourselves and our families, and freedom to live as we choose. We also strive for happiness. People throughout the world go about fulfilling these needs in a variety of ways. Some have many resources from which to draw, while others have little or nothing and must depend on others, especially in times of crisis.

It is my hope that this book will take readers on a journey that raises consciousness. Bringing quality multicultural literature into schools and libraries requires leadership, activism, commitment, and continuity. Multicultural education must become part of the school philosophy. We all have a stake in the future of our youth, and we must do whatever we can to develop empathy and compassion.

In closing, I would like to share some thought-provoking words from Newbery Award–winning author, Katherine Paterson, taken from her plenary address at the Young Adult Institute during the 1999 International Reading Association Meeting: "Be sure that the children and young people receive the gift . . . that only books can bestow. If they cannot connect deeply with the past, the treasure and wisdom of humankind that is found in books, they probably will not be able to connect with their deepest selves or with other persons different from themselves, and all our futures are in jeopardy."

# How to Use This Book

This book is intended to be a reference tool for raising multicultural awareness. It is useful for teachers, librarians, teacher education and library science faculty, parents, and anyone who influences children's lives. I have researched and gathered a multitude of multicultural literature that can be used on a daily basis within a unit or theme of study or to support a particular content area. Each section has a brief introduction with ideas and information on how to apply the literature discussed. I also have concluded each section with book connections and extensions, as well as personal experiences. My intent is to increase the use of multicultural literature in homes and libraries, infusing school curricula on a regular basis. These books are too beautiful to be saved for special occasions or celebrations; I encourage you to include them in library collections so children have the opportunity to learn about all peoples in this world. It is my hope that all of us begin to see the world as a global village, where every person is a contributor.

Each of the book's first four parts consists of an annotated list of books, including as many genres as possible. Recommended reading includes picture books, poetry, nonfiction, folklore, and fiction for audiences of all ages, from preschool to adult. Included in the lists of literature are a wide variety of topics for varied interests. A wide assortment of literature can help achieve a fuller understanding of diversity because one book may represent only one cultural perspective. This resource includes books and application strategies for preschool level through junior high school students. You may use the themes presented in the book as the basis of a program of study, or you may choose to select portions that fit into an existing curriculum.

If you want to start by seeking daily resources, I would draw your attention to Parts I and IV, which include many possibilities. In these two sections, you will find lists of folktales and stories from around the world, books that highlight universal similarities and world celebrations, and books connected to content areas. There are many individual books that can be used to start, culminate, or enhance a lesson or unit of study. Some books also may be used to teach a specific point or content, to trigger a discussion, or for critical analysis; they may also be useful resources to demonstrate a writing style, model an idea, or simply read for the enjoyment of hearing a good story. Even if the story collection is the only list you use, there are enough entries for an entire school year.

This reference volume includes a variety of literature from many genres. Each theme section in this volume includes picture books, novels, poetry, and nonfiction. The rule of thumb I use for thematic units is to have twice as many books as there are students in the class. Having more choices gives greater assurance that the list will include something for everyone, promoting student participation. The unique contribution from each student will provide a more thorough understanding of the theme. I find this works better than the practice of having every student read the same book. Additionally, when students read the book of their choice, they become experts on the information they have learned. Providing students with an opportunity to share information builds confidence, allowing them to contribute to the classroom community.

Along with the books discussed in this volume it takes little effort to find recipes and games from other countries, and these provide enjoyable motivators for multicultural learning. By experimenting with cooking and games, students will experience firsthand the richness of another culture. Life celebrations are universal, and there are many books listed here that offer ways to create celebrations in your community. I also have included a section featuring books in a series, which supply possibilities for learning about individual countries, cities, commerce and industry, recreation, plants, customs, the arts, and lifestyles.

The annotated lists of books include recommended grade levels for use, but do not let these parameters limit you. Teachers know their students' abilities and interests better than anyone. Be resourceful and go beyond the book list I have provided. Up to 6,000 new titles are published each year in the United States, and it would be impossible to include every book here. While writing this resource, I checked the availability of texts through *Books in Print* or with the publishers to make sure they were still available. I have listed a few out-of-print books that are likely to be available at public or school libraries.

Each part of the book concludes with a section called book extensions. These include suggested activities with chosen books, as well as other possible projects related to the theme. Additional book titles, connected to the content of the book being discussed, are found in both the annotations and the book extension section. There are content and subject applications for every book listed in this resource, but I have limited my suggestions to encourage readers to generate their own ideas. You will find my subject applications in bold at the end of each extension. As you explore this volume, you may think of new ways to include books into your lessons. When we look at literature in this way, the only limitation is our imagination. I offer the suggestions as springboards for your imaginative applications.

I hope you enjoy reading the variety of books and possibilities as much as I did during my ongoing reading journey across the globe. If you want to share or discuss any thoughts and ideas with me through e-mail or other means I would love to hear from you. My e-mail addresses are:

ssteiner@email.boisestate.edu   OR   ssteine@boisestate.edu

I can be reached at Boise State University by calling 1-208-426-3962 or 1-800-824-7017 ext. 3962. You can also contact me through my Web page at http://education.boisestate.edu/ssteine.

# 20 Reasons Why We Need Multicultural Literature

1. It provides an opportunity for all children to see themselves in the literature.

2. It fosters development and positive self-esteem.

3. It strengthens the significance of personal heritage.

4. It helps raise personal aspirations.

5. It provides a means for everyone to learn about people all over the world.

6. It recognizes and values the contributions of all people.

7. It broadens understanding of history and geography.

8. It cultivates respect, empathy, and acceptance of all people.

9. It helps build a global community.

10. It prevents people from feeling isolated.

11. It allows differences and promotes harmony.

12. It provides a multitude of opportunities to discuss similarities and differences.

13. It promotes social consciousness of people afflicted with social problems.

14. It helps overcome denial and fears of differences.

15. It provides daily opportunities to talk about diversity and current events.

16. It promotes positive actions to rectify unjust behaviors and events.

17. It blends easily into themes of study found in schools.

18. It provides the needed balance of literature representative of many cultures.

19. It offers a good option for locating well-written literature.

20. It prepares us for the future.

# Criteria for Building a Collection of Multicultural Literature Promoting a Global Community

**Strong Characters.** Look for books with strong characters keeping ethnic and gender diversity in mind.

**Authenticity.** Look for books with accurate representations of the cultural attitudes, feelings, and perspectives, both visually and literally.

**Interconnections.** Look for books that bring diverse people together in realistic ways and ones that reflect universal similarities of all cultures.

**Historical Representation.** Look for books that dispel misconceptions by reflecting truths.

**Balance.** Continually strive for a balance of diversity in the literature, both ethnically and across the genres of children's literature, so all students can relate to classroom activities.

**Become Proactive.** Read and recommend quality multicultural literature to students, teachers, librarians, curriculum committees, administrators, and your students' parents.

Stan Steiner © 2001

# Useful Facts to Know and Share

The following demographic information is valuable for educators and, more generally, for all citizens of the United States. It may also be helpful to people in places with little diversity or in communities where decision makers tend to overlook the wide variety of people living around them.

## Thinking about Diversity

If we could, at this moment, shrink the Earth's population to a village of precisely 100 females and males while maintaining the existing human ratios, it would look like this:

- There would be 61 Asians, 12 Europeans, 14 North and South Americans, and 13 Africans.

- Of these 100 individuals, 70 would be nonwhite, and 30 would be white.

- Of these individuals, 70 would be non-Christian, and 30 would be Christian.

- Among these 100 people, 70 would be unable to read, 50 would be malnourished, and 80 would live in substandard housing.

- Only one of these people would be a university graduate.

- Half of the entire world's wealth would be in the hands of 6 people, all citizens of the United States.

Consider the following information as well:

- The three most common languages spoken in the world, in descending order, are Mandarin, Spanish, and English.

- On October 12, 1999, the world population reached 6 billion.

- The 10 most populous countries, in descending order, are China, India, the United States, Indonesia, Brazil, Pakistan, Russia, Bangladesh, Japan, and Nigeria.

*Information extrapolated from the United Nations demographic data as of October 1999.*

# Part I

# Part I

## Ties That Bind:
## Celebrating Life around the World

*By the year 2020, one of every two students will be a person of color.*

—James Banks, Professor of Multicultural Studies
at the University of Washington

We live in an incredible age. The world's population exceeds six billion. Evidence of growing interdependence among nations can be seen in summits and gatherings such as the World Trade Organization meeting in Seattle and the activities of the World Bank organization, including the international protesters who remind us that we still have much work to do in reaching global equity. It is no longer adequate to view the world from the perspective of our own narrow community. Satellite transmissions and the Internet have profoundly improved our ability to communicate with people around the world. Never has the need to learn about people beyond our own culture been so strong. Never has the need to develop empathy and understanding been more urgent. Well-written books can answer these needs. Our classrooms, libraries, and homes can nurture the seeds of knowledge and understanding.

Recently, my family began to explore diverse cultures, both far away and in our own land. Our journey lasted several months, but we never tired, nor did we need anyone to collect the mail or cut the grass. We took the whole family on a journey, but travel fare was free. Ours was "armchair traveling," accomplished through books that were filled with color and vitality, books that made us want to taste and see things for ourselves.

So we did. We tasted and played and told stories. The books we found were not only filled with beautiful pictures, but marvelous ideas as well. When food was mentioned in the books, the authors often included recipes for us to try. If our cooking skills were too challenged, we visited the ethnic restaurants available in our community. We especially enjoyed *Celebration, Festivals, Carnivals, and Feast Days from around the World* by Anabel Kindersley and Barnabas Kindersley for its month-by-month listing. Children love to take part in cultural celebrations and games. Try some of the games and activities in your school, community, or family. You might recognize a few of the games or learn new versions of old favorites. Children take special delight in ethnic activities and games their young bodies can do with ease, leaving the grown-ups to catch their breath.

As we learned about the foods, celebrations, and play associated with a culture we took a rest break to read its folklore. It would be difficult to study or fully understand a culture without experiencing some of the folktales, legends, and myths that are central to its traditions. Folklore also provides an opportunity to learn about values and religious beliefs because it is often closely interwoven and passed down through the generations. Invite storytellers specializing in cultural tales into your schools and libraries. There are many volumes of cultural tales available, however I decided to feature multicultural story collections only. Also included are several books that feature brief histories of the world's largest religions in one volume. Celebrations, food, play, folklore, and religion contribute to a greater understanding of each culture.

Certainly the most fascinating discoveries in my family's book travels were the people. We saw abundant examples of people living their lives in the best way they could. Hairstyles, clothing, and housing reflect climactic conditions or a sense of belonging. People are clearly diverse in their worldview, but they share similar needs the world over. We all share a zest for life and a love of play and communication. Smiles are universal.

The increasing appearance of multicultural trade books has encouraged more teachers and librarians to balance their literature collections. Many classroom and school libraries include books by authors from many nations that depict children from a variety of ethnic backgrounds. Despite the growing awareness of the importance of multicultural literature, a limited approach to learning about diversity is all too common. Some schools dedicate only one day or several days to a cultural group. We observe classrooms around the country recognizing the birthday of Martin Luther King Jr. or *Cinco de Mayo* celebrations with their displays of African American and Latino/Latina books. The observance of these two occasions is commendable, but we have to ask, is this enough? Does this limited attention given to an ethnic group reach an overall goal of promoting awareness and harmony among all peoples? What do we really mean when we talk about multicultural awareness? Is it weekly recognition? Is it yearly recognition? I believe not. Multicultural literature as a means to enhance understanding the world's cultures needs to be available every day.

I have provided this list of multicultural literature in the hope that it will help educators celebrate diversity on a daily basis. Use the list to add many perspectives to the usual teaching themes. Rethinking a theme to include a global perspective is something toward which educators must strive. Americans may perform a task one way, but how is it done in other parts of the world? Gaze and learn about the wonders of the world. Expand young minds. There are so many books available, and many publishers have multicultural themes in their list of trade books. The list in this chapter provides books that offer a wide view of several world cultures under one cover.

I want readers of this volume to experience the wonder and excitement my family felt while traveling the globe through literature. When your students ask you, "Have you been there?" as they do in Gloria Houston's, *My Great Aunt Arizona,* you might say, "No, but you can go there someday!" Bon voyage!

# Life around the World

**Ajmera, Maya, and Anna Rhesa Versola.** *Children from Australia to Zimbabwe: A Photographic Journey around the World.* Charlesbridge, 1997. 64p. All ages.

For each of the countries featured, this alphabet book includes colorful photos, interesting facts, and a brief summary. Also included is a list of other countries beginning with the same letter of the alphabet. The format of this book lends itself to replicating an alphabet book in your classroom.

**Ajmera, Maya, Olateju Omolodun, and Sarah Strunk.** *Extraordinary Girls: A Celebration of Girlhood around the World.* Charlesbridge, 1999. 48p. All ages.

Beautiful photos celebrate girls worldwide. The tone is exuberant and uplifting. Two excellent companion books are *Girls Think of Everything: Stories of Ingenious Inventions by Women* by Catherine Thimmesh (published by Houghton Mifflin), and *Girls Who Rocked the World 2* by Michelle Roehm (published by Beyond Words).

**Ajmera, Maya, and John D. Ivanko.** *To Be a Kid.* Charlesbridge, 1999. 32p. All ages.

Ajmera and Ivanko capture the wonder of children from throughout the world. Photos feature children smiling, playing, going to school, eating, dancing, painting, helping, and hugging.

**Baer, Edith.** *This Is the Way We Go to School: A Book about Children around the World.* Illustrated by **Steve Bjorkman.** Scholastic, 1990. 40p. Pre K–2.

Some children walk to school; others ride a bus. Children go to school by ferry in New York, by *vaporetto* in Venice, by trolley car in San Francisco, and by helicopter in the Alaskan tundra. Discover how much fun getting to school can be with this book. How many different ways do children in your class go to school? Does it change with the seasons?

**Bernhard, Emery, and Durga Bernhard.** *A Ride on Mother's Back: A Day of Baby Carrying around the World.* Gulliver, 1996. 32p. Pre K–2.

As the mothers do their daily chores and routines, infants sleep peacefully or observe their new world. The informative, simple text and warm illustrations support the bonding between mother and child.

**Brandenberg, Aliki.** *Hello! Good-Bye.* Greenwillow Books, 1996. 32p. Pre K–2.

There are many ways to say hello and good-bye. Aliki captures the emotions behind the greetings with her trademark illustrations and word choice. Learning to greet new students and parents in their native language makes them feel welcome. To further explore the way people greet one another, see the nonfiction title, *Greetings of the World* by Richard Kozar (published by Chelsea House).

**Clay, Rebecca.** *Ties That Bind: Family and Community.* Blackbirch Press, 1996. 80p. Grades 5 and up.

Families and communities shape who we are. This book shares a global perspective on family and community. It offers thought-provoking insights into varied family structures found throughout the world.

**Copsey, Susan E.** *Children Just Like Me: A Unique Celebration of Children around the World.* DK, 1995. 80p. All ages.

This photographed compilation of children from around the world is based on Barnabas and Anabel Kindersley's worldwide travels and interactions with young people. This is an excellent contemporary resource full of cultural information, including how to set up universal pen pals. A nice feature is the portrayal of the many similarities children have throughout the world.

**Delafosse, Claude.** *Atlas of People: A First Discovery Book.* Illustrated by **Denise Millet.** Cartwheel Books, 1996. 30p. Pre K–3.

This beginners' guide to people and places of the world provides fascinating facts about people, customs, cultures, and countries. Another book by Delafosse in this series is *Atlas of Countries.*

**Dorros, Arthur.** *This Is My House.* Scholastic, 1992. 32p. Pre K–2.

All over the world, people make houses from the materials they have available to them. Readers experience the differences and similarities between housing structures in various countries. They also learn how to write and say "This is my house" in 17 languages.

**Fox, Mem.** *Whoever You Are.* Illustrated by **Leslie Staub.** Harcourt Brace, 1997. 32p. All ages.

Mem Fox celebrates the similarities in people all over the world. Smiles and loving hearts are the same no matter where they come from.

**Frasier, Debra.** *On the Day You Were Born.* Harcourt Brace, 1991. 32p. Pre K–1.

Regardless of where we were born, people on Earth all have the same sun, moon, and sky. Earth is our common home. Frasier also worked with the Minnesota Orchestra on a video adaptation of this award-winning book (available by calling toll-free 1-888-MN-NOTES).

**Gaskins, Pearl Fuyo.** *What Are You? Voices of Mixed-Race Young People.* Henry Holt, 1999. 288p. Grades 5 and up.

Young adults speak from the heart about their life as a mixed-race person. This is a great idea for a book that was long overdue. In America, cross-cultural marriages have occurred for well over 100 years, but public acknowledgement of these unions and their offspring often receives negative reaction. Now, at the threshold of the 21st century, 45 mixed-race youth share their thoughts and feelings about their status in this world. A great book connection is *Molly Bannaky* by Alice McGill.

**Gray, Nigel.** *A Country Far Away.* Illustrated by **Philippe Dupasquier.** Orchard, 1989. 32p. Pre K–3.

This book is a clever narrative coupled with playful illustrations of two young boys living a typical day in separate communities. Readers will experience similarities in two distant locations, North America and Africa. It provides an opportunity to brainstorm; encourage students to make comparisons between two other regions.

**Hausherr, Rosmarie.** *Celebrating Families.* Scholastic, 1997. 32p. Pre K–5.

This book is a wonderful reflection of families today that cuts across race, ethnicity, class, and gender. Bright photos on each page show the beauty of diverse family structures.

**Hollyer, Beatrice.** *Wake Up, World! A Day in the Life of Children around the World.* Henry Holt, 1999. 40p. Grades K–6.

Readers follow the eight characters in this book from the moment they wake up until the time they go to bed, taking part in all their activities. Brightly colored photos feature children from Australia, Brazil, England, Ghana, India, Russia, the United States, and Vietnam.

**Kissinger, Katie.** *All the Colors We Are: The Story of How We Get Our Skin Color.* Photography by **Wernher Krutein.** Redleaf Press, 1994. 32p. Pre K–3.

There are three things that determine our skin color: our ancestors, the sun, and melanin. Skin color is one of the things that makes us special and different from one another. To support this idea, there are wonderful sets of multicultural markers available for children when drawing human figures.

**Knight, Margy Burns.** *Who Belongs Here?* Illustrated by **Anne Sibley O'Brien.** Tilbury House, 1993. 36p. Grades 3 and up.

This is a poignant and realistic view of a young immigrant coming to the United States. As the new boy's classmates begin to explore their heritage, they realize an important lesson about the origins of all Americans. There is an accompanying teachers' guide full of activities for discovering heritage and breaking down stereotypes (available by contacting Tilbury House; see the list of publishers at the end of the book).

**Kroll, Virginia.** *When God Made the Tree.* Illustrated by **Roberta Collier-Morales.** Dawn Publications, 1999. 32p. Pre K–3.

In this book, Kroll beautifully demonstrates the reasons why animals and humans share trees. A closing section further describing trees, animals, and geography strengthens the message of ecological balance.

**Lakin, Patricia.** *Family: Around the World.* Blackbirch Press, 1995. 32p. Grades 2–5.

This book is part of an exceptional series that explores cultural identity and similarities shared by people all over the world. The needs for shelter, nourishment, and clothing are universal. Other books in the *We All Share* series include play, food, creativity, growing up, and grandparents.

**Lakin, Patricia.** *Grandparents: Around the World.* Blackbirch Press, 1999. 32p. Grades 2–5.

In many cultures, grandparents play a major role in raising the young. There is an African proverb that states, "When an old person dies, it is as though an entire library goes up in flames." This book supports that honorable tribute to our elders.

**Lewin, Ted.** *Market!* Lothrop, Lee & Shepard, 1996. 48p. Grades 3–6.

This intriguing book by an award-winning author and illustrator depicts the exuberance of markets across the continents. Many communities in America have seasonal "farmer's markets," flea markets, and livestock markets; in several coastal cities, there are open markets for fish and produce. Teachers can use this book to initiate a discussion comparing and contrasting markets and defining what constitutes a market. Don't overlook stock markets.

**McDonald, Megan.** *My House Has Stars.* Illustrated by **Peter Catalanotto.** Orchard, 1996. 32p. Grades K–3.

Children from eight geographic locations describe their homes, with one similarity: Children throughout the world see stars in the sky. Do you suppose children everywhere are curious about stars?

**Morris, Ann.** *The Baby Book.* Photos by **Ken Heyman.** Silver Burdett, 1996. 32p. Pre K–1.

Babies throughout the world are the same: They eat, sleep, snuggle, crawl, play, and cry. No matter where they live, their need for love is the same.

**Morris, Ann.** *The Daddy Book.* Photos by **Ken Heyman.** Silver Burdett, 1996. 32p. Pre K–1.

This heartwarming look at fathers worldwide and their special qualities is one of the books in the *World's Family* series.

**Morris, Ann.** *Families.* Lothrop, Lee & Shepard, 2000. 32p. Pre K–3.

This book depicts families working, playing, and interacting with each other and is part of the *Around the World* series.

**Morris, Ann.** *The Grandma Book.* Photos by **Ken Heyman.** Silver Burdett, 1998. 32p. Pre K–1.

Like Morris's other books, readers take a look at grandmothers all over the world.

**Morris, Ann.** *The Grandpa Book.* Photos by **Ken Heyman.** Silver Burdett, 1998. 32p. Pre K–1.

Just as mommies and daddies are universal, so are grandparents. What role they play in the nurturing of children differs from one culture to another. Some grandparents take an active role in raising their grandchildren; others enjoy special visits during the holidays and vacations.

**Morris, Ann.** *Hats, Hats, Hats.* Photos by **Ken Heyman.** Lothrop, Lee & Shepard, 1989. 32p. Pre K–3.

A hat can say a lot about where people come from, what they do, and who they are. Full-color photos reveal how people worldwide use hats.

**Morris, Ann.** *Houses and Homes.* Photos by **Ken Heyman.** Lothrop, Lee & Shepard, 1992. 32p. Pre K–3.

This book celebrates the many different kinds of homes around the world.

**Morris, Ann.** *Loving.* Photos by **Ken Heyman.** Lothrop, Lee & Shepard, 1990. 32p. Pre K–3.

People all over the world show their love for others in similar ways: by holding, helping, talking, listening, teaching, and sharing.

**Morris, Ann.** *The Mommy Book.* Photos by **Ken Heyman.** Silver Press, 1996. 32p. Pre K–1.

Mommies take good care of their babies, both before they are born and when they are tiny. Whether they work in fields or offices, they are available for loving talk, hugs, and smiles when their children need them.

**Morris, Ann.** *On the Go.* Photos by **Ken Heyman.** Lothrop, Lee & Shepard, 1990. 32p. Pre K–3.
> This book discusses the ways in which people worldwide move from place to place. Examples include walking, riding on animals, and traveling on wheels and water.

**Morris, Ann.** *Shoes, Shoes, Shoes.* Lothrop, Lee & Shepard, 1995. 32p. Pre K–3.
> An around-the-world tour demonstrates how footwear can reflect universal similarities, but also differences. This book features shoes from many countries as people wear them performing a variety of activities.

**Morris, Ann.** *Teamwork.* Lothrop, Lee & Shepard, 1999. 32p. Pre K–3.
> Working and playing together are important wherever you live. This book reflects the universal nature of teamwork with children and adults.

**Morris, Ann.** *Tools.* Photos by **Ken Heyman.** Lothrop, Lee & Shepard, 1992. 32p. Pre K–3.
> Morris describes a variety of tools and their many uses around the world.

**Morris, Ann.** *Work.* Lothrop, Lee & Shepard, 1998. 32p. Pre K–3.
> Men, women, and children all engage in various types of work. Sometimes the work is outside the house; other times, they do their work at home. Work is universal to all cultures.

*My Wish for Tomorrow: Words and Pictures from Children around the World.* William Morrow, 1995. 48p. All ages.
> To help celebrate the 50th birthday of the United Nations, children from every part of the world were asked, "If you were granted one wish to make the world a better place, what would it be?" Here are their answers, along with their remarkable illustrations. Use this book to encourage children in your community to write and illustrate their wish for the world. The book features introductions by Nelson Mandela and Boutros Boutros-Ghali.

**Pickering, Marianne.** *Lessons for Life: Education and Learning.* Blackbirch Press, 1996. 80p. Grades 5 and up.
> The lessons we learn in life occur in our homes, schools, and neighborhoods. This beautiful book looks at the universal nature of education.

**Powell, Jillian.** *Body Decorations: Traditions around the World.* Thomson Learning, 1995. 48p. Grades 5 and up.
> In a time when tattooing and body piercing have become fads in America, this book offers a world perspective on body art. It tours the world to look at the traditions and fads associated with body decorations. A bibliography of additional reading is included.

**Rotner, Shelley.** *Faces.* Photos by **Shelley Rotner and Ken Kreisler.** Macmillan, 1994. 32p. Pre K–1.
> This book features a collage of faces of young and old people from all over the world. Have children collect and take photos of the people in their community to make a bulletin board.

**Rotner, Shelley, and Sheila M. Kelly.** *Lots of Dads.* Dial Books for Young Readers, 1997. 24p. Pre K–1.
   This collection of photographs celebrates fathers and the things that make them special.

**Rotner, Shelley, and Sheila M. Kelly.** *Lots of Moms.* Dial Books for Young Readers, 1996. 24p. Pre K–1.
   Mothers live all over the world. This collection of photographs depicts many of the special things that mothers do, from playing with their young to comforting them.

**Sanders, Eve.** *What's Your Name? From Ariel to Zoe.* Photos by **Marilyn Sanders.** Holiday House, 1995. 30p. Grades K–3.
   Knowing the history behind one's name can lead to some wonderful discoveries and family stories. This alphabet book is a gem for introducing this concept into a classroom. Readers will meet 26 children and learn the history behind their names.

**Schuett, Stacey.** *Somewhere in the World Right Now.* Alfred A. Knopf, 1995. 32p. Grades K–3.
   Through this book readers travel the globe and are introduced to the many events involving everyday people at the same moment. The illustrations have maps worked into the drawings.

**Singer, Marilyn.** *Nine O'Clock Lullaby.* Illustrated by **Frané Lessac.** HarperCollins, 1991. 32p. Grades K–3.
   It's 9:00 o'clock in Brooklyn, New York, and Mama is singing a lullaby. What is the rest of the world doing? Singer's book tracks a 24-hour period around the world and back again. If you have access to the Public Broadcasting System's *Millennium Celebration,* from New Year's Day 2000, you can show students an example of this concept.

**Singer, Marilyn.** *On the Same Day in March: A Tour of the World's Weather.* Illustrated by **Frané Lessac.** HarperCollins, 2000. 32p. Pre K–5.
   We talk about traveling across time lines, but what about lines of latitude? This unique book takes readers on a weather tour from one polar cap to another. At each location readers experience weather conditions through bright illustrations and playful narrative. A great companion series is the six-book set, *Extreme Weather* (published by PowerKids Press).

**Sis, Peter.** *Madlenka.* Farrar, Straus & Giroux, 2000. 44p. Grades K–2.
   Madlenka has a loose tooth. Like most kids her age, she is obsessed with the fact that it's loose. She wants to tell the world and walks around her multicultural neighborhood to let all of her friends know. They greet her in their native languages. When her mother finally finds Madlenka, she says she has been around the world and lost her tooth. A charming story!

**Swain, Gwenyth.** *Smiling.* Carolrhoda Books, 1999. 24p. Pre K–2.
   Smiles are universal! This book is part of the four-book *Small World* series that features a universal look at themes including smiling, eating, carrying, and celebrating. A nice feature is the "More about the Pictures" section that provides a location and brief description of each photo.

**Weiss, Nicki.** *The World Turns Round and Round.* Greenwillow Books, 2000. 32p. Grades K–3.

In this nifty book grandmothers, grandfathers, aunts, and uncles from around the world send gifts, including articles of traditional clothing, to their grandchildren or nieces and nephews living elsewhere. There is a glossary for language and meaning translation along with a location map. The border on each page showing the origin of the gifts is decorated with postage stamps from that country.

# Food around the World

**Baer, Edith.** *This Is the Way We Eat Our Lunch.* Illustrated By **Steve Bjorkman.** Scholastic, 1995. 32p. Pre K–3.

Eating is something we all do, but what and how we eat may vary, as this book reveals in its description of lunches around the world.

**Cook, Deanna.** *The Kids' Multicultural Cookbook: Food and Fun around the World.* Illustrated by **Michael Kline.** Williamson, 1995. 160p. Prc K–5.

This book is a bountiful international experience with food as the common bond. Try the 50 great multicultural dishes yourself.

**Dooley, Norah.** *Everybody Bakes Bread.* Illustrated by **Peter J. Thornton.** Carolrhoda Books, 1996. 32p. Grades K–3.

When Carrie is sent to borrow a three-handled rolling pin, she learns that everyone in her culturally diverse neighborhood bakes bread in a unique way. Recipes are included.

**Dooley, Norah.** *Everyone Cooks Rice.* Illustrated by **Peter J. Thornton.** Carolrhoda Books, 1991. 32p. Grades K–3.

We all eat, and rice is a staple in many cultures. Young Carrie searches for her brother in their multiethnic neighborhood and learns that everyone is having rice for dinner, prepared with a unique flavor for each family. Recipes are included.

**Gay, Kathlyn.** *Keep the Buttered Side Up: Food Superstitions from around the World.* Illustrated by **Debbie Palen.** Walker, 1995. 102p. Grades 3 and up.

For those looking for another way to be creative at mealtime, this book will help you fill up on laughs—or suffer from a ruined appetite! A great book to have around for the curious appetite.

**Harbison, Elizabeth.** *Loaves of Fun: A History of Bread with Activities and Recipes from around the World.* Illustrated by **John Harbison.** Chicago Review Press, 1997. 112p. Grades K–6.

From the pitas of ancient Mesopotamia to the white breads of the modern bakery, kids can explore the globe with more than 30 exciting recipes and activities. Use Ann Morris's book *Bread, Bread, Bread* as an introduction and follow with the activities and baking in this book.

**Hughes, Meredith Sayles, and Tom Hughes.** *Buried Treasure: Roots and Tubers.* Lerner, 1998. 80p. Grades 3 and up.

This book is part of a wonderful 10-book series, called *Plants We Eat*, which covers the array of foods from roots and tubers to fruits from shrubs and vines. Each book has a global perspective of the featured food, from planting the seeds to harvesting the products, and then processing them for our meals. Health facts and tips and recipes are included.

**Lakin, Patricia.** *Food: Around the World.* Blackbirch Press, 1999. 32p. Grades 2–5.

The food that is available to people varies in different parts of the world. This beautiful book explores growing and cooking food as well as traditions and rituals associated with it.

**Morris, Ann.** *Bread, Bread, Bread.* Photos by **Ken Heyman.** Lothrop, Lee & Shepard, 1989. 32p. Pre K–3.

Bread is a staple in many lands. This book celebrates the different kinds of bread all over the world. It can lead to a discussion of other foods that are found in places around the globe. Norah Dooley's books listed above can be used in conjunction with this text.

**Pizarro, Joanne Alfonso.** *Coming Home.* Igloo, 1997. 240p. Grades 5 and up.

If I were to buy one multicultural cookbook, this would be the one. Not only does it include recipes, it also offers rich stories and photographs of people across 44 cultures. The format of this cookbook would be fun to replicate in your classroom or school.

**Priceman, Marjorie.** *How to Make Apple Pie and See the World.* Alfred A. Knopf, 1996. 40p. Pre K–3.

An apple pie may be easy to make, provided you have the ingredients. But where do these ingredients come from? This book takes the reader around the world to gather ingredients for an apple pie.

**Robins, Deri.** *The Kids' around the World Cookbook.* Illustrated by **Charlotte Stowell.** Kingfisher Books, 1994. 40p. Grades 3–7.

Gathered from all over the globe, the easy-to-make recipes in this book include such treats as Caribbean-inspired pineapple ice cream, hummus from Turkey, Swiss fondue, paella from Spain, Indonesian satay, African bobotie, and pizza from Italy.

**Shelby, Anne.** *Potluck.* Illustrated by **Irene Trivas.** Orchard, 1991. 32p. Pre K–2.

Preparing and eating ethnic foods is a natural means of acculturation between people, but there is no meal quite like this alphabet potluck in which everyone brings a special item to share. Other alphabet books with this theme are *Eating the Alphabet* by Lois Ehlert, *An Edible Alphabet* by Bonnie Christensen, and *The Spice Alphabet Book* by Jerry Pallotta. Alphabet master Jerry Pallotta created *The Make Your Own Alphabet Book* for guidance.

**Vezza, Diane.** *Passport on a Plate: Around the World Cookbook for Children.* Illustrated by **Susan Greenstein.** Simon & Schuster, 1997. 160p. Grades 4 and up.

Here's a cookbook that is a social studies, geography, and world history lesson, all rolled into one delicious package! This book offers easy-to-follow recipes while teaching youngsters about food customs from around the globe.

**Webb, Lois Sinaiko.** *Multicultural Cookbook of Life-Cycle Celebrations.* Oryx Press, 2000. 544p. Grades 3 and up.

This is a huge resource for bringing food into the curriculum. There are more than 500 recipes from 135 countries.

**Wells, Rosemary.** *Yoko.* Hyperion, 1998. 32p. Pre K–2.

This is a charming story about Yoko, a cat with Japanese heritage. Her mother sends traditionally prepared sushi for Yoko's lunch. The other students react to it, and the teacher decides to hold an international food festival to help her students become more accepting of others. Even though the characters in this book are personified animals, the reality of the lunchroom scene is a good springboard for a discussion of food choices with children in any school.

**Young, Caroline.** *Round the World Cookbook.* Usborne, 1993. 48p. All ages.

There is never a shortage of participants when it comes to eating food. If you involve children in cooking, they are more likely to try new foods. This is a good book to test their taste buds. Other nice features are maps showing where the ingredients come from; information on basic cooking tips, vocabulary, and safety; detailed illustrations with brief descriptions; and briefs on each country. If you are introducing children to serious cooking for the first time, you might want to consider the helpful tips this book has to offer.

**Zanger, Mark H.** *The American Ethnic Cookbook for Students.* Oryx Press, 2000. 288p. Grades K and up.

Approximately 400 recipes are arranged alphabetically by ethnic group. Each of the more than 120 ethnic groups represented in this book is introduced with background and food history followed by two to four recipes.

# Multicultural Games and Activities from around the World

**Ajmera, Maya, and Michael J. Regan.** *Let the Games Begin.* Charlesbridge, 2000. 32p. All ages.

Play is a universal pastime. Children engage in the thrill and excitement of sports all over the world for the same reasons. They like the camaraderie a sport has to offer, the challenge of learning something new, and the fun of participation. This book includes a foreword by former basketball star and senator Bill Bradley.

**Ancona, George.** *Let's Dance.* William Morrow, 1998. 32p. Pre K–3.

Simple text along with inserts and Ancona's eye for photos briefly portray a variety of dances from around the world. A nice companion to this book that takes you from learning about the dances to actually performing them is *International Playtime: Classroom Games and Dances from around the World,* listed below, by Wayne E. Nelson and Henry "Buzz" Glass.

**Dunn, Opal.** *Acka Backa Boo! Playground Games from around the World.* Illustrated by **Susan Winter.** Henry Holt, 2000. 48p. Grades K–3.

This book offers possibilities for celebrating diversity through play. You may recognize some of the games and now you will have a reference for where they originated. Playing a familiar game with a new student is one way to make them feel welcome.

**Erlbach, Arlene.** *Sidewalk Games around the World.* Illustrated by **Sharon Lane Holm.** Millbrook Press, 1997. 48p. Grades K–6.

This book is filled with some great games—hopscotch included—from 26 different countries. Clear directions and illustrations make it possible to try these games in your community. Sidewalks or hard surfaces are needed for most of the games.

**Hall, Godfrey.** *Games: Traditions around the World Series.* Raintree, 1995. 48p. Grades 4-6.

This book includes directions for dozens of games played around the world, including card games, dice, and dominoes. Adding Mary Lankford's book *Dominoes around the World* can expand on the domino possibilities.

**Lakin, Patricia.** *Play: Around the World.* Blackbirch Press, 1995. 32p. Grades 2–5.

Play is filled with laughter and good times wherever you live. This book (along with Ann Morris's book *Play)* shows the universal nature of play through photo images.

**Lankford, Mary.** *Dominoes around the World.* Illustrated by **Karen Dugan.** William Morrow, 1998. 40p. Grades 1 and up.

This book features directions and graphics for playing eight different versions of dominoes. The countries included are Cuba, France, Malta, The Netherlands, Spain, Ukraine, the United States, and Vietnam.

**Lankford, Mary.** *Hopscotch around the World.* Illustrated by **Karen Milone.** William Morrow, 1992. 48p. Pre K and up.

Included in this book are 19 hopscotch games from 16 different countries with complete rules, illustrations, and interesting facts. A nice bonus to this book is the physical exercise involved from actually playing the game.

**Lankford, Mary.** *Jacks around the World.* Illustrated by **Karen Dugan.** William Morrow, 1996. 40p. Grades 1 and up.

The format of this book contains a wealth of cultural facts and images for learning new ways of playing jacks from 14 countries.

**Miller, Thomas.** *Taking Time Out: Recreation and Play.* Blackbirch Press, 1996. 80p. Grades 5 and up.

Taking time to play is a necessary part of balancing our lives. People everywhere make time for leisure and play, and Miller takes us around the world to observe recreation in this action-filled book.

**Morris, Ann.** *Play.* Photos by **Ken Heyman.** Lothrop, Lee & Shepard, 1998. 32p. Pre K–3.

Readers have the opportunity to observe children around the world as they enjoy themselves.

**Nelson, Wayne E., and Henry "Buzz" Glass.** *International Playtime: Classroom Games and Dances from around the World.* Fearon Teacher Aids, 1992. 240p. Grades K–9.

This teacher resource bursts with dances and games. Clear illustrations and instructional guides for each dance are easy to follow. Also included is a brief description of the country of origin for each dance. The extensive bibliography of game resources is a good reason for teachers to keep this book handy.

# Celebrations around the World

**Angell, Carole S.** *Celebrations around the World: A Multicultural Handbook.* Fulcrum, 1996. 218p. All ages.

This is a great resource to have in a school or library. A daily list for each month's celebrations around the world is the core of the book. Also included are a section dedicated to holidays with no fixed date; indexes for quick referencing by country, holidays, activities, music, and recipes; and suggestions for further reading.

**Anno, Mitsumasa.** *All in One Day.* Illustrated by artists from around the world. Philomel, 1986. 32p. Pre K–5.

Artists from different locations on Earth illustrate scenes of children every hour on January 1. This is a unique book because it shows children as they might be celebrating, playing, eating, or sleeping on this day, depending on location.

**Beeler, Selby B.** *Throw Your Tooth on the Roof: Tooth Traditions from around the World.* Illustrated by **G. Brian Karas.** Houghton Mifflin, 1998. 32p. Pre K–2.

Two universals among children are teeth and the certainty of losing them. How do cultures around the world acknowledge this rite of passage? Beeler has researched this question and presents what she learned to readers.

**Bernhard, Emery.** *Happy New Year.* Illustrated by **Durga Bernhard.** Lodestar, 1996. 32p. Pre K–4.

The mark of a new year does not go unnoticed in any culture. This book provides the origins and celebrations of the New Year from around the world. Audiences may recognize some of their family and community traditions as they enjoy the lively illustrations.

**Chandler, Clare.** *Harvest Celebrations.* Millbrook Press, 1997. 48p. Grades 3–6.

Bright color photos embellish the historical information about contemporary harvest celebrations from around the world.

**Corwin, Judith Hoffman.** *Harvest Festivals around the World.* Silver Burdett, 1995. 48p. Grades 1–6.

All crop-producing peoples celebrate the harvest, the season of reward, and diverse cultural traditions make each celebration unique. Many activities and recipes are included. Lois Markham's *Harvest: World Celebrations and Ceremonies* and Clare Chandler's *Harvest Celebrations* are excellent companions to this title.

**Elliott, Kate, and Emma Danes.** *Round the World Song Book.* Usborne, 1996. 48p. All ages.

Song can be an important part of celebrations. The music and words for more than 30 songs are included in this resource, as are guides for pronunciation and accompaniments for piano, keyboard, and guitar.

**Erlbach, Arlene.** *Happy Birthday Everywhere.* Illustrated by **Sharon Lane Holm.** Millbrook Press, 1997. 48p. Pre K–5.

This book describes birthday customs from 19 countries and teaches students a special birthday greeting in the native language of each land. A map allows students to locate the countries as well.

**Feldman, Eve B.** *Birthdays! Celebrating Life around the World.* Illustrated by children from 24 different nations. Bridge Water, 1997. 32p. Pre K–2.

This book, describing birthday celebrations from around the world, is written in rhyming text with playful illustrations contributed by children from many nations. Part of the proceeds support Paintbrush Diplomacy, an organization that promotes international communication through the exchange of children's letters and artwork. Information about Paintbrush Diplomacy is included.

**Gilchrist, Cherry.** *A Calendar of Festivals.* Illustrated by **Helen Chan.** Barefoot Books, 1998. 80p. Grades 3–6.

This collection includes Gilchrist's retelling of eight stories from Jewish, Hindu, Buddhist, Japanese, Celtic, Christian, Caribbean, and Russian traditions. Readers learn about the historical and cultural context of the festivals.

**Henderson, Helene, and Sue Ellen Thompson (editors).** *Holidays, Festivals, and Celebrations of the World Dictionary* (2nd edition). Omnigraphics, 1997. 822p. Grades 5 and up.

This wonderful reference tool includes brief descriptions of international celebrations. Each entry is listed alphabetically and cross-referenced by state and country. A directory of tourism information includes addresses, phone numbers, and Web sites.

**Jackson, Ellen.** *The Autumn Equinox: Celebrating the Harvest.* Illustrated by **Jan Davey Ellis.** Millbrook Press, 2000. 32p. Grades 1–3.

Jackson does a nice job of traveling the globe in a continuous flowing narrative, unlike other formats that break the text for each location or culture. Colorful illustrations are found on every page, and the final section of the book includes classroom activities with a bibliography.

**Jackson, Ellen.** *Here Comes the Brides.* Illustrated by **Carol Heyer.** Walker, 1998. 32p. Pre K–3.

Weddings are special events in most cultures, and this multicultural showcase features brides from around the world. Noted artist Carol Heyer contributed lavish illustrations for each bride.

**Kindersley, Anabel.** *Celebrations! Festivals, Carnivals, and Feast Days from around the World.* Photos by **Barnabas Kindersley.** DK, 1997. 64p. Grades 2–6.

In the tradition of this well-known publisher, hundreds of colorful photos and brief captions capture the spirit of celebrations worldwide. Readers can spend hours admiring, learning, and dreaming about faraway places. This book also includes a calendar of celebrations to help plan special activities.

**Knight, Margy Burns.** *Welcoming Babies.* Illustrated by **Anne Sibley O'Brien.** Tilbury House, 1994. 32p. Pre K–2.

In this book, readers experience the celebration of birth in 14 different cultures. It acts as a springboard for children to find out how their own families celebrated birth.

**Langen, Annette.** *Felix's Christmas around the World.* Illustrated by **Constanza Droop.** Abbeville Press, 1998. 32p. Grades K–5.

A rabbit named Felix meets Santa and then travels from country to country with him, delivering presents along the way. Felix writes to Sophie from each place, telling her about its special Christmas traditions.

**Lankford, Mary D.** *Christmas around the World.* Illustrated by **Karen Dugan.** William Morrow, 1995. 48p. All ages.

This book is a sampler of the foods, symbols, and celebrations that make Christmas special in 12 nations around the world.

**Markham, Lois.** *Harvest: World Celebrations and Ceremonies.* Blackbirch Press, 1999. 24p. Grades 3–5.

As people reap the benefits from their crops, harvest celebrations take place in many countries. This book provides a global view of the harvest.

**Morris, Ann.** *Light the Candle! Bang the Drum!: A Book of Holidays around the World.* Dutton, 1997. 32p. Pre K–2.

Cultural and religious holidays are important to children. This book mixes new holidays with old traditions, marking festive occasions both at home and at school.

**Morris, Ann.** *Weddings.* Lothrop, Lee & Shepard, 1995. 32p. All ages.

Weddings are special celebrations, and this text invites readers to a Shinto rite in Japan, an orthodox Jewish service in Russia, and a Catholic mass in Slovakia. These full-color photo-essays take children on a trip around the world, providing a glimpse into rich traditions.

**Osborne, Mary Pope.** *One World, Many Religions: The Ways We Worship.* Alfred A. Knopf, 1996. 86p. Grades 5 and up.

This book features seven world religions: Judaism, Christianity, Islam, Hinduism, Buddhism, Confucianism, and Taoism. Included is a time line tracing the history of each religion and a world map showing the dominant religion that is practiced on each continent.

**Pirotta, Saviour.** *Joy to the World: Christmas Stories from around the World.* Illustrated by **Sheila Moxley.** HarperCollins, 1998. 46p. All ages.

This collection of five stories from Syria, Malta, Mexico, Ghana, and Russia is a fine addition for Christmas celebration.

**Rohmer, Harriet (editor).** *Honoring Our Ancestors: Stories and Pictures by Fourteen Artists.* Children's Book Press, 1999. 32p. Grades 3 and up.

This book honors ancestors that influenced its 14 featured artists. It celebrates the many ways that other people, especially people from another generation, can influence our lives. Some of these people are our ancestors; others are people about whom we have read or studied. All of these "ancestors" can help shape who we are.

**Siegen-Smith, Nikki.** *Songs for Survival: Songs and Chants from the Tribal Peoples around the World.* Illustrated by **Bernard Lodge.** Dutton, 1996. 80p. Grades 5 and up.

Siegen-Smith compiled these songs and chants with themes that include genesis, animals, the elements, and survival. Also included is a brief summary of the indigenous peoples from six regions across the globe.

**Sita, Lisa.** *Coming of Age: World Celebrations and Ceremonies.* Blackbirch Press, 1999. 24p. Grades 3–5.

Each culture celebrates coming of age differently. Open your students' world to the ways in which various cultures recognize the importance of growing. This book lends itself to a discussion of what happens in the United States, where many traditions from immigrants have been abandoned. What are Americans doing to celebrate coming of age?

**Sita, Lisa.** *Worlds of Belief: Religion and Spirituality.* Blackbirch Press, 1996. 80p. Grades 5 and up.

This text teaches readers how people practice their faith, emphasizing both differences and similarities.

**Spirn, Michele.** *Birth: World Celebrations and Ceremonies.* Blackbirch Press, 1999. 24p. Grades 3–5.

Although each culture may celebrate birth differently, each admires the wonder of a new life.

**Spirn, Michele.** *New Year: World Celebrations and Ceremonies.* Blackbirch Press, 1999. 24p. Grades 3–5.

A new year brings many wonderful events. Readers learn how other cultures celebrate the New Year as they travel the world with this book.

**Steele, Philip.** *The World of Festivals.* Rand McNally, 1996. 48p. Grades 3 and up.

This book compares festivals throughout the year from many nations. Festival themes found in this book focus on religious celebrations, death, seasons, independence, family, rites of passage, and more.

**Van Straalen, Alice.** *The Book of Holidays around the World.* Dutton, 1986. 192p. All ages.

Lively illustrations and summaries of holiday festivals celebrated around the world are featured in this large collection.

**Wong, Janet S.** *This Next New Year.* Illustrated by **Yangsook Choi.** Farrar, Straus & Giroux, 2000. 32p. Grades K–2.

This is a delightfully unique story in which a young boy of Korean and Chinese ancestry observes the Chinese New Year celebration in his neighborhood. His family follows many of the Chinese traditions, but they also have modified them to honor their Korean side, too. His multicultural neighbors adopt some of the Chinese traditions into their own celebrations.

*A World in Our Hands.* Written, illustrated, and edited by young people of the world. Tricycle Press, 1995. 96p. Grades 5 and up.

This book was created and written to honor the 50th anniversary of the United Nations. This helpful resource is filled with facts, stories, poems, illustrations, and commentary on the function and effects of the United Nations.

# Poetry around the World

**Ada, Alma Flor, Violet J. Harris, and Lee Bennett Hopkins (editors).** *A Chorus of Cultures: Developing Literacy through Multicultural Poetry.* Hampton-Brown Books, 1993.
> This is a wonderful collection of multicultural poetry, including many poems written by children. The format lends itself to a classroom, school, or community interested in creating a collection of poetry that is reflective of their rich ethnicity.

**Hamanaka, Sheila.** *All the Colors of the Earth.* William Morrow, 1994. 32p. Pre K–2.
> This book provides a unique and colorful celebration of cultural diversity. Children from all over the world smile, dance, play, and help make the Earth a better place.

**Kroll, Virginia.** *Hats off to Hair!* Illustrated by **Kay Life.** Charlesbridge, 1995. 32p. Pre K–2.
> This book is a tribute to hair, its many colors, and the various hairstyles people wear. Kay Life's illustrations add a playfulness to Kroll's lively verse.

**Kroll, Virginia.** *She Is Born: A Celebration of Daughters.* Illustrated by **John Rowe.** Beyond Words, 2000. 32p. All ages.
> The graceful and touching lyrics in this book celebrate the birth of girls. Kroll draws parallels to daughters worldwide, from cultural birth rituals, growing up, and then moving full circle to potential motherhood. Thoughtful concluding notes by Kroll further illuminate the similarities of daughters everywhere. The elegant illustrations by Rowe in his first picture book are breathtaking and truly capture the universal beauty of women.

**Kroll, Virginia.** *With Love, To Earth's Endangered People.* Illustrated by **Roberta Collier-Morales.** Dawn Publications, 1998. 48p. Grades 3–8.
> This book is a tribute to seven tribes around the world that are in danger of becoming extinct. Kroll conveys a thought-provoking message about the potential effects on the environment and on human beings if we were to lose these civilizations.

**Lundgren, Mary Beth.** *We Sing the City.* Illustrated by **Donna Perrone.** Clarion Books, 1997. 32p. Pre K–3.
> An eclectic group of children celebrates every aspect of their city. They consider diverse names, the tastes and smells of ethnic foods, and varied occupations. They celebrate places of worship, schools, and transportation. This book could provide a model to explore the rich qualities of diversity in other cities.

**Maguire, Arlene.** *Special People, Special Ways.* Illustrated by **Sheila Lucas.** Portunus, 1999. 32p. Pre K–4.
> This book is a sensitive way to help students understand disabilities. Maguire brings attention to an often-misunderstood group of people. Their diversity, among other characteristics, includes physical challenges.

**Maguire, Arlene.** *We're All Special.* Illustrated by **Sheila Lucas.** Portunus, 1995. 32p. All ages.
> This is a poetic description of how each of us has unique, yet universal, qualities. The warm illustrations depict diversity in a broad sense.

**Mavor, Salley (compiler).** *You and Me: Poems about Friendship.* Illustrated by Salley Mavor. Orchard, 1997. 32p. Pre K–3.

Mavor compiled these poems that focus on friendship, which have a universal appeal.

**Neaman, Evelyn.** *Folk Rhymes from around the World.* Pacific Educational Press, 1993. 64p. Grades 1–3.

This book includes folk rhymes from more than 20 cultures. Each rhyme is presented in the language of origin, along with an English translation. The collection includes riddles, tongue twisters, and rhymes to recite while skipping, counting, or playing games.

**Nikola-Lisa, W.** *Bein' with You This Way.* Illustrated by **Michael Bryant.** Lee & Low, 1994. 32p. Pre K–3.

This upbeat book is full of happy children. It was written as a poetic street rhyme chant and celebrates the physical characteristics that make us who we are.

**Nye, Naomi Shihab.** *This Same Sky: A Collection of Poems from around the World.* Four Winds Press, 1992. 212p. Grades 5 and up.

This is a unique thematic collection of poetry from 68 countries around the world. It includes poems on topics such as families, loss, human mysteries, and places where people live.

**Osborne, Mary Pope (editor).** *The Calico Book of Bedtime Rhymes from around the World.* Illustrated by **T. Lewis.** Contemporary Books, 1990. 64p. Pre K–2.

Throughout history, adults have sung, recited, read, and lulled children to sleep with bedtime rhymes. This book is a marvelous anthology of some of the best bedtime rhymes. Enjoy the universal delight of people from a variety of ethnic backgrounds when they recognize a rhyme from their childhood that was lost in their "memory bank."

**Philip, Neil.** *It's a Woman's World: A Century of Women's Voices in Poetry.* Dutton, 2000. 93p. Grades 3 and up.

This collection includes the work of more than 50 female poets from diverse backgrounds. The poems are grouped according to the following themes: Dear Female Heart, News of a Baby, A Freedom Song, Domestic Economy, Power, I Live with a Bullet, and The Old Women Gathered.

**Rosen, Michael J. (editor).** *The Greatest Table.* Illustrated by various artists. Harcourt Brace, 1994. 16p. All ages.

This 12-foot accordion book has a message about world hunger. The illustrations of food are exceptional. Part of the proceeds go to support Share Our Strength's projects. More interesting information on this organization and the author and illustrators is included in the book extension section in Part II.

**Rosenberg, Liz (editor).** *Light-Gathering Poems.* Henry Holt, 2000. 146p. Grades 5 and up.

This book is a powerful collection of poems from poets with roots all over the world. Some are still living; others are from the past. The theme encompasses a broad interpretation of light and its metaphors, from the lifting of burdens to "seeing the light."

**Ryder, Joanne.** *Earth Dance.* Illustrated by **Norman Garbaty.** Henry Holt, 1996. 32p. Pre K–3.

No matter where or who we are, human beings share the same precious Earth. Verse and illustration dance across the pages in tribute to the planet.

**Siegen-Smith, Nikki (compiler).** *Welcome to the World: A Celebration of Birth and Babies from Many Cultures.* Orchard, 1996. 48p. All ages.

Beautiful black-and-white photos complement the work of 12 poets (and several anonymous ones) from around the world that celebrates babies and birth.

**Yolen, Jane (editor).** *Mother Earth, Father Sky: Poems of Our Planet.* Illustrated by **Jennifer Hewiston.** Boyds Mills Press, 1995. 64p. Grades 4 and up.

Thirty-five poets write about our planet. This collection speaks of the Earth's beauty and what is necessary to sustain it. Many of the poets have written other poems about the Earth that may be worth locating for related units of study. In particular, Lee Bennett Hopkins has published many books of poetry that could offer useful resources to the classroom.

**Yolen, Jane (editor).** *Sleep Rhymes around the World.* Illustrated by 17 international artists. Boyds Mills Press, 1994. 40p. Pre K–2.

Young people everywhere enjoy sleep rhymes. Mothers and fathers remember and pass on the oral tradition of reciting or singing the rhymes to their little ones as they put them to bed. A nice companion to this book is *The Calico Book of Bedtime Rhymes from around the World,* edited by Mary Pope Osborne (published by Contemporary Books).

**Yolen, Jane (editor).** *Street Rhymes around the World.* Illustrated by 17 international artists. Boyds Mills Press, 1992. 40p. Pre K–5.

Children everywhere engage in play, and Yolen has edited a multicultural masterpiece with artists from around the world. This book features songs, rhymes, and chants in native language and in English.

# Story Collections from around the World

**Andrews, Jan.** *Out of the Everywhere: Tales of the New World.* Illustrated by **Simon Ng.** Groundwood Books, 2001. 80p. Grades 1 and up.

Andrews weaves tales from around the world into a new world setting. The stories are poignant and filled with wisdom. The origins for the stories are Chile, France, Greece, India, Finland, and Russia.

*Ask the Bones: Scary Stories from around the World.* Selected and retold by **Arielle North Olson, and Howard Schwartz.** Illustrated by **David Linn.** Viking, 1999. 148p. Grades 3–8.

Scary stories have a place in nearly every culture worldwide. Some offer pure entertainment, and others teach a lesson. This collection includes 22 frighteningly fun short stories.

***The Barefoot Book of Brother and Sister Tales.*** Retold by **Mary Hoffman.** Illustrated by **Emma Shaw-Smith.** Barefoot Books, 2000. 64p. Grades 3–7.

    Anybody who has a sibling knows a story or two. This book filled with stories from seven cultures from around the world may work to jog your memory. In this book the siblings complement each other and work together as heroes and heroines. Stories come from German, Cheyenne, Moroccan, Armenian, Russian, Japanese, and Sudanese roots.

***The Barefoot Book of Father and Son Tales.*** Retold by **Josephine Evetts-Secker.** Illustrated by **Helen Cann.** Barefoot Books, 1999. 80p. All ages.

    Male reading role models are desperately needed for so many young men in this world. These stories can provide a chance for fathers and sons, as well as other family members, to share and experience literature. Everyone can enjoy these stories from Greece, Germany, Egypt, Chile, Polynesia, Serbia, Scotland, Italy, and from the Chippewa tribe of North America. A great companion book is *The Barefoot Book of Mother and Son Tales,* also by these authors.

***The Barefoot Book of Giants, Ghosts and Goblins.*** Retold by **John Matthews.** Illustrated by **Giovanni Manna.** Barefoot Books, 1999. 80p. All ages.

    The theme of this book certainly will appeal to young, curious minds. There are nine stories in this collection, including tales from Norway, Australia, Ireland, China, Denmark, Scotland, and from the Hausa of West Africa, the Evenk in Siberia, and the Cheyenne of North America.

***The Barefoot Book of Mother and Son Tales.*** Retold by **Josephine Evetts-Secker.** Illustrated by **Helen Cann.** Barefoot Books, 1999. 80p. All ages.

    This book celebrates the unique bond between mother and son with beautiful stories from Nepal, France, Iceland, Siberia, Germany, Wales, and Greece, as well as from the Wabanaki Native American tribe and the Maori of Australia. A natural companion book from these authors is *The Barefoot Book of Father and Son Tales.*

***The Barefoot Book of Pirates.*** Retold by **Richard Walker.** Illustrated by **Olwyn Whelan.** Barefoot Books, 1998. 64p. All ages.

    Aye mates, this book is filled with a treasure of stories, which features mysterious tales about the pirates of the high seas. What is truth and what is fiction does not get in the way of a good story, be it from Scandinavia, Japan, or countries in between the two.

***The Barefoot Book of Princesses.*** Retold by **Caitlin Matthews.** Illustrated by **Olwyn Whelan.** Barefoot Books, 1997. 64p. All ages.

    The book presents seven delightful princess tales from around the world, with information on the origin of the story at the end. The tales are of Danish, Persian, Akamba, Kalmuck, Chinese, Iroquois, and German origin. As with other Barefoot books, each story can be read in one sitting.

***Book of Little Folk: Faery Stories and Poems from around the World.*** Collected, retold, and illustrated by **Lauren Mills.** Dial Books for Young Readers, 1997. 134p. All ages.

    Fairy stories have held a mystique aura for ages. Mills's enticing cover illustrations alone will encourage young readers to read this collection of 29 stories.

**Brill, Marlene Targ.** *Tooth Tales from around the World.* Illustrated by **Katya Krenina.** Charlesbridge, 1998. 32p. All ages.
Whether superstition or celebration, losing a tooth captures the attention of every child. This interesting book explains how past and present cultures have dealt with this natural phenomenon.

*Creation: Read-Aloud Stories from Many Lands.* Retold by **Ann Pilling.** Illustrated by **Michael Foreman.** Candlewick Press, 1997. 96p. All ages.
This collection of 16 pourquoi stories is packaged under three categories: The Creation of the World, Warmth and Light, and Creatures Great and Small. It is a nicely balanced collection from around the world.

*Dial Book of Animal Tales from around the World.* Retold by **Naomi Adler.** Illustrated by **Amanda Hall.** Dial Books for Young Readers, 1996. 80p. All ages.
Animals have been a part of the pourquoi stories of many cultures. This collection of nine stories is beautifully illustrated with the culture of origin in mind.

*Don't Read This! And Other Tales of the Unnatural.* Stories written by **Margaret Mahy, Charles Mungoshi, Susan Cooper, Roberto Piumini, Klaus Kordon, Eiko Kadono, Paul Biegel, Kit Pearson, Bjarne Reuter, Uri Orlev, and Jordi Sierra i Fabra.** Illustrated by **The Tjong Khing.** Front Street, 1998. 216p. Grades 3 and up.
This collection of 11 stories from around the world will keep readers on the edge of their seats. The work of these award-winning authors ranges in length from 10 to 25 pages and has much to offer reluctant readers.

*The Fabrics of Fairytale: Stories Spun from Far and Wide.* Retold by **Tanya Robyn Batt.** Illustrated by **Rachel Griffin.** Barefoot Books, 2000. 80p. All ages.
Stories from seven nations are found in this beautiful volume. Each page is adorned with quiltlike artwork. The stories focus on magical garments from around the world. Countries and cultures represented are Armenia, China, Hawaii, Indonesia, Jewish, Swahili, and Swedish.

**Ganeri, Anita.** *Out of the Ark: Stories from the World's Religions.* Illustrated by **Jackie Morris.** Harcourt Brace, 1996. 96p. All ages.
In this book are many wonderful stories from the most prominent religions of the world. The possibilities for understanding world cultures through contrast and comparisons abound. This is a wonderful source for including religion as part of understanding cultures.

**Gilchrist, Cherry, and Amanda Hall.** *Sun-Day, Moon-Day: How the Week Was Made.* Barefoot Books, 1998. 80p. All ages.
Since the beginning of human history, people have been curious about the origin of the sun and moon, and this book includes thoughts from cultures around the world. In addition, it explains how many cultures established the days of the week. The collection includes stories from the ancient Greeks, the Old English, the Romans, the Norse, and the Babylonians.

***The Golden Axe: And Other Folk Tales of Compassion and Greed.*** Retold by **Ruth Stotter.** Stotter Press, 1998. 184p. All ages.

This book is overflowing with worldwide stories based on the classic story, "The Kind and Unkind Girl." Besides girls, main characters in the stories may include neighbors, brothers, grown women and men, or even animals. At the end of each story are activities and a motif section to help readers make moral lesson connections.

***Grandmothers' Stories: Wise Women Tales from Many Cultures.*** Retold by **Burleigh Mutén.** Illustrated by **Sian Bailey.** Barefoot Books, 1999. 80p. All ages.

In many parts of the world, it is the women who retell stories and pass wisdom down through the ages. One need only listen to grandmothers to know that this is as true today as it was in ancient times. In this unique collection, readers will find stories from Senegal, Japan, Russia, Hawaii, Mexico, Ireland, Germany, and Sweden.

**Hausman, Gerald, and Loretta Hausman.** *Cats of Myth: Tales from around the World.* Illustrated by **Leslie Baker.** Simon & Schuster, 2000. 88p. All ages.

Cats have held a position of elegance among some cultures for centuries. Their charm can be found throughout the 10 stories in this collection. Themes include: The Creation Cat; The Trickster Cat; The Goddess Cat; The Monster Cat; and The Guardian Cat.

**Hausman, Gerald, and Loretta Hausman.** *Dogs of Myth: Tales from around the World.* Illustrated by **Barry Moser.** Simon & Schuster, 1999. 84p. All ages.

Dogs have a long and important history in many cultures. After reading these delightful stories, there is little reason to wonder why people are attracted to these animals. These tales are divided into six themes: creation, trickster, enchanted, guardian, super, and treasure.

**Hazell, Rebecca.** *The Barefoot Book of Heroic Children.* Illustrated by **Helen Chan.** Barefoot Books, 2000. 96p. All ages.

Rebecca Hazell has done a great service in creating such a timely book. If children have ever needed heroes in their lives, it surely is today. This collection includes 12 stories about heroic children from around the world, focusing on themes of bravery and determination.

**Hoffman, Mary.** *Earth, Fire, Water, Air.* Illustrated by **Jane Ray.** Dutton, 1995. 76p. All ages.

This book has an interesting format in which Hoffman covers the four elements through narrative vignettes. She combines her storytelling talents and understanding of world myths and legends with facts, story, and reflections on the future of the Earth's natural resources.

**Hoffman, Mary.** *Sun, Moon and Stars.* Illustrated by **Jane Ray.** Dutton, 1998. 76p. All ages.

Learning myths from around the world about the sun, moon, and stars enhances the study of astronomy. This collection of stories is a good resource to connect mythology and astronomy.

*In the Beginning: Creation Stories from around the World.* Told by **Virginia Hamilton.** Illustrated by **Barry Mozer.** Harcourt Brace, 1988. 176p. All ages.

This Newbery Honor book of 25 stories is as timely today as when it was released in 1988. Creation has always been a wonder, a controversy, and a mystery to people all over the world.

**Kindersley, Anabel, and Barnabas Kindersley.** *Children Just Like Me: Our Favorite Stories from around the World.* DK, 1997. 48p. Grades 1–5.

These authors truly have a lust for adventure, and this book features popular stories from 10 countries that they have visited. Perhaps it is the stories the authors have heard and collected along the way that fuel their wanderlust. These culturally embedded stories display their ability to interact with the people they meet on their journeys.

**Krull, Kathleen.** *Lives of Extraordinary Women: Rulers, Rebels on What the Neighbors Thought.* Illustrated by **Kathryn Hewitt.** Harcourt Brace, 2000. 96p. Grades 3 and up.

Women from around the world who made a difference is the central theme in this book. Each biography is brief and includes a caricature drawing. Other books in this clever series for the curious and reluctant readers are: *Lives of the Writers: Comedies, Tragedies, and What the Neighbors Thought; Lives of the Artists: Masterpieces, Messes, and What the Neighbors Thought; Lives of the Musicians: Good Times, Bad Times, and What the Neighbors Thought; Lives of the Athletes: Thrills, Spills, and What the Neighbors Thought.* A good series connection found in Part V is *Rulers and Their Times,* published by Benchmark Books.

*Listen to the Storyteller: A Trio of Musical Tales from around the World.* Illustrated by **Kristen Balouchi.** Viking, 1999. 28p. All ages.

Wynton Marsalis states in his introduction that stories are told "with words, with music, or with both, all we need to do is use our ears and our imagination." The original stories in this book are of Native American, Celtic, and Afro-Caribbean origins.

**MacDonald, Margaret Read.** *Celebrate the World: Twenty Telltale Folktales for Multicultural Festivals.* Illustrated by **Roxanne M. Murphy.** H. W. Wilson, 1994. 225p. Grades 5–12.

Celebrations abound throughout the world. This is a great collection to have available for a multicultural celebration. Everyone loves a good story. Read them with students so they can share storytelling as part of the program.

**MacDonald, Margaret Read.** *Earth Care: World Folktales to Talk About.* Illustrated by **Zobra Anasazi.** Linnet, 1999. 146p. Grades 5 and up.

In a time when conscious stewardship of the Earth is so important, MacDonald's stories are a welcome addition for any classroom or library. There are 36 folktales to read aloud to young and old. A nice companion to these stories is a poetry collection, *Mother Earth, Father Sky: Poems of Our Planet,* edited by Jane Yolen.

**MacDonald, Margaret Read (editor).** *Folklore of World Holidays.* Gale Research, 1991. 739p. Grades 5 and up.

This reference anthology of story origins, presented by days and months, is a good investment for any library. Each entry includes the traditions and historical practices associated with a given holiday. MacDonald also has included suggested resources for further exploration, and it provides useful information for the study of holidays and celebrations.

**MacDonald, Margaret Read.** *Peace Tales: World Folktales to Talk About.* Linnet, 1992. 116p. All ages.

The theme in this collection of stories is to promote peace awareness throughout the world. Each story offers the audience something to think about and discuss with others. Also included are strategies for creating peace and additional reading suggestions. Because of the popularity of this book, MacDonald created two companion videos, *Folktales of Peace* and *Folktales of Peace II,* also available through Linnet.

**MacDonald, Margaret Read.** *Tuck-Me-In Tales: Bedtime Stories from around the World.* Illustrated by **Yvonne Davis.** August House, 1996. 64p. Pre K–2.

Nationally known storyteller Margaret Read MacDonald has pulled together a very nice collection of bedtime stories from six countries around the world. Yvonne Davis's warm illustrations work as a beautiful complement to this collection for reading aloud and snuggling young audiences at bedtime.

*Magical Tales from Many Lands.* Retold by **Margaret Mayo.** Illustrated by **Jane Ray.** Dutton, 1993. 128p. All ages.

The word *magic* is most fitting for this book, which includes stories to read aloud or to retell. The 14 magical tales in this collection will mesmerize an audience.

**McCaughrean, Geraldine.** *The Crystal Pool: Myths and Legends of the World.* Illustrated by **Bee Willey.** Simon & Schuster, 1999. 144p. All ages.

This book is the fourth installment in the Myths and Legends of the World series. Like their previous books, these stories have wide appeal rooted in the rich oral traditions from many cultures. The author included explanatory endnotes to each story. Willey's playful illustrations enhance the 100 stories. Other titles included in the series are *The Bronze Cauldron, The Silver Treasure,* and *The Golden Hoard.*

*Mythical Birds and Beasts from Many Lands.* Retold by **Margaret Mayo.** Illustrated by **Jane Ray.** Dutton, 1996. 108p. All ages.

Margaret Mayo loves a good story. Together with illustrator Jane Ray, she has a special way of bringing magic to readers. This lively collection of 10 stories from around the world features birds and beasts, along with information on the origin of each story.

*Nursery Tales around the World.* Selected and retold by **Judy Sierra.** Illustrated by **Stefano Vitale.** Clarion Books, 1996. 114p. All ages.

These stories provide messages of bravery, wit, determination, and problem solving that will be meaningful to young and older readers alike. Her retellings are arranged within enticing themes, including Runaway Cookies, Incredible Appetites, Victory of the Smallest, Chain Tales, Slowpokes and Speedsters, and Fooling the Big Bad Wolf. The childlike characters take control of their situations using wit and charm instead of by force.

**Osborne, Mary Pope (compiler).** *Mermaid Tales from around the World.* Illustrated by **Troy Howell.** Scholastic, 1993. 96p. All ages.

Many a sailor has been lured by the mystique of mermaids, the sea-dwelling creatures who have fascinated people the world over for centuries. Osborne's compilation shows evidence of such claims. Readers may recognize a story or two, but they will surely enjoy those that are new to them.

**Pellowski, Anne.** *Hidden Stories in Plants: Unusual and Easy-to-Tell Stories from around the World Together with Creative Things to Do While Telling Them.* Illustrated by **Lynn Sweat.** Macmillan, 1990. 176p. All ages.
   This book is a collection of stories about plants, with possible activities to accompany them and a good bibliography. It offers a nice connection to plant studies for beginning gardeners, future botanists, or naturalists who like to tell a good story.

**Pellowski, Anne.** *The Story Vine: A Source Book of Unusual and Easy-to-Tell Stories from around the World.* Macmillan, 1984. 128p. All ages.
   Pellowski's knack for finding unique stories provides refreshing entertainment. Her stories enhance a lesson and pique interest among the curious.

**Pellowski, Anne (editor).** *A World of Children's Stories.* Illustrated by **Gloria C. Ortiz.** Friendship Press, 1993. 192p. Grades 3–6.
   Good stories need to be shared and passed down through the generations. Like Pellowski's other books, this is a nice collection of entertaining stories from around the world, edited by a master storyteller.

**Pooley, Sarah (compiler).** *Jump the World: Stories, Poems, and Things to Make and Do from around the World.* Dutton, 1997. 76p. All ages.
   This book offers enough activities to keep readers and children entertained for hours. Illustrated instructions are clear and easy to follow.

**Pullein-Thompson, Diana (editor).** *Classic Horse and Pony Stories: The World's Best Horse and Pony Stories in Their Real-Life Settings.* Illustrated by **Neal Puddephatt.** DK, 1999. 96p. All ages.
   Horse lovers can be found all over the world. This collection features 11 wonderful horse stories, both fanciful and realistic. Most are captivating scenes that have been abstracted from an original story. Two unique features of this collection are that the stories are placed in real-life settings, supported by beautiful illustrations, and that each is accompanied with a page of color photos and related horse facts. The six-book series *Magnificent Horses of the World* (published by Gareth Stevens) are good companion books.

**Ragan, Kathleen.** *Fearless Girls, Wise Women, and Beloved Sisters: Heroines in Folktales from around the World.* W. W. Norton, 1998. 352p. All ages.
   A definitive sourcebook of folktales and fairy tales, this volume is the first of its kind in featuring a variety of multicultural heroines. Its 100 stories celebrate strong female heroines across time and space. A nice companion book is *Extraordinary Girls: A Celebration of Girlhood around the World* by Maya Ajmera, Olateju Omolodun, and Sarah Strunk.

**Rosen, Michael.** *How the Animals Got Their Colors: Animal Myths from around the World.* Illustrated by **John Clementson.** Harcourt Brace, 1992. 32p. Pre K–3.
   Rosen blends his wit and humor in this collection of tales explaining how various animals got their colors. He concludes the book with source information on each story and a scientific brief about each animal.

***The Serpent Slayer: And Other Stories of Strong Women.*** Retold by **Katrin Tchana.** Illustrated by **Trina Shart Hyman.** Little, Brown, 2000. 113p. Pre K and up.

There is always a place and need for strong female characters in literature and this collection of 18 stories from around the world is a nice addition. Caldecott medalist Trina Shart Hyman's illustrations for this book add a lavish quality and strength to the women protagonists. These stories speak to young and old, female and male.

***The Seven Wise Princesses: A Medieval Persian Epic.*** Retold by **Wafá Tarnowska.** Illustrated by **Nilesh Mistry.** Barefoot Books, 2000. 96p. Grades 5 and up.

A unique and beautiful adaptation of stories from one of Persia's most famous poets, Nizami. This particular version of the poem "Haft Paykar" maintained his image of strong, virtuous, witty, and tender, passionate women, which was against the literary treatment of women at the time. A good read for older readers.

**Sierra, Judy.** *Multicultural Folktales for the Felt Board and Readers Theater.* Oryx Press, 1996. 197p. Pre K–3.

This folktale collection is a handy resource for young children that includes patterns for the felt board characters. It is a good source for beginning storytellers of all ages.

**Sierra, Judy, and Kaminski, Robert.** *Multicultural Folktales: Stories to Tell Young Children.* Oryx Press, 1991. 136p. Pre K–3.

This is a book for the inquisitive potential storyteller and for people who love to read and share stories. It includes stories, tips for good storytelling, and additional resources.

***The Songs of Birds: Stories and Poems from Many Cultures.*** Collected and retold by **Hugh Lupton.** Illustrated by **Steve Palin.** Barefoot Books, 2000. 80p. Grades 3 and up.

The combination of interesting stories with the illustrations of a noted bird illustrator provides all the ingredients of a great book for budding ornithologists, bird enthusiasts, and people who like to hear a good story. The stories are from around the world and retold through the words of an active storyteller.

***The Starlight Princess and Other Princess Stories.*** Retold by **Annie Dalton.** Embroideries by **Belinda Downes.** DK, 1999. 112p. All ages.

Few girls have never dreamed of being a princess. This book includes eight princess stories from around the world. The embroidery illustrations are incredibly detailed and a unique feature. With these precious tales, readers can keep their imaginations alive, relive a hopeful dream, compare and contrast variations, or analyze their character qualities.

***Tales for Telling from around the World.*** Selected by **Mary Medlicott.** Illustrated by **Sue Williams.** Kingfisher, 1991. 96p. Pre K–5.

This is a collection of 15 stories, some old and others new. A unique feature of these stories is that they come from cultures with oral traditions that are still active.

**Verniero, Joan, and Robin Fitzsimmons.** *One Hundred and One Read-Aloud Myths and Legends: Ten-Minute Readings from the World's Best-Loved Literature.* Black Dog & Levanthal, 1999. 192p. Grades 3 and up.

This book has enough multicultural stories for 101 days or nights. The stories are brief and concise making this a great source when time is an issue. The relatively few pictures make this collection more appealing to an older audience of children.

**Walker, Paul Robert.** *Little Folk: Stories from around the World.* Illustrated by **James Bernadin.** Harcourt Brace, 1997. 72p. Pre K–5.

From leprechauns to Inch Boy, this book includes eight stories about little characters. New and familiar tales come from Denmark, Germany, Hawaii, Ireland, Japan, North America, South Africa, and Wales.

**Waters, Fiona.** *Fairy Tales from Far and Wide.* Illustrated by **Lisa Berkshire.** Barefoot Books, 1999. 40p. Pre K–3.

This collection includes seven traditional multicultural stories from "Little Red Riding Hood" to "Anansi."

**Webber, Desiree, Ann Corn, Elaine Harrod, Donna Norvell, and Sandy Shropshire.** *Travel the Globe: Multicultural Story Times.* Illustrated by **Sandy Shropshire.** Libraries Unlimited, 1998. 275p. Grades Pre K–3.

This marvelous resource features stories from Australia, Brazil, the Caribbean islands, China, the Commonwealth of Independent States (formerly the Soviet Union), Egypt, Ghana, Greece, India, Ireland, Italy, Mexico, Vietnam, and Native American tribes of the United States. Included are stories for reading and storytelling, craft activities, finger plays, songs, rhymes, games, and media suggestions. Craft activities and flannel board stories come with directions and patterns. The authors also include annotated literature suggestions.

*When the World Was Young: Creation and Pourquoi Tales.* Retold by **Margaret Mayo.** Illustrated by **Louise Brierley.** Simon & Schuster, 1995. 76p. Pre K–5.

One of the beauties of pourquoi stories is their universality. Since the beginning of time, cultures have had a need to explain and understand the world around them and how it came into being. This collection includes 10 stories about how natural objects, phenomenon, and living things came to be.

*While the Bear Sleeps: Winter Tales and Traditions.* Retold by **Caitlin Matthews.** Illustrated by **Judith Christine Mills.** Barefoot Books, 1999. 80p. All ages.

Surviving the long days of winter is reason for celebration—especially among people who live in colder climates. The appreciation of winter, when life seems to slow down, is centuries old, as readers will see from this unique multicultural collection of stories.

*World Treasury of Myths, Legends, and Folktales: Stories from Six Continents.* As told by **Renata Bini.** Illustrated by **Mikhail Frodorow.** Harry N. Abrams, 2000. 128p. All ages.

First published in Milan, this book has 33 stories from around the world. Some stories are familiar retellings and many are new tales. Every page is filled with enticing illustrations to support the story. At the end of the book is an overview of people and places in mythology along with a list of books for further reading.

**Yolen, Jane.** *The Fairies' Ring: A Book of Fairy Stories and Poems.* Illustrated by **Stephen Mackey.** Dutton, 1999. 96p. All ages.

Mackey's fine illustrations and Yolen's eye for collecting and adapting wonderful stories and poems give readers hours of enjoyment. Yolen's introduction provides all the background you will need to enter the enchanted land of fairies.

**Yolen, Jane (editor).** *Favorite Folktales from around the World.* Pantheon Books, 1988. 448p. All ages.

Edited by a prolific writer and master storyteller, this wonderful anthology of children's favorite folktales from around the world is a priceless resource. Yolen also has produced a recording with 11 of the most popular fairy tales from around the world for pre-K through fourth-grade audiences (available through Fabulous Records, P.O. Box 8980, Minneapolis, MN 55408, fabrecords@aol.com).

**Yolen, Jane (editor).** *Gray Heroes: Elder Tales from around the World.* Penquin, 1999. 234p. All ages.

There are more than 75 tales in this collection. Some are very short, and others are lengthy. But each is filled with insight and wisdom to answer universal questions or give lessons on how to live a good life. The stories are gathered into categories such as wisdom, trickery, adventure, and a little bit of love.

**Yolen, Jane.** *Not One Damsel in Distress: World Folktales for Strong Girls.* Illustrated by **Susan Guevara.** Harcourt Brace, 2000. 116p. Grades 3–8.

This is a refreshing collection of 13 folktales in which girls are praised for their bravery and wit. As the author notes, you won't find any damsels in distress in this collection.

**Zeitlin, Steve.** *The Four Corners of the Sky: Creation Stories and Cosmologies from around the World.* Illustrated by **Chris Raschka.** Henry Holt, 2000. 144p. Grades 6–9.

This collection provides a look at the myths, legends, folklore, and theories associated with creation. A very nice inclusive book for all children in the classroom.

## Travel and More from around the World

**Ada, Alma Flor.** *Gathering the Sun: An Alphabet in Spanish and English.* Illustrated by **Simón Silva.** Lothrop, Lee & Shepard, 1997. 40p. Grades K–5.

This book is a tribute to Spanish migrant workers and an important consciousness-raising book. It helps readers recognize the all-to-often forgotten labor behind the fruits and vegetables we purchase from grocery stores. The tone and message in this poetic alphabet book speaks to all people, those who work in the fields and those who reap the benefits.

**Caballero, Jane.** *Children around the World.* Humanics, 1994. 192p. Pre K–4.

This comprehensive book introduces readers to people from around the world using native foods, music, games, and activities as resources. Caballero presents a rich variety of cultures, supported with color photos.

*A Children's Chorus.* **UNICEF.** Illustrated by 11 international artists. Dutton, 1989. 26p. Pre K–5.

This book pays respect to the rights of children throughout the world, supported with illustrations from 11 international artists. Included are the 10 principles adopted by the United Nations in 1959 that are worth reading and discussing with your students.

**Collard, Sneed B., and Action for Nature.** *Acting for Nature: What Young People around the World Have Done to Protect the Environment.* Illustrated by **Carl Dennis Buell.** Heyday, 2000. 112p. Grades 3–8.

Just as the title notes, this book is about young people making environmentally conscious decisions. Their environmental activism may inspire other students. The authors include contact information for environmental organizations.

**Danes, Emma.** *Round the World Songbook: Music and Words for Over 30 Songs.* Usborne, 1995. 48p. All ages.

Music is a universal language. Readers can travel the world through song with this handy resource, which also includes useful suggestions and notes for learning the music and guitar chords.

*For Every Child, a Better World.* **United Nations.** As told to **Louise Gikow and Ellen Weiss.** Illustrated by **Bruce McNally.** Golden Press, 1993. 24p. Pre K–4.

This book respectfully illustrates the basic human rights of children throughout the world. Part of the proceeds goes to support all of the United Nations projects listed at the end of the book.

**George, Lindsay Barrett.** *Around the World: Who's Been Here?* Greenwillow Books, 1999. 40p. Grades 1–5.

This picture book is an example of possibilities for teachers or librarians who are lucky enough to travel. Miss Lewis travels the globe while communicating with her students in an enticing format. Letters with clues encourage her students to search for the location of the animals she sees in her travels.

**Hathorn, Libby.** *The Wonder Thing.* Illustrated by **Peter Gouldthroupe.** Houghton Mifflin, 1995. 32p. Grades K–3.

This book shows how the people of the world are connected through one of our greatest natural resources: water. As readers travel through the illustrations, they will journey to all corners of the Earth.

**Hirst, Robin.** *My Place in Space.* Illustrated by **Roland Harvey.** Orchard, 1992. 40p. Pre K–5.

This is a unique book for teaching students about location and geography. Henry tells the bus driver exactly where he lives, positioning himself precisely in the universe. This book has universal connections and possibilities wherever you are located.

**Hobbie, Holly.** *Toot & Puddle.* Little, Brown, 1997. 32p. Pre K–3.

Toot and Puddle live together. Puddle likes the comforts of home, while Toot loves adventure. Toot travels the world and sends postcards back to Puddle.

**Hubbard, Woodleigh Marx.** *All That You Are.* Putnam, 2000. 24p. All ages.

Hubbard conveys a positive message, encouraging readers to follow their dreams and live their lives in a socially conscious manner. The combination of expressive illustrations and carefully chosen text carries a strong message.

**Knight, Margy Burns.** *Talking Walls.* Tilbury House, 1992. 36p. Grades 3 and up.

*Talking Walls* introduces young readers to different cultures by exploring the stories associated with walls from around the world. Knight masterfully communicates how walls can separate or hold communities together. Tilbury House also published a useful teacher's guide to accompany this book.

**Knight, Margy Burns.** *Talking Walls: The Stories Continue.* Tilbury House, 1996. 36p. Grades 3 and up.

Walls can function as a metaphor in our mind for blocking different points of view, as well as a visible physical barrier. Knight has fashioned another unique book that introduces young readers to the walls of different cultures. Fourteen vibrantly colored pastels, across two pages, take readers inside the world of each wall. This is the companion book to the first *Talking Walls* and also includes an optional teacher's guide.

**Krupinski, Loretta.** *Bluewater Journal: The Voyage of the Sea Tiger.* Harper, 1995. 32p. Grades 1–6.

This work of fiction presents another possibility of world travel. Set in the 1860s, the story is in the form of journal entries from a boy who sets sail on the *Sea Tiger* with his father.

**Krupp, Robin Rector.** *Let's Go Traveling!* William Morrow, 1992. 40p. Grades 2 and up.

This book has an adventurous format for kids with an itch to travel. Rachel Rose travels around the world through diary entries, postcards, maps, photographs, and souvenirs.

**Langen, Annette.** *Felix Explores Planet Earth.* Illustrated by **Constanza Droop.** Abbeville Press, 1997. 32p. Grades K–5.

Felix, the travel-happy rabbit, is on another world-trekking adventure. Like the other Felix books, Felix writes letters to his owner, Sophie. This book also has a fold-out map showing Felix's travel locations.

**Langen, Annette.** *Letters from Felix: A Little Rabbit on a World Tour.* Illustrated by **Constanza Droop.** Abbeville Press, 1994. 32p. Grades K–5.

This book is written in letter form and includes envelopes. Felix the rabbit sends letters to Sophie from his travels around the world while he tries to return home. The book comes complete with luggage stickers.

**Lester, Alison.** *Celeste Sails to Spain.* Houghton Mifflin, 1999. 32p. Pre K–2.

Celeste and her friends go on a series of adventures. One adventure takes place through dreams, which involve traveling to a favorite location in the world. Dreaming is one form of travel in which all can participate.

**Lewin, Ted.** *Touch and Go: Travels of a Children's Book Illustrator.* Lothrop, Lee & Shepard, 1999. 68p. Grades 5 and up.

This book is a biography filled with stories, photos, and illustrations about the places award-winning illustrator Ted Lewin has traveled. A good read for potential travelers, illustrators, photographers, and writers.

**Lobel, Anita.** *Away from Home.* Greenwillow Books, 1994. 32p. Grades 1–6.

Readers can take an alphabetic tour around the world from city to city. Each boy's name begins with the same letter as the city they are visiting. The format has many possibilities for replication in classrooms.

**Maestro, Betsy.** *The Story of Clocks and Calendars: Marking a Millennium.* Illustrated by **Giulio Maestro.** Lothrop, Lee & Shepard, 1999. 48p. Grades 5 and up.

A timely book (pun intended) for this new millennium. The historical context in this book serves as a good resource for students.

**Maestro, Betsy.** *The Story of Money.* Illustrated by **Giulio Maestro.** Clarion Books, 1995. 48p. Grades 1 and up.

With this book, readers can explore the many different forms money has taken around the world throughout history. A wonderful companion to this book is *Money* (an Eye Witness book from DK Publishing, 1990).

**Maestro, Betsy.** *The Story of Religion.* Illustrated by **Giulio Maestro.** Clarion Books, 1996. 48p. Grades 5 and up.

This book provides a nice overview of seven religions in the world. Maestro includes information about each religion's sacred book, its festivals and holidays, and the "golden rule" that is central to the faith.

**Morgan, Rowland (compiler).** *In the Next Three Seconds . . .* Illustrated by **Rod and Kira Josey.** Lodestar, 1997. 32p. Grades 3 and up.

What a cool book! Have you ever wondered how they make those amazing projections, such as it would take 17,393,459,104 jelly beans lined up end to end to circle the globe? This is the book that walks readers through the process of extrapolating numbers. I included this unusual book because of the math and science connections, along with endless global-projection possibilities when statistics reflect the Earth and its characteristics.

**Sikundar, Sylvia.** *Windows on the World: Plays and Activities Adapted from Folk Tales from Different Lands.* Illustrated by **Diane Williams.** Pacific Educational Press, 1997. 128p. Grades 4–7.

A hands-on resource for teachers, this book is a wonderful way to combine art and drama using multicultural folktale plays from Scotland, Australia, India, Korea, and Indonesia.

**Steele, Philip.** *Grasslands.* Carolrhoda Books, 1996. 32p. Grades 3–6.

Do grasslands of North America look like the grasslands of Australia? This book is part of a unique *Geography Detective* series. Each of the eight books takes readers on a journey around the globe while they learn about one geographic feature.

**Verne, Jules.** *Around the World in 80 Days.* Viking, 1996 (first published in 1873). 300p. Grades 5 and up.

For Phileas Fogg, an Englishman, the challenge to be the first person to travel around the world in 80 days results in an exciting journey, sparking enough stories for a lifetime. This classic adventure story still captures the wonder of travel, and the highly attractive Viking version is updated with pictures reflective of the times.

**Wood, Douglas.** *Making the World.* Illustrated by **Yoshi Miyazaki and Hibiki Miyazaki.** Simon & Schuster, 1998. 40p. Pre K–3.

Wood conveys a beautiful message about how the world continually depends on contributions from every living thing, including people. Each of us have a role in the world.

**Yorinks, Arthur.** *The Alphabet Atlas.* Illustrated by **Adrienne Yorinks,** with letter art by **Jeanyee Wong.** Winslow Press, 1999. 60p. Grades 3–6.

This is truly a unique atlas. The lavish illustrations bring each location to life through Adrienne Yorinks's careful choice of color and representative features of the locations Arthur Yorinks brings to life through words. Wong's lettering works well with the illustrations. This book is a starting place to learn more about geography. Visit the Winslow Press Web site for more information: www.winslowpress.com.

# Book Extensions

*A Children's Chorus* published by Dutton was a tribute to the 30th anniversary of the Declaration of the Rights of the Child by the United Nations. The book is beautifully illustrated by 11 international artists. There are 10 principles included in this Declaration of Rights for children. Each is illustrated, and a copy of the entire declaration is included at the end of the book. I emphasize one principle in particular: "The child shall be protected against all forms of neglect, cruelty, and exploitation. He shall not be the subject of traffic, in any form. The child shall not be admitted to employment before an appropriate minimum age; he shall in no case be caused or permitted to engage in any occupation or employment which would prejudice his health or education, or interfere with his physical, mental or moral development." This principle, along with the other nine, is worth sharing and discussing with your students.

The Declaration of the Rights of the Child was unanimously adopted on November 20, 1959. According to UNICEF, 2 million children have been killed in armed conflict over the last 10 years. We also know that many other violations against children have occurred around the world. The fact that nearly 250 million children work for meager wages is another statistic from the International Labor Organization worth discussing. Posting these principles at school may help others to recognize the universal rights of children and alert adults to this international effort. A useful teachers' handbook called *Human Rights for Children: A Curriculum for Teaching Human Rights to Children*

*Ages 3–12* (published by Hunter House) is a useful aide to educators who wish to teach their students about human rights for children. The United Nations also offers a variety of teaching materials at little or no cost. Contact the United Nations at 1-212-963-4475 or http://www.un.org. Contact the International Child Labor office at www.dol.gov/dol/ilab/public/media/reports/sweat/main.html. A book connection that specifically portrays child labor around the world is *Listen to Us: The World's Working Children* by Jane Springer, who worked for UNICEF for more than 10 years (published by Groundwood Books). Another is *Stolen Dreams: Portraits of Working Children* by David L. Parker, Lee Engfer, and Robert Conrow (published by Lerner). Both books work well for middle grades and up. **Social Studies, Sociology, History, Political Science**

Many of the books in this list feature people from around the world. To enhance a geography lesson, use a world map and find the location and settings mentioned in the descriptions and pictures. For more geography skills, create a map that pinpoints all the continents, nations, countries, states, provinces, cities, and towns where members of the class have friends and family. Another angle to this activity could be generating maps that show birthplaces, ancestry, or all the places your students have lived, comparing them to the present location. These activities could be done individually or as a school community. The awareness of global connections resulting from these latter two activities is enlightening. Book connections include *Who Belongs Here?* by Margy Burns Knight, and two complementary book series published by Carolrhoda Books, *Globe-Trotters Club* and *A Ticket to . . .* A great Web connection for tracking global adventures is The Odyssey at www.worldtrek.org. **Social Studies, History, Geography, Political Science**

For a math connection, calculate the air and surface miles from place to place as students move from country to country through the books. Try to follow actual routes that might be taken where airplane service is not available. At the end of your calculations, compare this to the circumference in miles and kilometers of the Earth. Do some comparative projections between the distances students travel to school, to see friends and relatives, or to go shopping or to work with the distance to another country. How many trips would students need to make from home to school compared with a trip to Moose, Wyoming? There is also a great math connection through a multibook series, *Count Your Way Through* (Lerner). These are great dual-language counting books from a host of countries around the world. This series offers the opportunity to learn how to count to 10 in another language, along with information about each country. Sweet Honey on the Rock has a marvelous recording for children, *I Got Shoes,* which has a counting song that repeats in five languages. **Math, Social Studies, Geography, Language Arts, Music**

Educators can create another math connection using the statistics we read on global happenings or phenomena. When students read a statistic, such as "the human population will increase by nine people in the next three seconds," do they wonder how the statisticians can make such a statement? The world is full of such provocative statistics. Nonfiction books are especially good sources for finding numbers. Numbers are used to bring attention to problems and issues, as well as to entertain people with trivial but interesting information. The book, *In the Next Three Seconds . . .*, compiled by Rowland Morgan, is filled with statistics and how to make numerical projections. It doesn't take long to imagine the possibilities of playing with numbers in a fun way with this book. **Math, Social Studies, Sociology, Psychology**

Teachers can demonstrate global interdependence in their classrooms. Have students check clothing and product labels in the classroom and then graph the results by country. This activity could be extended to individual homes and collectively shared and graphed on a subsequent day at school. Set up displays of items people have in their homes that were made in other countries. Students can also compare items collected during their own (or their teachers' and librarian's) foreign travels. Take time to re-create and listen to the stories that accompany the artifacts acquired firsthand. There is a good book connection found in the *Look What Came From* series (published by Franklin Watts), discussed in Part V of this book, that features products from a number of countries around the world. **Social Studies, Economics, Geography, Math**

Books such as Shelby and Trivas's *Potluck,* Morris's *Bread, Bread, Bread,* Dooley and Thornton's *Everybody Cooks Rice,* and Diane Vezza's *Passport on a Plate: A Round-the-World Cookbook for Children* can be used to discuss, cook, and demonstrate the acculturation that has taken place in our world. Food festivals or multicultural potlucks in schools are one way to celebrate a global community. Caroline Young's book *Round the World Cookbook* has some nice safety and cooking vocabulary features to consider when introducing children to serious cooking for the first time. Two great resources to add are *Multicultural Cookbook of Life-Cycle Celebrations* by Lois Sinaiko Webb and *The American Ethnic Cookbook for Kids* by Mark H. Zanger. A fun book series that focuses on ethnic cooking is *Kids in the Kitchen: The Library of Multicultural Cooking* (published by PowerKids Press). **Social Studies, Sociology, Culinary Arts, Science, Math**

The opportunity to experience ethnic food is abundant in today's transient society. What city does not have ethnic restaurants? But better still is to invite neighbors into the home. One of the most glorious times in our lives was the three years that my wife, Joy, and I were attending graduate school. As students, we lived in university housing. The apartment-like structures were meager at best, but comfortable. The best part of living there was our neighbors. Families from China, Germany, India, Iraq, Ireland, Italy, Japan, Kenya, Senegal, and elsewhere lived around us. We shared the same courtyard, clothesline, self-service laundry, and community center. The air at dinnertime was heavenly, filled with spice smells from around the world. Curiosity about all these beautiful people made us think about the best way to meet them. So we made a practice of having the families into our home to share a meal with us on a monthly basis. In return, we were invited into their homes to experience ethnic foods firsthand. What a treat! We met many wonderful people and heard some wonderful stories. Many of the people we met are still friends today that we visit or communicate with on a regular basis. Ask students, teachers, and librarians to share their stories about meeting people across cultures. Think of ways to invite ethnic groups into your school. **Social Studies, Communication, and Potentially All Subjects**

If you look closely at the format in Joanne Alfonso Pizarro's cookbook *Coming Home,* there is potential to use it for a variety of language arts activities and more. Students may conduct oral interviews and collect family stories, practicing their listening skills. Test the recipes to practice measurement, cooking, and reading. Record the recipes and stories as a way to demonstrate two styles of writing. Take photos or make illustrations to accompany the book as part of an art lesson. Design, edit, and publish the book to learn about the publishing process. Sell the book for lessons in marketing, money management, and accounting. Host an international food festival to learn organizational skills, food safety, and book promotion. Bring in adults who are experts in each of the respective fields implied in this project to enhance the learning process. **Language Arts, Social Studies, Economics, Sociology, History, Culinary Arts, Math, Science, Art**

Learning from our ancestors is one of the most important activities we can do to help understand who we are. Harriet Rohmer's edited book, *Honoring Our Ancestors,* is one of the finest tributes to this idea I have ever seen. In her book, 14 artists illustrate and write about the ancestors that have influenced their way of thinking today. Applying this concept in a classroom has great potential for student understanding of heritage and diversity. Getting students to research their heritage is a win-win situation for all the people involved. An excellent resource on how to collect family stories is *Through the Eyes of Your*

*Ancestors: A Step-by-Step Guide to Uncovering Your Family's History* by Maureen Taylor (Houghton Mifflin, 1999). If you want to simplify the task for young children, check out Eve Sanders's alphabet book, *What's Your Name? From Ariel to Zoe,* for some ideas. If you want to look at some other great examples of acknowledging ancestors, try *Sisters in Strength: American Women Who Made a Difference* by Yona Zeldis McDonough, *My Name Is Not Gussie* by Mikki Machlin, or *Seven Brave Women* by Betsy Hearne. **Social Studies, Anthropology, History, Language Arts**

Using Maya Ajmera and Anna Rhesa Versola's alphabet book, *Children from Australia to Zimbabwe: A Photographic Journey around the World,* Arthur Yorinks's, *The Alphabet Atlas,* or Anita Lobel's *Away from Home* can help classrooms research additional countries as listed under the letters of the alphabet. Students could also replicate the formats of these books as a great extension of geography skills and learning about additional cultures around the world. This activity also lends itself to student-generated illustrations. **Language Arts, Social Studies, Geography, Art**

Use Mitsumasa Anno's *All in a Day* and Marilyn Singer's *Nine O'Clock Lullaby* to help explore and study time. You can also chart the time zone changes as you travel through the countries featured in many of the books. Explore the history of time with Betsy Maestro and Giulio Maestro's *The Story of Clocks and Calendars: Marking a Millennium.* If possible, combine this with a videotape of the Public Broadcasting System's *Millennium Celebration.* **Social Studies, History, Geography, Math**

*Children Just Like Me,* by Sue Copsey, has information on establishing international pen pals. Help students set up pen pals with children around the world. Under the right conditions, this writing relationship could occur through e-mail. Also learn about Paintbrush Diplomacy, an organization that promotes international communication through the exchange of children's letters and artwork from Eve B. Feldman's book, *Birthdays! Celebrating Life around the World.* If you want to extend the art concept check out the series *Young Artists of the World* (published by PowerKids Press). **Language Arts, Art, Social Studies, Geography**

Children have always been curious about other children. Viewing pictures and reading about people their own age in faraway lands fascinates youngsters. To think that other kids might do some of the same things they do is thought-provoking. There are great ways to extend this natural curiosity and wonder. Check out the books included in this part under "Life around the World," and check out Part IV, especially those listed under "Universal Similarities." Some of my favorites include *Children Just Like Me* by Sue Copsey; *My House Has Stars* by Megan McDonald; *Whoever You Are* by Mem Fox; and *To Be a Kid* by Maya Ajmera and John D. Ivanko. For an even more fascinating connection, look for copies of the *Kids throughout History* series (published by PowerKids Press). This unique series allows young people to look back through history and compare lifestyles of today with the past. **Social Studies, History, Sociology, Geography**

Encourage students to write to people and organizations in the countries they discover in these books. Ask for free materials, such as maps and tourism information about the country. Don't forget Internet searches for additional information. Books such as *To Be a Kid* by Maya Ajmera and John D. Ivanko or *A World in Our Hands* (published by Tricycle Press) include additional resources for further information. Contact these valuable resources to extend your knowledge and understanding of the world community. **Language Arts, Social Studies, Geography**

There is a natural connection between the sciences and the study of other countries. Students can have fun researching the origins of plants, rocks, minerals, animals, and foods. Compare and contrast synthetic and natural products (for example, homeopathic remedies and synthetic prescriptions or hemp and wood products). A resource that could get students started is the *Plants We Eat* series by Lerner or Philip Steele's *Grasslands*. If you want to enhance your science units with stories or poetry, try Anne Pellowski's *Hidden Stories in Plants: Unusual and Easy-to-Tell Stories from around the World Together with Creative Things to Do While Telling Them;* Mary Hoffman's *Earth, Fire, Water, Air* and *Sun, Moon and Stars;* or Jane Yolen's *Mother Earth, Father Sky: Poems of Our Planet.* **Science, Language Arts, Geography**

Compare and contrast various countries' methods used to create toys, instruments, and clothing. Which ones use the available natural resources? Which ones require special equipment or tools to manufacture? Which ones are imports or exports? This could also lead to a discussion of the World Trade Organization and its policies on labor and the environment related to people and working conditions. Three nice book connections from the fifth part of this text are the *Crafts of the World* series (published by PowerKids Press) and *Worldwide Crafts* and *Williamson Kids Can* (both published by Gareth Stevens). **Social Studies, Geography, Economics, Art, Science**

Apply the concept of global travel to the sciences. Identify locations of plants, rocks and minerals, rivers, lakes, and animals. The possibilities abound when students look at things through a global lens. Some book connections are *Geography Detective* series (published by Carolrhoda Books) and *Plants We Eat* series (published by Lerner). The first series suggested is about similar geographical features found throughout the world, including deserts, islands, rivers, valleys, mountains, rain forests, oceans, tundra, and grasslands. *Explore the Science of Nature* series (published by Gareth Stevens); it offers individual themes such as rocks, eggs, flowers, fossils, patterns, seeds, shells, bubbles, wings, and more to explore in 36 books on nature. To make weather connections try the *Extreme Weather* series (published by PowerKids Press) or their *Natural Disasters* series; the graphic photos will capture students' attention immediately. For an animal theme, try the *Bears of the World* series (published by PowerKids Press) or *Magnificent Horses of the World* (published by Gareth Stevens). **Science, Social Studies, Geography, Sociology, Math**

Another extension could be a theme focused on endangered species. As they research and explore the information, ask students questions. Is protecting endangered species a global problem? Should we be responsible for endangered animals living on another continent? If so, why? What protection efforts are in place? Are they effective? Why was the Endangered Species Act put into effect? Has enacting the Endangered Species Act helped animals? Who were some of the people (and countries) behind this legislative act? Do you know of any animals in the United States that have been impacted by the Endangered Species Act? What North American bird was removed from the Endangered Species List in 1999? Do you live in a location that has endangered species? Can you identify them? A resource to get the class started is the January 17, 2000, issue of *Time Magazine*. This issue has a feature article on 25 of the most endangered primates: www.time.com. For some book connections, review *Endangered Animals of the Islands/Northern Continents,* a two-book set, and *Endangered,* a four-book set, both published by Gareth Stevens. Charlesbridge has two wonderful books worth exploring: *Will We Miss Them? Endangered Species* by Alexandra Wright, and *Can We Save Them?* by David Dobson. **Science, Geography, Political Science, Language Arts, Economics, Math**

Ever thought of offering students a worldview by studying record breakers? Have students read about the tallest, the shortest, the hottest, and so forth. A fascinating, full-color book series is available through Gareth Stevens. *Record Breakers* will help get students started on a world tour for the curious. There are four books in this set with the following titles: *Earth and Universe, The Living World, Machines and Inventions,* and *People and Places.* Don't forget to include the *Guinness Book of World Records*. **Science, Social Studies, Economics, Sociology, Geography, Math**

Another fascinating (and sometimes sobering) look at our multicultural world is through the environmental effects on this Earth. One great series (published by Chelsea House) is *Earth at Risk.* Titles in that series include *Acid Rain, The Automobile and the Environment, Clean Air, Clean Water, Degradation of the Land, Economics and the Environment, Environmental Action Groups, Environmental Disasters, Extinction, Global Warming, The Living Ocean, Nuclear Energy/Nuclear Waste, Overpopulation, The Ozone Layer, The Rainforest, Recycling, Solar Energy, Toxic Materials,* and *Wilderness Preservation.* Included in the series is a list of environmental organizations and contact information. **Science, Social Studies, Economics, Sociology, Geography, Math**

If you have students from many cultural backgrounds, which is common in today's classrooms, the likelihood of finding a book about each individual's culture is greater now than ever before, thanks to the publishers who have created series for this purpose. One series featuring individual countries, such as *Cultures of the World* (published by Marshall Cavendish), has more than 90 books in the set. *Major World Nations* (published by Chelsea House) has more than 80 titles. *Countries of the World* (published by Gareth Stevens) has 64 titles. *Enchantment of the World* (published by Children's Press) includes more than 50 books. For a different approach, the *Geography Detective* series (published by Carolrhoda Books) highlights geographical features found throughout the world. Some of their titles include *Grasslands, Deserts, Islands, Rivers and Valleys, Mountains, Rain Forests, Oceans,* and *Tundra.* PowerKids Press publishes *Peoples and Their Environment,* a six-book set. Charlesbridge has an incredibly illustrated set of nine books with titles including *Our Wet World, The Forest in the Clouds, Our Natural Homes, At Home in the Rain Forest, Desert Discoveries, Tundra Discoveries, At Home in the Coral Reef, This Is Our Earth,* and *At Home in the Tide Pool.* **Science, Social Studies, History, Geography, Anthropology**

One of the many wonderful teaching experiences I have had took place in an elementary school with which I collaborated. Our goal was to develop cultural understanding among the students and staff. This particular school is one that receives many new immigrants. At one point, a young Haitian refugee girl recently had arrived with her family. It wasn't long before she approached her teacher about classmates unfairly blaming her for something she didn't do because of her skin color. The young girl's self-esteem was challenged. The teacher took the time to read and discuss *The Palm of My Heart,* a book of African American poems written by kids and edited by Davida Adedjouma. The young girl took the book home over the weekend. She shared it with her siblings, wrote some of her own poetry, and proudly announced, "I felt good about being black." For another written account of this incident and more information, read "Books

That Bind: Children Use Reading to Understand Cultural Differences" by Ellie Rodgers (an article from *Idaho Statesman,* February 21, 1999, pp. 1E, 10E; www.idahostatesman.com). When children find their own life experiences mirrored in books, they receive affirmation of themselves and their culture. A natural extension is to write poetry. Before starting, I suggest reading some of the poetry from *It's a Woman's World: A Century of Women's Voices in Poetry,* edited by Neil Philip; *Mother Earth, Father Sky: Poems of Our Planet,* edited by Jane Yolen; and *This Same Sky: A Collection of Poems from around the World,* edited by Naomi Shihab Nye. **Social Studies, Geography, Sociology, Language Arts**

Displays are always attention getting, and when you make a conscious effort to have a multicultural theme, it is even better. As students decorate their school or library, encourage them to create a collage of photos, pictures, and artifacts that show people of all ages from around the world. Themes could include people smiling, working, or playing. Examples of this concept are Ann Morris's books listed under "Life around the World" and *Smiling* by Gwenyth Swain. This type of display can send a message that all people are welcome. **Social Studies, Geography, Art, Psychology**

International festivals are one way to celebrate and recognize the rich diversity in your community. There are many things to consider as students prepare for a festival. Encourage them to include as many parts of a culture as they can, from games and activities, dance, and music, to dress, food preparation, native speakers, and artifacts. A useful 48-book series to help with planning is *Festivals of the World* (published by Gareth Stevens). **Social Studies, Geography, Music, Physical Education, Culinary Arts, Science, Math, Language Arts**

Encourage children to adventure beyond food that comes from their local grocery store or restaurant. For this activity, ask students to keep track of the meals they eat over the course of one week. While recording their meals, have them list the ingredients or bring in the content labels from the packaging. Research the origins of these ingredients. If you want to limit your search, choose one ingredient such as fats, oil, or spices. One series of books to help in the geographical food search is *Plants We Eat* (published by Lerner). Another great source is *Round the World Cookbook* by Caroline Young. Eating ethnic food is one of the quickest ways to demonstrate and discuss acculturation. Don't overlook the graphing possibilities with all of the meals to record and sort. Bon Appetite! **Math, Geography, Culinary Arts, Science, Language Arts**

It is increasingly possible for students to travel around the world during holiday breaks and other times during the school year. Have students keep a journal during their travels. Encourage them to collect artifacts in print, take pictures, pick up postcards, and so forth. Have them send a postcard or letter to the class from location. If you have a highly mobile class, create a special place to display the materials. Applications abound to the language arts, geography, and other subjects. Consider models for travel writing, such as Marissa Moss's *Amelia Hits the Road,* Robin Rector Krupp's *Let's Go Traveling!,* Annette Langen's *Letters from Felix: A Little Rabbit on a World Tour,* Anni Axworthy's *Anni's Diary of France* (and the companion volume about India), and Hollie Hobbie's *Toot & Puddle* for starters. A book model for teachers is Lindsay Barrett George's book, *Around the World: Who's Been Here?* Another fascinating read is Ted Lewin's biography, *Touch and Go: Travels of a Children's Book Illustrator.* For additional formats, review these two book series: *Postcards From . . .* (published by Steck-Vaughn) and *Letters Home From . . .* (published by Blackbirch Press). **Language Arts, Social Studies, Geography, Art**

Many teachers give their students journal assignments that are associated with time travel. This can be a meaningful task, but it can also become a frustrating and confusing experience for children. I offer this bit of advice based on my personal teaching experience. Children can only write about something they know. When we assign a student to write a journal as though they were actually traveling the Oregon Trail, for example, we can't expect them to write with description and voice unless they are intimately familiar with the subject. How can you write about the Oregon Trail if you have never been there? It is possible, but not until students have read and researched the topic. Provide lots of context. Then give the writing assignment along with some models. Donald Graves, one of the founding fathers of research on children's writing, would refer to it as "setting the stage": supplying the writer with images, vocabulary, and possibilities before the pen ever touches the paper. A few book connections using a journal format are *Bluewater Journal: The Voyage of the Sea Tiger* by Loretta Krupinski, *Rachel's Journal: The Story of a Pioneer Girl* by Marissa Moss, *The Journal of Joshua Loper: A Black Cowboy* by Walter Dean Myers, *A Journey to the New World: A Diary of Remember Patience Whipple* by Kathryn Lasky, *A Gathering of Days: A New England Girl's Journal 1830–32* by Joan W. Blos, *Catherine, Called Birdy* by Karen Cushman, *The Journal of James Edmond Pease, A Civil War Union Soldier* by Jim Murphy, and *The Children of Topaz* by Michael Tunnell. There are many more examples of journal writing available. These contemporary authors carefully researched their material before writing. **Language Arts, Social Studies, History, Geography**

The books by Ann Morris, Shelley Rotner, and Gwenyth Swain have universal themes that could be replicated into a book describing your community. Children could write descriptions of the town, take pictures, and interview people in the area. For example, given a theme such as tools, students can identify the variety of tools in their home or community with photos and descriptions. They also can put them in categories such as household tools, kitchen tools, construction tools, sewing tools, and farming tools. **Language Arts, Art, Social Studies, Geography, Sociology, Anthropology, Economics, Science, Math**

Early-childhood specialist Gordon Wells stated in his book, *Meaning Makers,* that "you can predict a child's literary success in schools by the number of stories he or she has heard." This can include both storytelling and reading stories aloud to children. With this in mind, the section in this chapter on stories from around the world offers the possibility of much more than a year's supply of daily stories. A person could literally read a new story every day from the books listed and never have to repeat the same story. You might get some variations of the same folktale, but you would never have to worry about duplicating yourself. As a cautionary note from my storytelling wife Joy, don't let the fear of duplication interfere with hearing or reading a good story more than once. After all, the oral tradition is based on the premise of duplicating stories through the ages. It is good to make comparisons. A funny picture book that illustrates this point is *Wolf!* by Becky Bloom. **Language Arts, Social Studies, Anthropology, History**

One area of the curriculum that can be controversial is the study of religion. Teachers who have had success in bringing religion into their curricula have approached it in the context of studying a culture or including a balanced look at many religions from the world. One example of an all-inclusive book that looks at creationism from myth, legend, folklore, and theory is *The Four Corners of the Sky* by Steve Zeitlin. Many of the books in Part V afford the opportunity to discuss religion embedded in a culture by using multiple books. Another opportunity is to approach religion through books that handle many religions in one volume. Some suggested one-volume titles are *Sacred Places* by Philemon Sturges, *Sacred Places* by Jane Yolen, *The Story of Religion* by Betsy Maestro, *One World, Many Religions: The Ways We Worship* by Mary Pope Osborne, and *Worlds of Belief: Religion and Spirituality* by Lisa Sita. Several-volume series are the *Cultures of the World* series (published by Marshall Cavendish) and the *Places of Worship* series (published by Gareth Stevens). The *Religions of the World* series (published by PowerKids Press) is unique because the information is shared through a child's voice. **Social Studies, Sociology, Anthropology**

In more recent years, world humanitarians have taken a closer look at the potential effects of Western influence and other forms of intrusion on various cultures around the world. The loss of a cultural group is a world problem to solve as Virginia Kroll so eloquently points out in her book *With Love, to Earth's Endangered People.* Another companion book showing the potential effects of losing the wisdom of tribal shamans is Lynne Cherry and Mark J. Plotkin's book, *The Shaman's Apprentice: A Tale of the Amazon Rain Forest.* Lynne Cherry's book, *The Great Kapok Tree,* is another poignant example. Reading these books and discussing the ramifications is one way to raise social consciousness to this global problem. If you and your students take time to research other organizations and groups who are making a difference, you will begin to see potential ways to help. A good place to begin is the December 14, 1998, February 28, 2000, or Special Earth Day 2000 issues of *Time Magazine:* www.time.com. Another useful resource is the Peace Corps. Visit its Web site to see all the materials it has to offer teachers and schools: http://www .peacecorps.gov. Also check out the Working Assets Web site: GiveForChange .com for more possibilities. **Social Studies, Anthropology, Economics, Geography, Science**

The strength and wisdom of girls and women can be found throughout history, but they have often been slighted in textbooks. As a way to elevate women's role in this multicultural world, I would suggest the following titles: *Girls Who Rocked the World 2* by Michelle Roehm, *Girls Think of Everything: Stories of Ingenious Inventions by Women* by Catherine Thimmesh, *Extraordinary Girls: A Celebration of Girlhood around the World* by Maja Ajmera, Olateju Omolodun, and Sarah Strunk. Two good poetry connections are *All by Herself* by Paul Ann Whitford and *It's a Women's World: A Century of Women's Voices in Poetry* by Neil Philip. **Social Studies, Science, Math, Art, Language Arts**

*Mother Earth, Father Sky: Poems of Our Planet,* edited by Jane Yolen, is an anthology of poems with a common focus. It occurred to me that many of the poets included in this anthology have written other poems about the Earth that may be worth including in related units of study. Writing poetry on a given theme gives teachers and students room to study connected ideas, as well as to brainstorm vocabulary. These themes also can have universal connections, as evidenced by Naomi Shihab Nye, Nikki Siegen-Smith, and Jane Yolen's other books listed in the "Poetry around the World" section. A writer who has mastered the theme poetry format is Lee Bennett Hopkins. A few of his titles include *Questions: Poems of Wonder; Blast Off! Poems about Space; Good Books, Good Times!; Small Talk: A Book of Short Poems; Ring Out, Wild Bells:*

*Poems about Holidays and Seasons;* and *Extra Innings: Baseball Poems.* To consider the theme of Earth through stories, I suggest Margaret Read MacDonald's book *Earth Care: World Folktales to Talk About.* **Language Arts, Geography, Science**

Three useful guidebooks worth reviewing for multicultural sources beyond books are *Culturally Diverse Videos, Audios, and CD-ROMs for Children and Young Adults* by Irene Wood; *Kids@School.on.the.net* by Karen Krupnick; and *New Kids on the Net: Internet Activities in Elementary Language Arts* by Sheryl Burgstahler and Laurie Utterback. The first book features 900 titles covering a wide range of cultures. The guide can be purchased from Neal-Schuman by calling 1-212-925-8650 or on the World Wide Web at http://www.neal-schuman .com. The second and third books include activities connected to Web sites. They have included activity pages with corresponding Internet sites. The second book is available through The Learning Works in Santa Barbara, California. The third book is available through Allyn & Bacon at 1-800-278-3525 or www.abacon.com. One other good resource is the annual list of the Notable Books for a Global Society selected by board members from the Children's Literature Special Interest Group in the International Reading Association. The list can be found through their Web site: www.csulib.edu/org/childrens-lit or by obtaining a copy of their journal, *The Dragon Lode.* Another source for award-winning multicultural literature is *Skipping Stones Magazine,* P.O. Box 3939, Eugene, OR 97403; 1-541-342-4956 or www.efn.org/~skipping. Also review the list of references found in the "Resources for Promoting Children's and Young Adult Literature" section at the end of this book. **Social Studies, Language Arts**

I have discovered another amazing resource that has a multitude of information for teachers and librarians, as well as Internet access. Classroom Connect is a relatively new company featuring theme materials found on Web sites. Subscribers receive updates and newsletters on a growing number of themes to support their curriculum. As with all Internet materials, educators need to select what is best for their needs. Reach Classroom Connect at www.classroom.com or 1-800-638-1639. **All Subjects**

Pearl Fuyo Gaskins's book *What Are You? Voices of Mixed-Race Young People* is a book that is long overdue. Mixed-race marriages are a phenomenon that have occurred for well over 150 years in this country, but the reception that many of these couples have received has been less than cordial. We are entering a new century and must ask ourselves and the youth of today if we still harbor some of the negative sentiments associated with mixed-race unions and their offspring. This book provides a wonderful opportunity for us to explore and discuss the heritage in our communities and throughout the world. Arnold Adoff's book of poetry, *Black Is Brown Is Tan,* considered a classic for understanding biracial marriages, is still timely today. Two nice companion books are *Molly Bannaky* by Alice McGill and *Who Belongs Here?* by Margy Burns Knight. Another good resource is *Raising Black and Biracial Children;* for more information, write to RBC, P.O. Box 17479, Beverly Hills, CA 90209. **Social Studies, Sociology, History, Political Science**

---

Teachers and librarians may want to research what other professionals across the country are doing to promote a global community. One resource is the Association for Supervision and Curriculum Development's (ASCD) Global Education Network by contacting Marilyn McKnight, Milwaukee Public Schools, Forest Home School, P.O. Drawer 10L, Milwaukee, WI 53201 (1-414-645-5200), or visit the ASCD home page at www.ascd.org. Other possible contacts include the United Nations (1-212-963-4475), www.un.org; the Peace Corps (1-800-424-8580, ext. 2283), www.peacecorps.gov; *Learning the Skills of Peacemaking,* available from Jalmar Press (1-800-662-9662); *Second Step: A Violence Prevention Curriculum*, available from the Committee for Children (1-800-634-4449), www.cfchildren.org; *Rethinking Our Classrooms: Teaching for Equity and Justice* from Rethinking Schools (1-414-964-9646), www.rethinkingschools.org; National Coalition of Educational Activists (NCEA) (1-914-876-4580) or http://members.aol.com/nceaweb/; Network of Educators on the Americas (NECA), www.teachingforchange.org; Teaching Tolerance, 400 Washington Avenue, Montgomery, AL 36104; UNICEF (1-212-922-2510); National Association for Multicultural Education (NAME), www.umd.edu/name; Teacher's PET Project, 1400 16th Street, NW, Suite 30, Washington, DC 20036 (1-800-POP-1956), www.zpg.org/education. To receive a catalog of hundreds of curriculum materials, contact Social Studies School Service (1-800-944-5432), http://socialstudies.com. **All Subjects**

# Part II

# Part II

## Refugees and Homeless: Nomads of the World

In America, you are not required to offer food to the hungry. Or shelter to the homeless. There is no ordinance forcing you to visit the lonely, or comfort the infirm. Nowhere in the Constitution does it say you have to provide clothing for the poor. In fact, one of the nicest things about living here in America is that you really don't have to do anything for anybody.

—*World Traveler,* January 1997 (Advertisement from the Ad Council and the Independent Sector)

Projections on homeless in the United States range from 350,000 to 3 million people. The United States has the greatest number of homeless people in any industrialized nation. Homelessness affects people throughout the world, irrespective of age, background, and race. Children are the fastest-growing population of homeless. It is estimated that 13 million children in the United States alone live in poverty; at any given time, 200,000 children are homeless. The United States is second only to Mexico among the industrialized nations with 22.4 percent of our children living in poverty. These alarming statistics, coupled with present welfare reforms in the United States, make it clear that student awareness of the issue is critical.

I found an enlightening body of literature that exposed my own naivete of this overwhelming social problem. More than ever, teachers, librarians, and students may be in a position to aid homeless people through learning the facts, generating classroom discussions, and taking action. Because welfare reform is shifting to more state and local control, informed citizens can have a voice in the decisions. Although homelessness addresses only one segment of the multitude of needy people, President Clinton has referred to it is as our nation's biggest social problem.

A closer look at this social problem reveals a long history of the homeless in America. Carole Seymour Jones's book, *Past and Present: Homelessness,* reveals evidence of homeless dating back to the colonial period. Over the years, the number of homeless people has increased. The single most important factor to homelessness in the United States is unemployment. Most recently, this translates to people losing their jobs because of cutbacks and corporate downsizing or the rising cost of living

**51**

in combination with income levels that cannot meet basic needs. *Bye, Bye, Bali Kai* by Harriett Luger and *Pickle Song* by Barthe DeClements paint realistic pictures of the impact of such actions on families.

Natural disasters have also left many people without homes. Examples from the 1990s are the floods in Venezuela and earthquakes in Turkey. Other homeless peoples are forced into refugee status because of war, famine, poverty, political ideology, and cultural oppression. Rwanda, Ethiopia, Guatemala, and Bosnia are only four of many contemporary examples. The problem of homelessness reaches far beyond U.S. borders. Refugees form the largest group of homeless people in the world. In the last 20 years alone, the number of refugees worldwide has quintupled to an overwhelming number of more than 20 million men, women, and children.

Often the realities of refugee conditions are masked in the United States. We notice these victims more often when they are in situations in which they receive help from church-sponsored organizations or other relief agencies. For the most part, our information comes from the news media and, in a few situations, through personal accounts in books and articles. We learn from books about the emotional trauma and incomprehensible hardships many refugees endure. Some books on the subject include *When I Left My Village* by Maxine Rose Schur, *Where the River Runs: A Portrait of a Refugee Family* by Nancy Price Graff, *Year of Impossible Goodbyes* by Sook Nyui Choi, and *I Dream of Peace: Images of War by Children of Former Yugoslavia.* Refugees who manage to come to the United States are given a chance for a new life, and in many cases, a chance for life itself. As I write this book, the issue of a better chance has reached national attention with the fate of Cuban-born Elián Gonzáles. What are the pros and cons to the decision that has been made? How will his story affect the future of others fleeing to the United States? One good book connection on refugees in the United States is *Who Belongs Here?* by Margy Burns Knight.

Perhaps one of the most well known refugee tragedies of all time was the Holocaust. In this chapter, I chose not to include any books dealing specifically with the Holocaust because of its unique place in history. For a book list dealing specifically with the Holocaust, I recommend *Remember to Never Forget*, found in the March 1993 issue of *Book Links,* and two excellent literature-based resources, the two-volume set, *The Spirit That Moves Us* by Laura Petrovello and Rachel Quenk (Tilbury House), and *The Holocaust in Literature for Youth: A Guide and Resource Book* by Edward T. Sullivan. My intention was not to marginalize the refugee situation that occurred during the Holocaust, but to raise awareness of refugee and homeless situations that have received limited attention in the media and literature.

In this collection, I have provided a reflection of historical events, along with contemporary realities that have created homeless situations. In most cases, the stories are written from the perspective of the young, which helps school-aged audiences relate to the story.

It is estimated that 1.2 billion people in this world live in poverty, and many of these individuals are homeless. This equates to one-fifth of the entire world population. This segment of the world population needs special attention. By developing the theme of homelessness, I hope to raise consciousness among the educators of our youth. I believe children hold the answers, but the world will never conceive solutions until we create dialogues with and among children. The following books may serve as catalysts to initiate such dialogue with your students and ultimately encourage them to change the plight of the homeless and of refugees. I introduce these books with words from renowned linguist Noam Chomsky, considered to be one of the world's greatest intellectuals: "We don't know that honest and dedicated effort will be enough to solve our problems; however, we can be quite confident that the lack of such efforts will spell disaster."

# Picture Books

**Balgassi, Haemi.** *Peacebound Trains.* Illustrated by **Chris K. Soentpiet.** Clarion Books, 1996. 48p. Grades 2 and up.

Sumi is lonesome for her mother who has joined the U.S. Army and is away on basic training. Her concept of sacrifice and separation changes when she learns about her mother and grandmother's escape from Korea and their arrival in the United States.

**Bunting, Eve.** *December.* Illustrated by **David Diaz.** Harcourt Brace, 1997. 34p. Grades K and up.

Simon and his mother live in a makeshift home of cardboard and plywood scraps. On Christmas Eve, they are determined to celebrate in their own special way. Then an unexpected visitor knocks on their shanty, and the evening's events take on a new meaning.

**Bunting, Eve.** *Fly Away Home.* Illustrated by **Ronald Himler.** Clarion Books, 1991. 32p. Grades K and up.

This story is told from the viewpoint of a young boy who is homeless and living with his father in the airport. They must never stay in the same place too long so as to avoid attention from the airport security. While the boy's father is working to save enough money for housing, others in the same predicament look out for the boy.

**DiSalvo-Ryan, DyAnne.** *Uncle Willie and the Soup Kitchen.* Morrow, 1991. 32p. Grades K–3.

Uncle Willie volunteers in a soup kitchen on a weekly basis. He also picks up his nephew from school every day. One day, when school is not in session, Uncle Willie takes his nephew to help in the kitchen, where an understanding of homelessness becomes a social consciousness-raising experience.

**Franklin, Kristine L., and Nancy McGirr (editors).** *Out of the Dump.* Lothrop, Lee & Shepard, 1995. 56p. Grades 3 and up.

This book is a collection of photos and narratives by children who describe their life in the Guatemala City dump. The vision for this book, which uses the children's pictures and descriptions, came when Nancy McGirr was taking photos of the dump. She noticed many children rummaging through the garbage when they should have been in school. The proceeds from this book allow many of these children to attend school and help to support their families.

**Hathorn, Libby.** *Way Home.* Illustrated by **Gregory Rogers.** Crown, 1994. 329p. Grades K–6.

 This powerful book is filled with images of streets and alleys as the reader travels with a young homeless boy. Shane befriends a kitten, and they make their way through the obstacles to "his home."

**Hughes, Monica.** *Handful of Seeds.* Orchard, 1996. 32p. Grades 2 and up.

 After Concepcion's grandmother dies, she must leave her home because her landlord knows he can find a family who will have more hands to do more work for him. Concepcion takes to the barrios the packet of seeds and the knowledge of gardening that she gained from her grandmother. Her gardening talents become a source of food for many other homeless children she meets.

**Kilborne, Sarah S.** *Leaving Vietnam: The Story of Tuan Ngo, A Boat Boy.* Illustrated by **Melissa Sweet.** Simon & Schuster, 1999. 32p. Grades 3 and up.

 Fleeing Vietnam during the 1970s required strength, courage, and hope for many refugees. This is a simplified version of the events that so many faced as they fled for freedom. The story line of helping and consideration for youth will appeal to a wide audience.

**Knight, Margy Burns.** *Who Belongs Here? An American Story.* Illustrated by **Anne Sibley O'Brien.** Tilbury House, 1993. 40p. Grades 3–8.

 This book serves as a reminder to Americans of their origins, from the first settlers to recent arrivals. Knight and O'Brien present a contemporary scenario for considering the issue of new arrivals to America.

**Kroll, Virgina.** *Shelter Folks.* Illustrated by **Jan Naimo Jones.** William B. Eerdmans, 1995. 40p. Grades 2–5.

 Joelle, her mother, and her younger brother, Eli, are forced to move into a shelter home. For the first time, Joelle realizes their new home is right in the neighborhood where she has always lived. Keeping her new living situation a secret from her classmates is difficult until she realizes that caring and family are most important.

**Marx, Trish.** *One Boy from Kosovo.* Photographs by **Cindy Karp.** HarperCollins, 2000. 24p. Grades 3 and up.

 In 1998 and 1999, war drove nearly 1 million Albanians out of their homes. This story is about one Kosovoan boy Edi and his family. The story is entirely set in the Brazda, a refugee camp in Macedonia. A moving story of present-day refugee conditions in a country that has a long history of struggle for independence.

**McCully, Emily Arnold.** *Little Kit, or The Industrious Flea Circus.* Dial, 1995. 32p. Grades 2 and up.

 Set in the 1800s, Kit passes herself off as a boy and agrees to work for a man to care for his "novelty act." Soon this homeless waif finds herself at the mercy of this tyrant but strikes out on her own once again, this time finding good fortune.

**Park, Frances, and Ginger Park.** *My Freedom Trip: A Child's Escape from North Korea.* Illustrated by **Debra Reid Jenkins.** Boyds Mills Press, 1998. 32p. Grades 3 and up.

This is a heartfelt, true story based on the authors' mother, who escaped from Korea as a small child. That night, Soo reached freedom and her father on the other side of the river, but her mother was left behind and became a victim of the Korean War. Soo never saw her again.

**Polacco, Patricia.** *I Can Hear the Sun.* Philomel, 1996. 32p. Grades 3 and up.

Fondo, a young boy who lives in a shelter home, befriends Stephanie Michele, a park naturalist. They develop a special relationship with the geese in the nearby park. Fondo has a way of communicating with a blind goose. His mysterious departure leaves readers pondering the fine line between truth and fiction.

**Rosen, Michael (editor).** *Home: A Collaboration of 30 Distinguished Authors and Illustrators of Children's Books to Aid the Homeless.* HarperCollins, 1992. 32p. Grades K and up.

This book is a collection of narratives and poetry about home. Each author and illustrator expresses through words and pictures his or her perception of home. This volume is another of Rosen's fine collaborative editions for humanity.

**Schur, Maxine Rose.** *When I Left My Village.* Illustrated by **Brian Pinkney.** Dial, 1996. 64p. Grades 3 and up.

Menelik, a young Ethiopian refugee tells the story of his family's flight to Israel. This award-winning book is a compelling drama of a family's race for survival.

**Sendak, Maurice.** *We Are All in the Dumps with Jack and Guy.* HarperCollins, 1993. 56p. All ages.

In his classic style, Sendak illustrated his version of two nursery rhymes that offer a satirical look at treatment and conditions of the homeless. The characters' faces and images are likely to create empathy among readers and listeners.

**Shea, Pegi Dietz.** *The Whispering Cloth.* Illustrated by **Anita Riggio.** Boyds Mills Press, 1995. 32p. Grades 3 and up.

Mai's *pa'ndau* (embroidered story blocks) illustrate the circumstances that brought her and her grandmother to the refugee camp. The Hmong were forced to leave their homeland in southwest China. Many have relocated in the United States, but others are still in transition in Southeast Asia. Another author/artist who uses story quilts is Faith Ringgold. For a journey connection, teachers might want to specifically check out Ringgold's *Aunt Harriet's Underground Railroad in the Sky.*

**Testa, Maria.** *Someplace to Go.* Illustrated by **Karen Ritz.** Albert Whitman, 1996. 32p. Grades 3–6.

With realistic and touching illustrations, this story is a snapshot of Davey's activities and thoughts one afternoon as he bides his time for the shelter to open. Avoiding drugs, playing with a friend, and sleeping in the library are all part and parcel of his long wait to meet his mother and older brother at the shelter.

**Wild, Margaret.** *Space Travelers.* Illustrated by **Gregory Rogers.** Scholastic, 1992. 32p. Grades K–3.

Zac and his mother, Mandy, sleep in a rocket ship. This playground equipment offers them some comfort in their imaginary space travels and dreams of their own home with a real bed and bath. When a temporary housing opportunity arises, they entrust their spaceship to a fellow homeless lady.

**Wyeth, Sharon Dennis.** *Something Beautiful.* Illustrated by **Chris K. Soentpiet.** Doubleday, 1998. 32p. Grades K–5.

A young girl searches her neighborhood for the meaning of the word *beautiful*. She sees trash, dark alleys, homeless people, and graffiti. When she asks the people in her neighborhood what beautiful is, they each have their own unique idea. Her self-discovery ends in a beautiful act of kindness.

# Fiction

**Ackerman, Karen.** *Leaves in October.* Atheneum, 1991. 128p. Grades 3–7.

Livvy is convinced that her dad, Poppy, will find work soon. If that happens, she, Younger (her brother), and Poppy will move out of the shelter home. When Poppy does find work, their situation changes, but not as Livvy had planned. A very heartfelt look at a family in a desperate situation.

**Bat-Ami, Miriam.** *Two Suns in the Sky.* Front Street/Cricket Books, 1999. 220p. Grades 6 and up.

This refugee story involves an American Jewish girl and a Yugoslavian refugee. The setting is right after World War II. The tension of a first love and ethnic barriers is captivating right to the end.

**Buss, Fran Leeper.** *Journey of the Sparrows.* Dutton, 1991. 160p. Grades 5 and up.

After she is smuggled into the United States as an illegal alien, 15-year-old Maria struggles to provide for her expectant sister and young brother. Other illegal aliens and a kind Catholic priest help Maria. She does her best to send money home to El Salvador to help the rest of her destitute family.

**Carlson, Natalie Savage.** *The Family under the Bridge.* Illustrated by **Garth Williams.** Harper & Row, 1958. 112p. Grades 4 and up.

Armand, a "confirmed" hobo in Paris, is won over by three children and their mother, who have recently become homeless. His knowledge of the streets helps to protect them, and in the end, their hopes for a better future touch his life in a way he never imagined. A timeless story.

**Choi, Sook Nyui.** *Year of Impossible Goodbyes.* Houghton Mifflin, 1991. 176p. Grades 5 and up.

This is an emotionally charged story of a North Korean family who must endure the military forces of Japan and Russia during and after World War II. Ten-year-old Sookan and her family encounter one hardship after another, as their people struggle under one dictatorship after another. Their only hope is to escape to American-controlled South Korea.

**Crew, Linda.** *Children of the River.* Bantam Doubleday, 1989. 213p. Grades 6 and up.

Cambodian refugees who came to work the land near the author's home inspired this captivating story. Through the eyes of a teenage girl, Crew describes the move to the United States and the conflict between Cambodian and American culture.

**Curtis, Christopher Paul.** *Bud, Not Buddy.* Delacorte Press, 1999. 243p. Grades 4 and up.

Winner of the Newbery Award in 2000, this book is charged with humor and emotion from the first page to the last. The year is 1936. Times are tough because of the Great Depression. Ten-year-old Bud has been bounced around between foster homes and the orphanage, and he has had enough of this life. His mother had given him a few clues about who his father might be, and Bud is determined to find out the truth. He sets out to find Herman E. Calloway, a bandleader and bass player.

**Cushman, Karen.** *Midwife's Apprentice.* Clarion Books, 1995. 122p. Grades 5 and up.

Known only as "Brat," a homeless girl during the medieval era has her share of troubles in this Newbery Award winner. After a midwife takes her in, Brat's life is filled with many challenges, but she has gained a home, food, midwifery skills, and the name Alyce, which gives her a new start in life.

**DeClements, Barthe.** *Pickle Song.* Viking, 1993. 160p. Grades 4–8.

Paula learns that her new friend, Sukey, has been sleeping in her car. She wants to help out but is faced with family problems of her own. A realistic look at difficult times of unemployed families.

**DeFelice, Cynthia.** *Nowhere to Call Home.* Farrar, Straus & Giroux, 1999. 200p. Grades 4 and up.

The story takes place during the Great Depression. Frances Elizabeth Barrow, "Frankie Blue," discovers the hobo lifestyle when she takes to riding the trains. DeFelice paints the realities of the homeless conditions during this period in an emotional page-turner.

**Doherty, Berlie.** *Street Child.* Orchard, 1993. 154p. Grades 5 and up.

Set in England during the 1860s, Jim Jarvis is forced to live in the streets after his mother dies. His older sister was fortunate enough to be hired out for room and board. Jim is left to wander the streets until he bands with other homeless youth. Their condition inspired a doctor to open the first children's refuge in London.

**Fenner, Carol.** *The King of Dragons.* Simon & Schuster, 1998. 160p. Grades 4–7.

Ian and his Vietnam-vet father have been living in the streets. Their residence is an abandoned courthouse. The disappearance of Ian's father will have readers riveted to the end.

**Fleischman, Sid.** *Whipping Boy.* Greenwillow Books, 1986. 96p. Grades 3–8.

Jemmy of the streets finds himself in a predicament in the king's palace, where he has been singled out to stand in as the "whipping boy" for the unruly Prince Brat. Through happenstance, they both wind up in the streets and fleeing for their lives. Jemmy's courage and knowledge of the street becomes a lesson in humility for the prince, and two unlikely companions become friends.

**Fox, Paula.** *Monkey Island.* Orchard, 1991. 160p. Grades 4–8.

Clay Garrity has been left to fend for himself. His father left one night after an argument with his mother, and Clay has not seen his mother for several days. The reality of living in the streets or of being taken away by social workers are Clay's options as he sees them. He chooses life in the streets. He meets two other people living without homes, Buddy, an adolescent African American, and Calvin, an older man. The compelling events and outcome of the story are very convincing.

**George, Jean Craighead.** *The Missing Gator from Gumbo Limbo.* HarperCollins, 1992. 148p. Grades 4–8.

Liza K. and her mother live in the Florida Everglades and cannot afford housing with her mother's limited income. While finding solace in the wildlife and fauna of the Everglades, Liza K. takes special notice of an old alligator. After the alligator turns up missing, she is determined to find out why.

**Hamilton, Virginia.** *The Planet of Junior Brown.* Macmillan, 1971. 240p. Grades 6 and up.

Three people from diverse lifestyles find solace in each other's company. Junior, an overprotected, overweight, musical prodigy spends his day in the school basement with Mr. Pool, a teacher turned janitor, and Buddy, a homeless teenager. Their varying personalities connect in this heartfelt drama of sanity, survival, and life. This is a Newbery Honor book.

**Ho, Mingfong.** *The Clay Marble.* Houghton Mifflin, 1991. 163p. Grades 5 and up.

This compelling drama of life set in a Cambodian refugee camp is told through the eyes of preadolescent Dara. Her hopes and dreams must override the hardships refugees face as they struggle to return to their homeland. Ho created this story from her experience doing volunteer work at the refugee camps.

**Holman, Felice.** *Slake's Limbo.* Simon & Schuster, 1974. 126p. Grades 5 and up.

Everyone pushes around Aremis Slake until he takes refuge in the subways of New York City and sets up housekeeping. By using his wits, Aremis satisfies most of his needs, including human contact and compassion with those who become regulars in his newspaper "business." This story is an all-too-real and accurate portrayal of the "unseen" in major metropolitan areas.

**Holman, Felice.** *Wild Children.* Puffin Books, 1985. 152p. Grades 5 and up.

This story is set in Moscow following the Russian Revolution of 1917. Alex returns home from an outing and finds his family gone. He is forced to live in the streets and becomes one among hundreds of homeless children. This is a captivating work of historical fiction.

**Holtwijk, Ineke.** *Asphalt Angels.* Front Street, 1995 (English translation, 1999). 184p. Grades 5 and up.

Alex has been thrown out of the house by his abusive father and must turn to living in the streets of Rio de Janeiro. He joins the Asphalt Angels, a gang living in the streets. This moving story puts readers face-to-face with realities of street life. Alex has a will to survive in a world with few opportunities.

**London, Jonathan.** *Where Is Home?* Viking, 1995. 89p. Grades 4–8.

Aaron and his father set out for California, hoping for a fresh start, but they end up on the street when Aaron's father is unable to secure work. They encounter many personalities among the homeless, both good and bad. In their struggle for survival, Aaron and his father become separated. The difficulties associated with finding homeless kin unfolds into a thought-provoking story.

**Luger, Harriet.** *Bye, Bye, Bali Kai.* Harcourt Brace, 1996. 150p. Grades 4–8.

Suzie's father is laid off from work, and her mother's income is not enough to pay the rent and put food on the table. While trying to keep their situation secret from her friends at school, Suzie's family soon finds themselves desperately living out of their car.

**Mikaelsen, Ben.** *Sparrow Hawk Red.* Hyperion, 1993. 185p. Grades 5 and up.

Ricky Diaz lost his mother in a mysterious plane crash, which results in his father leaving his job with the CIA. Ricky uncovers evidence that a drug-smuggling ring may have arranged his mother's death. In his search for the truth, Ricky leaves Texas headed for Mexico. He befriends homeless people, both out of need to survive and for information that may expose the smuggling operation.

**O'Dell, Scott.** *Sarah Bishop.* Houghton Mifflin, 1980. 184p. Grades 5 and up.

After the death of her family, Sarah Bishop is forced into exile when both sides of the Revolutionary War accuse her of being a spy. Sarah attempts to survive the winter in a mountain cave, and readers follow a compelling adventure of hope and life for a girl without a country.

**Orlev, Uri.** *Lady with the Hat.* Houghton Mifflin, 1995. 192p. Grades 6 and up.

As the only survivor from his family of the Holocaust, teenaged Yulek returns to his former home in Poland, only to find it occupied by a Communist Party leader. With mixed feelings, he and other Polish refugees are forced to seek refuge in Palestine. Later, his only living relative sees a newspaper photograph of the Polish refugees seeking freedom in Palestine. His aunt, who had moved away from Poland before the war, thinks one of the persons in the photo (Yulek) looks like a member of her family. Her search for the truth will keep readers on the edge of their seats.

**Schnur, Steven.** *The Shadow Children.* Illustrated by **Herbert Tauss.** Morrow, 1994. 88p. Grades 3–8.

This story is set in France and takes place after World War II. One summer, Etienne, a young boy, is visiting is grandfather near the town of Mont Brulant. While adventuring on horseback near the farm, Etienne discovers children living in the woods. This remarkable award-winning story will hold readers' attention to the end.

**Spinelli, Jerry.** *Maniac Magee.* Little, Brown, 1990. 184p. Grades 3 and up.

This Newbery Award winner deals with many social issues, including homelessness. Maniac Magee, an inner-city legend, is a friend to all regardless of what part of town someone comes from. His survival conditions make a great springboard for critical discussions about many present-day social issues.

**Wilson, Jacqueline.** *Elsa, Star of the Shelter.* Illustrated by **Nick Sharratt.** Albert Whitman, 1995. 208p. Grades 3–7.

This is an upbeat story of a homeless family told from the perspective of Elsa, a young girl. She loves to tell jokes (included in the text) and is constantly trying to win friends and help her mother, who experiences fits of depression. Although the setting is England, Wilson clarifies many explanations of British terminology with American words.

# Nonfiction

**Berek, Judith.** *No Place to Be: Voices of Homeless Children.* Houghton Mifflin, 1992. 148p. Grades 5–8.

    Poignant stories are unveiled in this thought-provoking book through the words of more than 30 children from New York City that Berek interviewed. The format states the problems and realities of and statistics about homelessness, flanked by student voices.

**Budhos, Marina.** *Remix: Conversations with Immigrant Teenagers.* Henry Holt, 1999. 145p. Grades 6 and up.

    Budhos spent several years traveling the United States, talking and collecting interviews with recent teen immigrants. The portraits she paints of 14 youth struggling to fit into a new country, while adapting to a new set of cultural values and a new school, are poignant and insightful. Selecting some of these vignettes to share with adults and teens who interact with new immigrants would help them to more fully understand their struggles.

**Graff, Nancy Price.** *Where the River Runs: A Portrait of a Refugee Family.* Photography by **Richard Howard.** Little, Brown, 1993. 72p. Grades 3–6.

    A Cambodian mother and her elementary-school-aged sons came to the United States to begin a new life. This story follows them through daily routines as they make the transition.

**Greenberg, Keith Elliot.** *Erik Is Homeless.* Photographs by **Carol Halebian.** Lerner, 1992. 40p. Grades 3–6.

    This book is a photographic narrative about a homeless boy and his mother who take part in the holistic Homes for the Homeless program in New York City. The program gives both parents and children educational opportunities to enable their future lives. Only 6 percent of the program's graduates become homeless again, compared with 40 percent in other programs available in the city.

**Greenberg, Keith Elliot.** *A Haitian Family.* Lerner, 1998. 56p. Grades 3–8.

    As citizens born in the United States, it is often difficult for us to imagine the hardships and dangers that refugees face once they leave their homeland. This is one family's story, depicting the events surrounding their journey to the United States. This book is part of a series, *Journey between Two Worlds*, that features refugee families from Armenia, Bosnia, Eritrea, Guatemala, the Hmong, Kurdistan, Liberia, Mien, Nicaragua, Russia, the Sudan, and Tibet.

**Hurwitz, Eugene, and Sue Hurwitz.** *Working Together against Homelessness.* Rosen, 1994. 64p. Grades 5 and up.

    The Hurwitzes use a provocative, consciousness-raising questioning format in their book. Scenarios, often presented in a dialogue style, reflect how many people are volunteering to help the homeless. Children and adults from any community can generalize the examples in this book to take action in their community.

**Hyde, Margaret O.** *The Homeless: Profiling the Problem.* Enslow, 1989. 96p. Grades 5 and up.

This book uses an ethnographic approach to describe people who are homeless, telling readers about where they live, the challenges they face, and the services available to them. Hyde also offers suggested courses of action to aid the homeless.

*I Dream of Peace: Images of War by Children of Former Yugoslavia.* **UNICEF.** Written and illustrated by children from the former Yugoslavia. HarperCollins, 1994. 80p. Grades K and up.

This is a moving book filled with stories, poems, and illustrations from many children who experienced war and refugee conditions firsthand. There clearly is an element of pain and sadness in many of the entries, but there is also hope for a brighter future.

**Kosof, Anna.** *Homeless in America.* Franklin Watts, 1988. 110p. Grades 5 and up.

This book describes the homeless in America. Included are sections on children, a day in the life of a homeless person, and the constant search for shelter. The Heights Project in New York City is profiled as one example of success; it provides living space and educational training for homeless people.

**Nichelason, Margery G.** *Homeless or Hopeless.* Lerner, 1994. 112p. Grades 5 and up.

In her approach to understanding the problem, Nichelason raises several important questions for readers to consider. Do we as a society have a moral obligation to help the homeless? If so, is it the responsibility of the government to help the homeless? Is it the job of private charities? Or is it time for the homeless to take responsibility for themselves?

**Olson, Tod.** *The Good Fight: Stories about Real Heroes.* Scholastic, 1999. 36p. Grades 3–6.

This is a collection of brief biographies of six heroic people from the past and present. The final entry is about Iqbal Masih, who only lived to the age of 13. Iqbal's work and tragic murder gained the world's attention toward forced child labor. Other heroes featured are Chief Joseph, Irene Gut Updyke, Rachel Carson, Barbara Johns, and Chico Mendes.

**Rozakis, Laurie.** *Homelessness: Can We Solve the Problem?* Henry Holt, 1995. 64p. Grades 5 and up.

A very informative book that identifies the problems associated with homelessness. Rozakis carefully identifies the causes, the people most affected, the myths associated with homeless victims, and the daily burdens homeless people face. She also shares many positive attempts at solving this social problem.

**Seymour-Jones, Carole.** *Past and Present: Homelessness.* New Discovery Books, 1993. 48p. Grades 5 and up.

This historical look at homelessness devotes much of the text to the causes of homelessness, such as war, natural disasters, accidents, and limited natural resources, that result from politics, acts of God, and the struggle for power. The information is presented in a straightforward, factual format.

**Trier, Jean.** *United Nations High Commissioner for Refugees.* New Discovery Books, 1994. 64p. Grades 6 and up.

This is an emotionally charged book with many photos and actual accounts gathered from refugees around the world. Also included are a time line of the United Nations' actions related to refugees, a glossary of terms, and sources for additional information.

**Walgren, Judy.** *The Lost Boys of Natinga: A School for Sudan's Young Refugees.* Houghton Mifflin, 1998. 44p. Grades 5 and up.

This is an informational book showing the plight of Sudanese refugees. The act of literacy has some serious implications for the children featured in this book. Raising social consciousness is their only hope.

**Weitzman, Elizabeth.** *Let's Talk about Staying in a Shelter.* PowerKids Press, 1995. 24p. Grades K–4.

This book can help young children understand the realities of living in a shelter. The language and information are intended to help ease students' concerns and fears. Kids learn they are not alone in the crisis situation they face.

**Wolf, Bernard.** *Homeless.* Orchard, 1995. 48p. Grades 3–6.

This story is narrated through the eyes of an eight-year-old boy whose family is experiencing a homeless crisis. Readers walk through the changing of schools, finding a place to live, getting help from the caseworker, accepting charity, and dreaming of becoming "somebody who really matters."

**Zamenova, Tatyana.** *Teenage Refugees from Russia Speak Out.* Rosen, 1995. 64p. Grades 7 and up.

This book is a collection of insightful vignettes through the words of teenage refugees from Russia. The true stories are based on their experiences, beginning with their departure from Russia through their transition to living in the United States.

# Book Extensions

Homelessness can happen to many different peoples anywhere in the world. Natural disasters such as floods, earthquakes, and tornadoes can destroy homes. Job loss can destroy a family's means of survival; it is estimated that nearly 50 percent of all Americans are one paycheck away from homelessness. The severity varies depending on the type of disaster, the location of the individuals, and the relief available to them. Three excellent book connections that reveal the difficult fact that stable families can lose their homes are *Bye, Bye, Bali Kai* by Harriet Luger, *Elsa, Star of the Shelter* by Jacqueline Wilson, and *Homeless* by Bernard Wolf. Have students collect news stories from newspapers, magazines, the Internet, and local relief organizations such as the Red Cross. With this information, they can do location checks, mathematical projections on affected people, and estimations of damage costs. They can also brainstorm about how they might help. **Social Studies, Geography, Economics, Sociology, Health**

Students can research the resources their community provides to aid the homeless. Based on their findings, they might come up with a plan of action that could become a community-service project. Two books that provide resource possibilities are *Homeless or Hopeless* by Margery G. Nichelason and *Working Together against Homelessness* by Eugene Hurwitz and Sue Hurwitz. One organization that can provide information is the National Coalition for the Homeless. In June 1999, it produced a provocative paper titled *Homeless Families and Children: NCH Fact Sheet #7*. The paper can be accessed at http://nch.ari.net/families.html. **Social Studies, Economics, Health**

Children are the fastest-growing segment of the worldwide homeless population. Some fascinating book connections include *Street Child* by Berlie Doherty, *No Place to Be: Voices of Homeless Children* by Judith Berek, *Nowhere to Call Home* by Cynthia DeFelice, the *Children in Crisis* series published by Blackbirch Press, and *Monkey Island* by Paula Fox. In addition to these books, read "10 Principles for Children" from the United Nations, which were adopted in 1959. You can read them in *A Children's Chorus* (published by Dutton) or by going to the United Nations Web site www.un.org. After students become informed of this global problem through their reading and classroom discussions, they can brainstorm possible solutions and plans of action to educate their legislators. For interesting examples, refer to the December 21, 1998, issue of *Time Magazine* www.time.com, which features a story, *The Children's Crusade,* about fourth- and fifth-grade social activists in Aurora, Colorado, who raised funds to buy the freedom of slaves in Sudan, Africa. A second story, published June 26, 2000, features a school in Phoenix, Arizona, that helped a homeless child from the streets get into college. For more examples of youth as social activists, read the book extensions in the fourth part of this text. **Social Studies, History, Geography, Political Science, Language Arts, Math**

When students hear about crisis situations, they might begin to think about the best ways to exercise their power. It may be through a variety of means, including letter or e-mail writing to people in power, food and clothing collection, donations, fund-raising, or by directly helping refugee families who have arrived in their schools and communities. Students can help in many ways right in their own towns. Have personnel from the Red Cross or other relief organizations come and speak to your students. Do not overlook church organizations that support mission work in other countries as a resource. Part of the fine print in the advertisement with which I opened this chapter included a number to call for volunteer or donation possibilities around the world (call 1-800-55-GIVE5). Given our living conditions we must ask if developing an empathy toward others is worth acquiring. Three books that offer more insight on the problems and possible solutions are *Homelessness: Can We Solve the Problem?* by Laurie Rozakis, *Working Together against Homelessness* by Eugene Hurwitz and Sue Hurwitz, and *United Nations High Commissioner for Refugees* by Jean Trier. **Social Studies, Political Science, Sociology, Economics, Math, Language Arts**

Students can interview refugees in their community and put together a class book of refugee stories. Interviewees could create original artwork to become part of the book. Check with state humanities councils for possible funding. A good book connection for this project is *I Dream of Peace: Images of War* by children of former Yugoslavia. **Social Studies, History, Language Arts, Art**

An insightful simulation experience can be created in your classroom by transforming the class into another country for a day. A different language can be spoken and ethnic food can be served. Modify instruction so all children in the room can begin to feel what it is like to be in a new country. Anyone who has traveled to another country where he or she did not speak the language can quickly relate to the intention behind this exercise. **Social Studies, Geography, Culinary Arts, Language Arts**

As students read the statistics on homelessness, they can make mathematical projections and ratio estimates on their community and state populations. For example, the projected number of refugees in the world is 20 times the entire population of Idaho. Many of the books in the nonfiction section of this chapter include statistics on refugees and the homeless. For information by state, contact the United States Conference of Mayors, 1620 Eye Street, NW, 4th Floor, Washington, DC 20006-4005 (1-202-293-7330) and ask for their publication, *A Status Report on Hunger and Homeless in America's Cities* (1998). There may be a charge for the document. Also check out The Hunger Site at www.thehungersite.com. **Math, Social Studies, Geography, Language Arts**

Children are the future, but we also have reached an interesting point in our history where the senior citizen population is now equivalent to the adolescent population. The ramifications of this statistic are worth discussing with the students in our classrooms. One statistic that may help you get started is the number of working-age people compared with nonworkers in the United States. Today that ratio is 3 to 1. By 2030, it is predicted that the ratio of workers to nonworkers, without any reform efforts, will be 1.5 to 1. What does this mean for immigrants who already are needed in the workforce? What does it mean for government spending on youth versus that spent for senior populations? To read more about these statistics, read the January/February 1999 issue of *Foreign Affairs.* **Social Studies, Economics, Sociology, Political Science, Math**

---

The refugee series, *Journey between Two Worlds* (published by Lerner) is unique in format. Each book in the series follows one family's plight from their homeland to America. Another compelling book that looks at refugee families is Nancy Price Graff's *Where the River Runs: A Portrait of a Refugee Family.* Tatyana Zamenova's book, *Teenage Refugees from Russia Speak Out,* is another source of refugee stories. The realities and stories that surround each family's circumstance are worth sharing and discussing with students. These books also encourage similar projects of collecting the stories from refugees who have relocated to your community. The more we hear these stories, the more empathy and understanding we gain toward events that seem distant from our homeland. I would like to share one example of how a book at the right moment and context made a difference in a classroom. My wife, Joy, was recently a resident storyteller and writer in a school close to our home. She and the students were talking about journeys in life and history. The conversation evolved to quilts that tell a story. Joy shared the embroidered story block she had purchased at an art fair from a Hmong woman who escaped the Vietnamese conflict with her family. She also shared books that were examples of story quilts, one of which was *The Whispering Cloth* by Pegi Dietz Shea (a refugee story). One of the students, a young girl of Vietnamese heritage, voluntarily told about her father's escape from Vietnam. Her father was the only survivor in the family and traveled alone as a young teen to America. The other students and adults were spellbound at first. Then the comments and questions began to fly among the group. The young Vietnamese American girl's story opened the eyes of all who were in attendance. One of the best results was the little girl finding her voice in that classroom. According to her teacher, she had never contributed to a classroom discussion until that day. The use of storytelling and books made a difference in the classroom that day. **Language Arts, Social Studies, Political Science, Art**

---

In 1999, the Nobel Peace Prize was awarded to the international aide group, Doctors without Borders. A worthy project would be to research the story behind the actions of these compassionate and courageous people. Many individuals over the years have been honored with the Nobel Peace Prize. A great research activity is to obtain the list of recipients and read up about their contributions to humanity. Report your findings to the community through articles, displays, media, or any other means. Receiving this prestigious international award is no small task and should be celebrated in any way possible. These are the true heroes of our time. A good book connection published by Crabtree is *Nobel Prize Winners* by Carlotta Hacker. **Social Studies, Political Science, Sociology, Health, Language Arts**

---

Have students identify some of the heroes in their community. Having students define a hero is a good place to start this task. We live in an interesting age in which media influences many of our opinions. When your students agree on a definition of the word, have them seek out heroes in their community. Give these people the attention they deserve. Articles in the newspaper or letters to the editor are ways to let more people know about their efforts. If you are working with students in grades 6 and up, I recommend reading *Hero* by S. L. Rottman (available through Peachtree). If nothing else, read the protagonist's essay at the end of the book as a seed for generating a discussion among your students about heroes. If you are looking for a collection of stories about heroic children, look at *The Barefoot Book of Heroic Children* by Rebecca Hazell, mentioned in the first section of this book under "Story Collections from around the World." Other places to look for books on heroes are publishers of reading series who have a heroes book as part of their series (i.e., Perfection Learning, the Wright Group, and Houghton Mifflin). Two other good book connections are *Something Beautiful* by Sharon Dennis Wyeth, and *The Good Fight: Stories about Real Heroes* by Tod Olson. The *Earth Day 2000 Special Edition* of *Time Magazine* featured a host of heroes to read about and explore; visit their Web site at www .time.com. Another Web site on heroes worth checking is www.makeadifferenceday .com. **Social Studies, Language Arts**

---

Michael Rosen, the editor of *Home* discussed in this chapter, is an amazing humanitarian. Part of the proceeds of this book go to the Share Our Strength (SOS) organization in Washington, D.C. From 1984 to the publication of his book (1992), the organization had distributed more than $7 million to food banks and homeless shelters in the United States and several relief centers around the world. Many of the proceeds from his other edited publications have gone to a variety of nonprofit organizations as well. The books may give educators ideas and sources for humanitarian acts in their schools. Some of the titles of his other books include *Food Fight: Poets Join the Fight against Hunger with Poems to Favorite Foods, The Greatest Table, Purr . . . Children's Book Illustrators Brag about Their Cats, Speak! Children's Book Illustrators Brag about Their Dogs,* and *Down to Earth.* **Social Studies, Art, Language Arts**

Volunteering in a soup kitchen is an eye-opening experience for children. DyAnne DiSalvo-Ryan's book, *Uncle Willie and the Soup Kitchen,* is a nice read for future soup-kitchen volunteers. Taking time to talk about the homeless in the community can lead to many good things. Invite speakers into your classroom who have experience working in underdeveloped nations. Possible candidates are Peace Corps workers, missionaries, members of Doctors without Borders, and disaster-relief volunteers. Visiting a labor camp or housing for migrant farm laborers is also worthwhile. Locate on a map the places that volunteers and speakers have helped people in need. Goals for these activities are to develop empathy and understanding for the less privileged people of our world, or those who have faced difficult political or natural disasters. **Social Studies, Geography, Economics, Language Arts, Health**

Kristine L. Franklin and Nancy McGirr edited a book called *Out of the Dump.* The book is a collection of photos, poetry, and narratives by children who literally live in or near the Guatemala City dump. Profits from the book sales are used to help the children featured in the book and their families. The children greatly benefited from its publication, but they had to agree to attend school, to take the photos, and to write the narratives. Another example of children's or young adult authors involved in amazing humanitarian acts is Ben Mikaelsen and his wife Melanie. They started, helped build, and funded a school near Guatemala City for children born with a cleft palate. Without people like the Mikaelsens, these children often are left to fend for themselves. Encourage your students to think of new ways to help people in desperate situations. **Social Studies, Economics, Language Arts, Math**

Homelessness has been a brutal reality for many people since the beginning of human civilization. Evidence of this fact abounds in many of the novels included here. The stories are based on real life. There are also picture books that can be woven into a lesson. One of the best resources for picture-book applications with older readers is *Worth a Thousand Words: An Annotated Guide to Picture Books for Older Readers* by Bette Ammon and Gale Sherman. Another source for using read-aloud with secondary students is *Read It Aloud: Using Literature in the Secondary Content Classroom* by Judy S. Richardson. Using a novel or picture book along with your history lessons can stir emotions that textbooks cannot. These stories are about children, often of the same age as your students. Placing the stories of children in a historical context is another advantage of novels and personal nonfiction accounts that textbooks cannot offer. I do not mean to imply that textbooks should be abandoned, but for teachers who want to capture students' attention and increase their understanding of history, literature provides a valuable resource. **Social Studies, Sociology, History, Language Arts**

Some additional resources for more information are UNICEF's education department, 333 E. 38th Street, New York, NY 10016 (1-212-922-2510); *New Internationalist,* 1011 Bloor Street West, Suite 300, Toronto, Ontario, M6H 1M1 (1-416-588-6478); Food First, 398 60th Street, Oakland, CA 94618 (1-510-654-4400); and Defense for Children International, USA, 210 Forsyth Street, New York, NY 10002 (1-212-353-0951). **Social Studies, Language Arts**

# Part III

# Part III

## Navigating the Road to Literacy

Whether in nature or in human relationships, few images are more compelling than that of an encounter: a butterfly and a flower come together in a brief burst of color, the sun's rays and raindrops joined in a rainbow, a mother reaching out for her newborn child, two pairs of eyes held in a deeply felt gaze, two hands clasped in friendship. And surely, among the most meaningful encounters, the one between a child and a book.

—Alma Flor Ada, author of *A Magical Encounter*

Reading impacts our lives every day. From recognizing print in the world around us to scanning the World Wide Web, we are a nation dependent on the ability to read and comprehend. When reading skills are not strong, we suffer in various ways. Ensuring that all children and adults engage in the act of reading is one of the biggest challenges to teachers, librarians, and parents. More distractions—television, computers, and electronic games, to name a few—confront our young people today than at any other time in the history of printed media, but fighting illiteracy and aliteracy is central to building lifelong readers. There are many ways to combat it. First, we must have abundant role models. Second, people of all ages must have access to books and printed media that reflect their interests. Equally important, we must create community environments where talking about books is a natural way of life.

Those of us who love reading must be role models for all the people we encounter. Spreading the word about the pleasures of reading takes a commitment. We need to talk to children, parents, educators, seniors, politicians, and civic groups about the importance of reading. Many people are good at this mission, but based on the climbing rate of aliteracy, more people must join forces to carry out the task. My intent in this section is to encourage others to help with this mission; I also provide tools to help. Over the years, I have found that one effective way to emphasize the importance of reading is through literature in which the act of reading is a central theme. The following annotated list of literature, including picture books, poetry, and novels, is a useful tool for promoting lifelong reading. I hope you find the books useful for opening discussions about the importance of reading with audiences of all ages.

Primary teachers know and have observed that reading to children before they begin formal schooling has a positive effect on their educational outcomes. On the first day of school, kindergarten teachers can tell which kids have been exposed to literature. Environments that do not continue to encourage reading contribute to a decline in literacy, and television often is cited as a major cause of this decline. As Aunt Chip from Patricia Polacco's book, *Aunt Chip and the Triple Creek Dam Affair,* states, "there will be consequences." Statistics reveal that by the age of five, children will have logged more time in front of the television than it takes to get a college degree or more time than they will spend in their entire lifetime in conversation with their parents. Depending on conservative or liberal estimates, students will have witnessed from 40,000 to 140,000 acts of violence on television by the end of their grade school experience. We can accept these alarming statistics as a sign of the times or share them with parents and children in our crusade toward creating a nation of readers. One way to confront the excessive viewing of violence is to get students involved in graphing their classroom viewing habits and also recording acts of violence they observe on the television programs they watch.

Of course, there are positive aspects of television, too. Programs such as *Sesame Street* and *Reading Rainbow* have made a mark on literacy. We also can see a rising number of book "talk groups" among adults, thanks to the media coverage that Oprah Winfrey and other socially conscious individuals have given to reading. Special-interest groups known as "Teachers as Readers" also have bolstered the pleasures and importance of reading.

The pleasures of reading can be contagious. Just ask avid readers about the urge to share a good book with somebody after they finish it. This same feeling is natural among students, too. They want to share what they read in ways different from traditional book reports, but we have to provide the time for this to happen. The influx of parents and various volunteers coming to schools and libraries taking part in literature groups with students is an all-out effort to combat the national threat of aliteracy. The number of people who *can* read but choose not to was projected to represent 50 percent of the U.S. population by the year 2000. That is a prediction of epidemic proportions. I long for the day when it becomes as natural to talk about books as to talk about the weather or sports.

There are many in the workforce who feel unaffected by a declining literacy rate because children have little connection to their respective fields. If these workers consider how many tax dollars go to paying for correctional institutions where the illiteracy rate is a whopping 85 percent among inmates, their opinions might change. Countries such as Japan have fewer problems with illiteracy because committing a crime can be a life sentence reducible only if the inmate learns to read. Repeat offenders are few in Japan. By contrast, the greater majority of U.S. inmates are repeat offenders.

There are organized groups around the country promoting literacy. Some of these are mentioned below as springboards for others to build local programs. Encouraging acts toward promoting literacy can be observed in unexpected places. Interesting books can be found in doctors' offices; some doctors even prescribe reading to their patients. Volunteers read to children in homeless shelters, hospital waiting rooms, schools, and community centers. Various community groups provide books as gifts to newborns, new parents, children and adults who are homeless, and refugees at home or abroad. School programs reward reading by giving away books. And there are a variety of tutorial and ESL (English as a second language) opportunities focused on helping others learn to read; some of the people who benefit from these programs are refugees, immigrants, and migrants. These are only a few examples of the many literacy efforts. People who volunteer to help in the quest for literacy know that access to books for all people is vital to our nation's health.

Like the children in *Running the Road to ABC* by Denize Lautre, there are also many obstacles that readers must maneuver as they navigate the road to literacy. Patricia Polacco created a stalwart, determined character in *Aunt Chip and the Great Cripple Creek Dam Affair,* who metaphorically repaired major road damage caused by television alone. Even well-meaning educators can cause detours to the real act of reading by excessively engaging in debates over phonics versus whole language. Clearing a path for a child to become a reader is eloquently portrayed in another Polacco book, *Thank You, Mr. Falker.* In this book, Polacco relates a personal story of her struggle with reading and declining self-esteem. This is a similar tale too often repeated with other emergent readers across our nation. Fortunately for Ms. Polacco, the road was cleared and paved by a wise and persistent teacher, Mr. Falker. Furthermore, new roads to literacy must be built to bridge the gap between the privileged and those living in oppressed environments where access to literacy is withheld. One example to make this point is the treatment of slaves in Gary Paulsen's book, *Nightjohn.* A contemporary parallel occurs in Sudan, as Judy Walgren describes in her book, *The Lost Boys of Natinga.* Our "reading highway" must provide literacy for all. Literacy is a global issue, and we must continue to encourage literacy programs close to home and abroad.

We have much work to do, but the rewards of our collective efforts will return twofold. As Grandpa says to Mary Ellen in Patricia Polacco's, *The Bee Tree,* "There is such sweetness inside of that book too! . . . Such things . . . adventure, knowledge and wisdom. But these things do not come easily. You have to pursue them. Just like we ran after the bees to find their tree, so you must also chase these things through the pages of a book!"

# Picture Books

**Berkeley, Laura.** *The Keeper of Wisdom.* Illustrated by **Alison Dexter.** Barefoot Books, 2000. 32p. Pre K–7.

An old women tries to sell her books of wisdom in a prosperous city, but the mayor turns her away because the citizens have everything they could possibly need. One winter, when times are rough, the mayor of the city has second thoughts about the books, but is it too late? A marvelous story about the importance of preserving the wisdom associated with books and story.

**Best, Cari.** *Red Light, Green Light, Mama and Me.* Illustrated by **Niki Daly.** Orchard, 1995. 32p. Pre K–1.

Lizzie's mother works in the children's section of the public library. One day Lizzie goes to work with her mother and helps in a variety of ways. She assists other employees, helps other children find books, listens to her mother tell a story, and then puts the books away before going home.

**Black, Irma Simonton.** *Little Old Man Who Could Not Read.* Illustrated by **Seymour Fleishman.** Albert Whitman, 1968. 32p. Grades K–3.

In this funny, poignant story, an illiterate old man realizes what can happen when you depend on someone else to do the reading for you. His wife leaves town for a few days, and he has to do the shopping and other household chores. You can imagine his surprise when he opens cans of what he thought were his favorite foods. Using this book can lead to an interesting discussion about environmental print and ESL strategies for learning the names of objects.

**Bloom, Becky.** *Wolf!* Illustrated by **Pascal Biet.** Orchard, 1999. 28p. Pre K–3.

This is a delightful and charming work of fantasy. A distraught wolf wanders into a town one day. He is after something to eat when he remembers a nearby farm. Upon his arrival, he finds several animals engaged in an odd activity—reading! The animals are so mesmerized with the books that they are unafraid of the wolf, so he decides to learn to read. After several attempts, he becomes quite a storyteller.

**Bradby, Marie.** *More Than Anything Else.* Illustrated by **Chris K. Soentpiet.** Orchard, 1995. 32p. Grades 1–5.

This is a fictionalized glimpse of Booker T. Washington's life at a time when he discovered the power of print. Through his persistence and the help of "the newspaper man," he learns the "song on paper." From that moment, we all benefited from his accomplishments. Have students research Booker T. Washington's contributions to the education of African Americans.

**Bunting, Eve.** *Wednesday's Surprise.* Illustrated by **Donald Carrick.** Clarion Books, 1989. 32p. Grades 1–5.

Teaching someone to read can happen at different levels. Anna teaches her grandmother to read. On her father's birthday, they surprise him with her new skill. Some nice companion books to this one are *When Jessie Came across the Sea* by Amy Hest, *I Speak English for My Mother* by Muriel Stanek, *Amber on the Mountain* by Tony Johnston, and *Read for Me, Mama* by Vashanti Rahaman.

**Cheng, Andrea.** *Grandfather Counts.* Illustrated by **Ange Zhang.** Lee & Low Books, 2000. 32p. Grades K and up.

Helen has been waiting for the arrival of Gong Gong (Grandfather). He was now going to live with them in the United States. When he arrives only speaking Chinese there is an unspoken tension that arises. In time Helen learns she has some common interests, and she and Gong Gong learn to communicate, teaching each other their native language. A nice companion book is *The Trip Back Home* by Janet S. Wong.

**Cohen, Barbara.** *Molly's Pilgrim.* Illustrated by **Daniel Mark Duffy.** Lothrop, Lee & Shepard, 1983; revised 1998. 32p. Grades 3–6.

This book has warmed hearts in many classrooms. An exceptional immigration story that shares the difficulty of a new school, a new language, and students who don't understand. The teacher handles the scenario in a way that becomes a lesson for all.

**Cummings, Julie.** *The Inside-Outside Book of Libraries.* Illustrated by **Roxie Munro.** Farrar, Straus & Giroux, 1996. 48p. All ages.

This is a good explanation of the workings of a library in a picture-book format. It could be used to introduce young and old to a library.

**Deedy, Carmen Agra.** *The Library Dragon.* Illustrated by **Michael P. White.** Peachtree, 1994. 32p. Grades K–6.

This is a must for school librarians who are more concerned with books than with getting them into the hands of readers. It is a charming and delightful read, sure to bring a smile to librarians' faces.

**Ernst, Lisa Campbell.** *Stella Lou Ella's Runaway Book.* Simon & Schuster, 1998. 32p. Grades K–3.

Stella tells everyone about the favorite part of a book she checked out from the library. But then she becomes frantic when the book is lost. She is convinced she will never be able to check out a library book again. When Stella finally goes to tell Mrs. Graham, the librarian, she learns the book has been found. Stella asks Mrs. Graham what her favorite part of the book is, and the librarian replies, as she always does, "When someone READS it!"

**Fleischman, Paul.** *Weslandia.* Illustrated by **Kevin Hawkes.** Candlewick, 1999. 32p. All ages.

This book is an amazing display of determination, imagination, and wit. Wesley was not your average child. He is a reader with a natural curiosity and unusually creative imagination about the world. Even his parents don't think he fits in with other children, and his peers are definitely anti-Wesley. The children in the neighborhood chase and taunt him at every opportunity until they discover that Wesley has something they lack. Once the other kids discover Wesley's imaginative world and wit, he has no shortage of friends.

**Godard, Alex.** *Mama, Across the Sea.* Adapted from the French by **George Wen.** Henry Holt, 1998/2000. 40p. Grades K–3.

Cecile's mother works across the sea. Her father drowned while fishing, and Cecile lives with her grandparents on Port Royal in the Caribbean. Because she knows how to read and write, Cecile can read the mail. Her literacy skills also come in handy when her grandmother wants to learn to read after she has to pay someone to help cash her social security check.

**Gruber, Wilhelm.** *The Upside-Down Reader.* Illustrated by **Marlies Rieper-Bastian.** North-South Books, 1998. 62p. Grades 1–4.

This is a delightful beginning chapter book about the trials of learning to read. Tim is learning to read. Through patience and an insightful grandmother, the challenges of decoding the printed word come together.

**Heide, Parry Florence.** *The House of Wisdom.* Illustrated by **Mary Grandpré.** DK, 1999. 40p. Grades 2–6.

In the city of Baghdad, in the year of A.D. 830, the Caliph al-Mámun built the House of Wisdom. It became a learning institution, a library, and a translation bureau. In this building, scholars and intellectuals contributed to and preserved the knowledge of the ancient world. This marvelous story conveys the magic of discovering the power of reading and books through a young boy, Ishaq.

**Heide, Parry Florence.** *The Problem with Pulcifer.* Illustrated by **Judy Glasser.** Mulberry, 1982. 64p. Grades 2–6.

What happens when your child is more interested in reading than watching television? In this parody, the whole school revolves around television, but Pulcifer marches to a different drummer.

**Heide, Parry Florence, and Judith Heide Gilliland.** *The Day of Ahmed's Secret.* Illustrated by **Ted Lewin.** Lothrop, Lee & Shepard, 1990. 32p. Pre K–3.

This lovely story takes place in Cairo, Egypt. Ahmed is proud that he can do father's job of delivering fuel for people's stoves. But he is even more pleased when he finishes his work and can share a new learning discovery with his family: He has learned to write his name. The excitement of learning to write for the first time is universal, regardless of age or geography.

**Hest, Amy.** *When Jessie Came across the Sea.* Illustrated by **P. J. Lynch.** Candlewick Press, 1997. 40p. Grades 3 and up.

Grandmother insisted that Jessie learn to read and write. Jessie, in return, taught her grandmother. "Sometime, you never know, you may want to read some things," Jessie said. "You may want to write." This moving story captures the essence of immigration to "America, land of plenty."

**Hill, Lee Sullivan.** *Libraries Take Us Far.* Carolrhoda Books, 1998. 32p. Pre K–2.

This is a nice look at libraries around the United States. While touring them, the text supports the uses and applications of a public library. And yes, the libraries take us far in more ways than one. A good companion book is Julie Cummings, *The Inside-Outside Book of Libraries.*

**Houston, Gloria.** *My Great Aunt Arizona.* Illustrated by **Susan Condie Lamb.** HarperCollins, 1992. 32p. All ages.

"Have you been there," asks the inquiring minds of students as Aunt Arizona reads aloud and stretches their imagination? "No, but you will someday," replies Arizona. This book promotes one of the many pleasures of reading—traveling anywhere a book takes you.

**Howard, Elizabeth Fitzgerald.** *Virgie Goes to School with Us Boys.* Illustrated by **E. B. Lewis.** Simon & Schuster, 2000. 32p. Pre K–3.

This is a moving story based on the author's ancestors. Shortly after the American Civil War, a group of Quakers in Jonesborough, Tennessee, started a school for Black children. It was in this school that her grandfather, his brothers, and his sister (Virgie) attended school. Howard built this incredible story around Virgie's determination to go to school. In her endnotes, Howard says that Virgie is a symbol of the former slaves, the new African American citizens, who endured many hardships to get an education. In Howard's closing comments, she states, "I imagine her [Virgie] as having left a legacy for all children, girls and boys, African American and not, that education will always be the first step in 'learning to be free.' "

**Hutchins, Hazel.** *Nicholas at the Library.* Illustrated by **Ruth Ohi.** Annick Press (Firefly Books), 1990. 32p. Pre K–2.

Fantasy and an abundance of imagination can be found in books at the library, and this book illustrates this point. Nicholas teams up with the librarian to help the little chimpanzee, who has literally fallen out of a story. A wonderful adventure takes place as they find his rightful home.

**Johnston, Tony.** *Amber on the Mountain.* Illustrated by **Robert Duncan.** Dial, 1994. 32p. Grades 1–4.

Amber lives high in the mountains isolated from most people. One day a man and his family show up to build a road. Amber befriends Anna, who can read. Anna shares the gift of learning to read with Amber.

**Lapointe, Claude.** *Out of Sight.* Creative Editions, 1995. Grades 1–5.

This nearly wordless book does not reflect reading directly but has a subtle message about time spent playing computer games. While three children are engrossed in the computer games, a world of action unfolds outside their window. In closing, the girl remarks about today being just another boring day. This book can be a reality check for busy parents, too.

**Lautre, Denize.** *Running the Road to ABC.* Illustrated by **Reynold Ruffins.** Simon & Schuster, 1996. 32p. Grades 1–4.

Learning to read in a Third World country often is a guarded privilege. The challenges are many, from few printed materials to physical hurdles: The children in this story need to get up early, run through the village, through the forest, and then up and down hills to get to school, but they are happy to have the opportunity.

**Levinson, Nancy Smith.** *Clara and the Bookwagon.* Illustrated by **Carolyn Croll.** Harper & Row, 1988. 64p. Grades 1–5.

This beginning chapter book is based on the true story of the first book wagon in the United States, pulled by horse. It was started in 1905 in the town of Hagerstown, Maryland. Clara is enamored with the idea of books, even though she cannot read. Her father says farmers don't have time for such distractions, but he changes his mind when the book-wagon lady comes to the farm.

**Marshall, Rita.** *I Hate to Read.* Illustrated by **Etienne Delessert.** The Creative Company, 1993. 32p. All ages.

Victor does well in school—except when it comes to reading. He hates to read. As characters from books come to life, they entice him into the adventures found in books. There is a lesson here for those of us who work with children and adults who do not like to read: Play to their interests.

**McGugan, Jim.** *Josepha: A Prairie Boy.* Illustrated by **Murray Kimber.** Chronicle, 1994. 32p. Grades 3–5.

This work of historical fiction, set in the late 1800s, shows the realities of children confronted with making a decision between attending school or working in the fields. It captures the sentiments of the teacher and peers who witness Josepha choosing work over an education. The position of being torn between two realities is one our ancestors often faced, and one that many underprivileged families around the world still face today.

**McPhail, David.** *Edward and the Pirates.* Little, Brown, 1997. 32p. All ages.

Adventure abounds in this swashbuckling tale. When the pirates in Edward's book come to life, there is only one thing that can save him—reading aloud to the pirates.

**McPhail, David.** *Fix-It.* Dutton, 1984. 24p. Pre K–2.

Emma bear gets up early to watch television, until one day the television is not working. She demands that her parents get it fixed now! After the repairman fails, her parents try to get Emma interested in something else. Reading aloud is the perfect antidote and remains the preferred choice when her dad discovers the television simply wasn't plugged in.

**Miller, William.** *Richard Wright and the Library Card.* Illustrated by **Gregory Christie.** Lee & Low Books, 1997. 34p. Grades 2 and up.

This biographical story is from Richard Wright's life. Miller tells of a time when Black people often could not have library cards. Wright shared his determination to read with an understanding white man, who allowed him to use his own card to check out books.

**Mora, Pat.** *The Rainbow Tulip.* Illustrated by **Elizabeth Sayles.** Viking, 1999. 32p. Grades 1–3.

At home she is Estelita; at school she is Stella. Estelita wants the most colorful tulip costume for the school play. Her Tía (Aunt) Carmen is a seamstress who will make the tulip skirt if her mother asks. Throughout the story, Estelita compares the way her family lives with the way she is learning in school. Mora poignantly describes the subtle conflicts that Estelita faces as a child who learned Spanish as her first language and the need to preserve cultural traditions.

**Mora, Pat.** *Tomás and the Library Lady.* Illustrated by **Raúl Colón.** Random House, 1997. 40p. Grades 1–5.

Tomás Rivera's grandfather and a librarian in Iowa encouraged him to read. The friendship with this lady changed his life. As history has proven, Rivera went on to accomplish great things and is revered as an important role model in the Latino community.

**Oppenheim, Joanne.** *The Story Book Prince.* Illustrated by **Rosanne Litzinger.** Harcourt Brace, 1987. 32p. Pre K–2.

This story is about a prince who cannot fall asleep. All the entertainers of the castle try to amuse him, but they all fail. One day, an old woman comes to the castle with "the very best thing" for bedtime: a book to read.

**Pak, Soyung.** *Dear Juno.* Illustrated by **Susan Kathleen Hartung.** Viking, 1999. 32p. All ages.

This is one of the best examples of "reading the world." Although Juno cannot read words, he can read the content clues his grandmother in Korea sends him in her letters. When his parents read the letters, they are surprised at his intuitive accuracy. Juno writes back to Grandmother in his own form of communication. A delightful book!

**Polacco, Patricia.** *Aunt Chip and the Great Cripple Creek Dam Affair.* Philomel, 1996. 40p. All ages.

"There will be consequences," blurts Aunt Chip to her nephew, as she shares the story of the dismantling of the town library. This is a heartfelt tale about the significant role libraries play in a community.

**Polacco, Patricia.** *The Bee Tree.* Philomel, 1993. 32p. All ages.

"I'm tired of reading, Grandpa," Mary Ellen sighs, "I'd rather be outdoors running and playing." Grandpa takes Mary Ellen outdoors on a honeybee chase that turns into a lesson about reading. Both looking for honey and reading take patience and persistence, but the rewards are worth the effort.

**Polacco, Patricia.** *Pink and Say.* Philomel, 1994. 48p. Grades 3 and up.

Learning to read for Pink, a slave, provides a freedom that can never be taken from him. This compelling story from the American Civil War, which was handed down through Polacco's ancestors, is about two young men who learn about friendship, love, freedom, and the power of reading.

**Polacco, Patricia.** *Thank You, Mr. Falker.* Philomel, 1998. 40p. All ages.

Perhaps no one knows better the challenges associated with learning to read than a person who has been through the struggle. Polacco shares a bit of her life in a moving story that all elementary teachers should read as a reminder of why we are in this profession.

**Radlauer, Ruth Shaw.** *Molly at the Library.* Illustrated by **Emily Arnold McCully.** Simon & Schuster, 1988. 32p. Pre K–1.

Little Molly learns about the library and the many benefits of checking out books on topics that interest her. Besides checking out books she has selected, her parents read them to her, too.

**Rahaman, Vashanti.** *Read for Me, Mama.* Illustrated by **Lori McElrath-Eslick.** Boyds Mills Press, 1997. 32p. Grades 1–5.

This is a great book about community literacy. Joseph loves library day more than any other school day because Mrs. Ricardo knows how to make the books come to life, and he gets to check out two books. He also loves the stories his mother tells him each evening. But when Joseph insists that she read to him, he discovers she cannot read.

**San Souchi, Robert D.** *A Weave of Words.* Illustrated by **Raúl Colón.** Orchard, 1998. 32p. Grades 1-5.

The somewhat spoiled Prince Vachagan discovers that not everything is at his disposal when he meets the weaver's daughter, Anait. She will marry him, but not until he learns a trade and also learns to read and write. In the end, his ability to write and Anait's bravery save the prince's life.

**Stanek, Muriel.** *I Speak English for My Mom.* Illustrated by **Judith Friedman.** Albert Whitman, 1989. 32p. Grades 1–4.

This book offers wonderful insight into understanding immigrants in America. Lupe must translate for her mother wherever they go, except at the Mexican store close to their home. There everyone speaks Spanish. Lupe's mother knows the only way she will get a better job is to learn English, but she cannot afford to pay someone to teach her. Finally, she learns of an opportunity for free English classes.

**Stewart, Sarah.** *The Library.* Illustrated by **David Small.** Farrar, Straus & Giroux, 1995. 32p. Grades K and up.

It seems as though every town has a librarian, past or present, who is the book person extraordinaire, a person who loves reading, who knows where to find books to match the interests of every patron, and who has devoted his or her life to the library. This book is about such a librarian, Elizabeth Brown.

**Viorst, Judith.** *The Good-Bye Book.* Illustrated by **Kay Chorao.** Atheneum, 1988. 32p. Pre K–2.

Little kids hate it when their parents go out and leave them behind. They think of everything to dissuade their parents. In this book, nothing makes a young boy content until the baby-sitter arrives with some new books and begins reading to him.

**Vivelo, Jacqueline.** *Reading to Matthew.* Illustrated by **Brigitta Saflund.** Roberts Rinehart, 1993. 40p. Grades 2–6.

This is a touching story about the power of reading aloud to siblings. Passing on the legacy of reading within the family may have saved Matthew's life.

**Williams, Suzanne.** *Library Lil.* Illustrated by **Steven Kellogg.** Dial Books for Young Readers, 1997. 32p. All ages.

There is no challenge too great for the librarian who knows how to promote reading. Not even Bust-'em-up Bill and his gang could get the best of Library Lil. There is a subtle message in this book about rough and tough characters and reading.

**Winch, John.** *The Old Woman Who Loved to Read.* Holiday House, 1996. 34p. All ages.

Life chores sometimes get complicated, but avid readers often will put their love for the printed word ahead of work. This story shows a creative way to surmount challenges and find time to read—when the chores are done, of course!

**Wittbold, Maureen K.** *Let's Talk about When Your Parent Doesn't Speak English.* PowerKids Press, 1997. 24p. Grades K–4.

Having parents who speak a language other than English can be difficult and confusing for children when they enter school. Wittbold helps children in this situation overcome their fears and uncertainty.

**Wong, Janet S.** *The Trip Back Home.* Illustrated by **Bo Jia.** Harcourt Brace, 2000. 32p. Grades 1–6.

This heartfelt story is a good example of grandchildren faced with a language barrier when visiting grandparents in another country. Something for educators worth pondering over in this book is children's natural ability to read the world through a desire to communicate. When the young girl and her mother visit Korea, they also take gifts. Among them are books with the English alphabet. On their departure they receive gifts, one a poem in Korean. This book works well with *Grandfather Counts* by Andrea Cheng in this section.

# Poetry

**Dakos, Kalli.** *The Goof Who Invented Homework: And Other School Poems.* Illustrated by **Denise Brunkus.** Dial Books for Young Readers, 1996. 80p. All ages.

Within this wonderful collection of school poems is a gem about reading good books, *The Book That Made Danny Cry.* Read this poem aloud and give students and adults a strong message about the impact of good literature.

**Diggory-Shields, Carol.** *Lunch Money: And Other Poems about School.* Illustrated by **Paul Meisel.** Dutton, 1995. 40p. All ages.

Among this fun collection of humorous poems is one that gets to the heart of the controversy between reading and technology. Read aloud *Who Needs School,* and let the debate begin.

**Feelings, Tom.** *Soul Looks Back in Wonder.* Dial Books for Young Readers, 1994. 40p. All ages.

Included in this award-winning collection of poems, written by African American poets, is one written by Maya Angelou that brilliantly juxtaposes reading and popcorn. Read aloud *I Love the Look of Words* or hang it up in a classroom or library—or at a concession stand.

**Hopkins, Lee Bennett.** *Good Books, Good Times.* Illustrated by **Harvey Stevenson.** HarperCollins, 1990. 32p. All ages.

This anthology of poetry depicts the joys of books and reading, as told by a variety of poets.

**Lewis, J. Patrick.** *The Bookworm's Feast: A Potluck of Poems.* Illustrated by **John O'Brian.** Dial Books for Young Readers, 1999. 32p. All ages.

This is a clever feast of poetic tidbits arranged like courses on a menu. You can select a favorite "entrée," garnished with clever illustrations. Bon appetite readers everywhere!

**Medina, Jane.** *My Name Is Jorge: On Both Sides of the River.* Illustrated by **Fabricio Vanden Broeck.** Boyds Mills Press, 1999. 32p. Grades 2 and up.

This poignant set of poems accurately captures the feeling of being caught between two worlds. Jorge, symbolic of all second-language learners, describes his feelings about attending school in a world that does not always honor his native language, Spanish. One of my favorite poems is *Recitation.* The book is bilingual, with English and Spanish text.

**Paraskevas, Betty.** *Gracie Graves and the Kids from Room 402.* Illustrated by **Michael Paraskevas.** Harcourt Brace, 1995. 32p. Grades 3–6.

This collection of poetry describes characters in a class from their teacher to the individual students. This book acts as a model for writing extensions in other classrooms. There is one poem, however, *Billy Boyle,* that educators may want to read the next time they consider assigning traditional book reports.

**Rosen, Michael (editor).** *Home: A Collaboration of Thirty Distinguished Authors and Illustrators of Children's Books to Aid the Homeless.* HarperCollins, 1992. 32p. All ages.

A poem by Karla Kuskin, *Comfortable Old Chair,* captures the feelings of a comfortable reading place, whether one is reading aloud or "escape reading."

# Novels

**Ada, Alma Flor.** *Where the Flame Trees Bloom.* Atheneum, 1994. 75p. Grades 3–8.

This wonderful collection of stories from Alma's childhood is filled with moving stories. The first story is about her grandmother, who founded a school. She felt the need to help children—and anyone else for that matter—to become literate. Having read about this incredible woman, it is no wonder that Alma has continued the cause in her ongoing work to end illiteracy. This book inspires others to write their family stories. Since the publishing of *Where the Flame Trees Bloom,* Alma wrote a companion book, *Under the Royal Palms,* which won the 2000 Pura Belpré Award, honoring Latino and Latina writers whose work best portrays, affirms, and celebrates Latino culture.

**Cart, Michael (compiler).** *Tomorrow Land: Stories about the Future.* Scholastic, 1999. 198p. Grades 5 and up.

Michael Cart compiled this thought-provoking collection of short stories by 10 well-known authors. One story in particular fits very well into this theme, *The Last Book in the Universe* by Rodman Philbrick (now a full-length novel published by Scholastic). What if there were no more books in the future, but only memories of a former reader? Philbrick's story keeps you wondering right to the end. Other contributors in this captivating collection are Jon Scieszka, Tor Siedler, Gloria Skurzynski, Ron Koertge, Lois Lowry, Katherine Paterson, Jacqueline Woodson, James Cross Giblin, and Michael Cart.

**English, Karen.** *Francie.* Farrar, Straus & Giroux, 1999. 199p. Grades 5–8.

Francie wants to leave Noble, Alabama, to join her father in Chicago. That's all she can think about as she and her mother work for the white families in their town. Her salvation is found in her school and teacher, in reading, and in helping 16-year-old Jessie learn to read. When Jessie is accused of knocking down his white employer and is forced to flee, Francie knows she must help him. But this puts her own family in danger.

**Garland, Sherry.** *Letters from the Mountain.* Harcourt Brace, 1996. 211p. Grades 6 and up.

To get away from a bad situation, Taylor Ryan's family sends him to stay with his great uncle and aunt for the summer. He meets a nomadic family of post cutters and discovers that Jesse Lee, a boy about his age, cannot read. Taylor makes a deal with him to trade what they know. If Jesse Lee teaches him to shoot a gun, Taylor will teach him to read. But the trade also uncovers some deep pain in Taylor's family.

**Gilson, Jamie.** *Do Bananas Chew Gum?* Lothrop, Lee & Shepard, 1980. 160p. Grades 5–7.

Sam Mott has struggled with reading and writing for as long as he can remember. A new town and school were supposed to be different, but his problems do not disappear. A baby-sitting job that requires minimal reading, a peer who happens to be both a girl and the class brain, and caring teachers who see something different about Sam influence his road to literacy.

**Hesse, Karen.** *Just Juice.* Illustrated by **Robert Andrew Parker.** Scholastic, 1998. 138p. Grades 4–7.

Nine-year-old Juice would rather be home with her dad than in school. Hiding the fact that she can't read is easier when she's not in school. She and her family learn some powerful messages about illiteracy and the hardships that it causes.

**Paulsen, Gary.** *Nightjohn.* Doubleday, 1993. 96p. Grades 5 and up.

This story is set in the American Civil War era. At the cost of risking his life, Nightjohn shows up at night to teach willing slaves to read and write. Young Sarney is one of his students. When her mother asks why he risks his life just to teach someone to read, Nightjohn's poignant response is, "We all have to read and write so we can write about this. What they doing to us. It has to be written."

**Paulsen, Gary.** *Sarney: A Life Remembered.* Delacorte Press, 1997. 192p. Grades 5 and up.

A sequel to *Nightjohn,* this book takes place near the end of the American Civil War. Sarney leaves her oppressive situation to search for her children, who were sold to another slaveholder. Sarney meets with opposition along the way, but persistence and the caring Miss Laura take her to New Orleans, where she finds her children. Sarney's continued friendship with Miss Laura and her determination to make things better for the freed slaves result in opening the first school for Black children.

**Rabe, Berniece.** *Tall Enough to Own the World.* Franklin Watts, 1989. 160p. Grades 4–6.

Ten-year-old Joey has been through several schools. Learning to read has eluded him at each one. Joey has a difficult time admitting his illiteracy and often ends up fighting anyone who reminds him of it. Things begin to look up for him when an understanding volunteer, a teacher, a neighbor, and several classmates help him in unique ways.

**Sanvoisin, Éric.** *The Ink Drinker.* Illustrated by **Martin Matje.** Delacorte Press, 1998. 40p. Grades 3–6.

"Ink drinkers" are people who love reading and suck up the printed word as if it were chocolate. They can be found in every library and bookstore. This wonderful fantasy metaphorically conveys the power of adventure reading. Look for the companion book, *A Straw for Two.*

**Scieszka, John.** *This Summer Reading Is Killing Me.* Illustrated by **Lane Smith.** Viking, 1998. 73p. Grades 3–6.

This is another adventure in the *Time Warp Trio* series. This time, the heroes get mixed up with characters from their summer reading list. Their only escape from the rival between good and evil characters is to get everyone back to their rightful book.

**Smith, Doris Buchanan.** *The Penny Whistle Tree.* Putnam, 1991. 144p. Grades 5–7.

Jonathon's neighborhood is pretty predictable until George moves in across the street. The first day he throws a brick at Jonathon and his friends. Jonathon can't ignore George because he is in his classroom, too. One day, George confides in Jonathon that he cannot read and wants help. Jonathon discovers some heart-wrenching insights and realities about George as he reluctantly befriends him.

**Snyder, Zilpha Keatley.** *The Runaways.* Delacorte Press, 1999. 188p. Grades 5–8.

The three characters in this book each deal with personal problems. They decide that one way out is to run away from their desolate desert town, Rattler Springs. Each of them is an avid reader, and their literacy skills hold answers to their seemingly desperate situation.

**Spinelli, Jerry.** *The Library Card.* Scholastic, 1997. 148p. Grades 6 and up.

This is a great collection of four stories, ranging from humorous to one that pulls at the heartstrings. The common theme among all the stories is the protagonist's adventures with a library card.

**Spinelli, Jerry.** *Maniac Magee.* Little, Brown, 1990. 184p. Grades 4–8.

    This Newbery Award–winning book deals with social issues in the United States, including literacy. Maniac and Amanda, from two different backgrounds, share a love for reading.

**Walgren, Judy.** *The Lost Boys of Natinga: A School for Sudan's Young Refugees.* Houghton Mifflin, 1998. 44p. Grades 5 and up.

    This is an informational book depicting the plight of Sudanese refugees. The act of literacy has some serious implications for the children in this book. Raising social consciousness among those who can help is their only hope.

# Book Extensions

The obvious, but often overlooked, point of a literacy theme such as this one is to find out how many of the children in your class possess a public library card. I have students who come to my university classes who do not have a library card. Ask students how many use the library. When was the last time you took students in your school on a field trip to the public library? If you have not been there for a while, go with a set of questions related to the curriculum themes you are studying. You might be surprised at the number of resources the library has. Many libraries offer free book-talk sessions in which library personnel visit the classroom with a box full of new and exciting books. Librarians could modify the book talk to fit the theme you are studying. Look in the first section of this chapter for a multitude of books connecting the functions of libraries with young patrons. **Language Arts, All Subjects**

The American Library Association (ALA) recommends that a school library should budget the cost of two books per child per year to simply maintain a library. Three books per child each year will expand it. In a similar vein, the International Reading Association (IRA) came out with a position statement on the importance of students having access to books. The IRA recommends 7 books per child in the individual classrooms and 20 per student in the school library. It also recommends adding one book per child in the classroom and two per child in the school library to promote yearly library growth. At this time, the average cost of a children's book is about $15. Compare the library budget with your student population. Is your school library budget for books close to the recommended amount? The last figure I read in 1998 on the national average spent on books per school library was $18 per child per year.

    Brainstorm what you can do to get more book choices for your students. There are many community organizations that are looking for service projects to help children. Getting more books in the hands of young people makes a difference. Contact IRA and ALA for materials and references to support your efforts. IRA at www.reading.org and ALA at www.ala.org. **All Subjects**

There are some great international and community book projects. It is worth researching to see if your community is taking advantage of everything available. A few organizations and programs to consider are the International Book Project; Reading Is Fun Week; Read across America; National Library Week; Family Literacy Day; Teen Read Week; Children's Book Week; International Literacy Day; National Poetry Month; National Young Reader's Day; Week of the Young Child; Freedom of Information Day; National TV Turnoff Week; National Book Month; Books for Babes; Operation Wishbook; Reach Out and Read (or A Literal Prescription for Reading); Read to Me; World Book and Copyright Day; and International Children's Book Day.

Check state and local library associations, as well as reading and parent associations. Don't overlook community groups that have targeted literacy-related activities as one of their goals. Business partners can help, too. If you are close to a university that offers an education or library science program, call the respective departments to find out what they have to offer in the way of outreach. At the university where I am employed, several of the faculty, as well as future teachers and librarians, conduct book talks and storytelling sessions. They organize book donations, literature circles, book groups, and offer countless hours of volunteer time to reading aloud at clinics, classrooms, homeless shelters, doctor's offices, day-care centers, after-school programs, and libraries. Educators should not be shy about asking for help to build their literacy programs. Practice with real children is good for our future teachers and librarians.

Some good contacts for more information are the International Book Project (1-606-254-6771), ibookp@iglou.com; National Book Award Organization (1-212-685-0261), www.nationalbook.org; National Education Association (1-202-822-7387), www.nea.org; the Academy of American Poets, www.poets.org; American Library Association, www.ala.org; Early Childhood Organization, www.naeyc.org; Reading Is Fundamental (1-877-RIF-READ), www.rif.org; TV-Free America, (1-800-939-6737), www.tvfa.org; International Literacy Organization, www.naa.org; International Reading Association, www.reading.org; National Council of the Teachers of English, www.ncte.org; National Center for Family Literacy (1-502-584-1133), www.familit.org; United States Board on Books for Young People (1-302-731-1600, ext. 229), www.usbby.org; BOOKIT (1-800-4-BOOK–IT), www.bookitprogram.com; U.S. Department of Education (1-877-433-7827), www.ed.gov; UNESCO, www.unesco.org; Idaho State Library Read to Me Project, www.lili.org/isl/readtome; Cooperative Children's Book Center, www.soemadison.wisc.edu/ccbc/; and Children's Book Council, www.cbcbook.org. **All Subjects**

One international library project in particular that is having great success is the Sister Library Program, started through the American Library Association. A quick overview of this project involves libraries in the United States taking on sister libraries from other countries. There are many possibilities with this project, including supplying books, interlibrary loan delivery, and exchange programs. The ALA has a database at intl@ala.org, or you can call 1-800-545-2433, ext. 3201 in the United States (the international phone number is +1-312-280-3201; fax 1-312-280-3256). You can also check the ALA International Relations Office Web page at www.ala.org/sisterlibraries.

Other organizations have Web sites that offer information about their international library projects: International Federation of Library Associations and Institutions (IFLA), www.ifla.org; Rotary International, www.rotary.org; Sister Cities International, www.sister-cities.org; U.S. Peace Corps, www.peacecorps.gov; and U.S. National Commission on Libraries and Information Science (NCLIS), www.nclis.gov//millennium/millenn.html. The NCLIS also can be contacted by phone (1-202- 606-9200) or fax (1-202-606-9203). **All Subjects**

---

Even those who live in isolated communities can have an impact on literacy abroad. It may be something as simple as a community book drive that sends books to a needy school in another state or country. A good place to start is by contacting the International Book Project, 1440 Delaware Avenue, Lexington, KY 40505 (1-606-254-6771); e-mail: ibookp@iglou.com. This nonprofit organization offers ideas and help to promote global literacy. The International Reading Association and the American Library Association are two additional places to look for international efforts, www.reading.org and www.ala.org. **Social Studies, Language Arts**

---

Many communities have refugee and immigration centers. In addition to the need for adequate housing, there are constant requests for tutors to help with English as a second language (ESL) programs. Your students and parents can be a part of this project. Most of the refugees and immigrants are families. Children helping children is a nice match. Students with a little ESL training can do wonders. **All Subjects**

---

Another resource found in many communities are adult literacy center projects, which are often housed in public libraries. These centers are always looking for volunteers and donations of books, writing materials, and technology. Three book connections to the topic of adult literacy are Vashanti Rahaman's *Read for Me, Mama,* Muriel Stanek's *I Speak English for My Mom,* and *Wednesday's Surprise* by Eve Bunting. **Language Arts, Social Studies**

Starting school in a new city or country can be an intimidating experience for the new child and his or her parents. One important thing educators can do is to make them feel welcome. Books can be useful tools in classrooms that have a new student with limited English proficiency. Some book suggestions are *I'm New Here* by Bud Howlett, *My Name Is Jorge: On Both Sides of the River* by Jane Medina, *When Jessie Came across the Sea* by Amy Hest, *La Mariposa* by Francisco Jiménez, *I Speak English for My Mom* by Muriel Stanek, *My Name Is Maria Isabel* by Alma Flor Ada, *Let's Talk about When Your Parent Doesn't Speak English* by Maureen Wittbold, *The Rainbow Tulip* by Pat Mora, *The Magic Shell* by Nicholasa Mohr, *Molly's Pilgrim* by Barbara Cohen, and *Who Belongs Here? An American Story* by Margy Burns Knight. Another important way of making these students feel welcome is to have books about their homeland or in their native language available to them. You can find some possibilities for this option in the "Multicultural Books in a Series" part and in the reference list for multicultural literature. **Social Studies, Geography, Language Arts**

As you promote literacy in your own classroom, first reflect on what is occurring there. What are the behaviors associated with your readers? With the nonreaders? With the struggling readers? With the unmotivated/reluctant readers? After you have observed and reflected on the behaviors of these children, there are other things to consider. First, let me state that I do not pretend to have all the answers for every child, because I do not know them well enough to give specific suggestions. I would, however, offer suggestions for you to consider, as well as recommending a closer look at some of the resources I have listed for further reading at the end of this book.

There are three things I look for in a successful literature-rich classroom. The first is role models. Who are the role models that students can observe reading? You may be the only one, so make sure to model reading. Share books and talk about what you are reading and what reading means to you. Allow children the pleasure of seeing you read. A second factor is that students must have access to books. Children must have access to a multitude of books on a variety of topics, from many genres, and at various reading levels. Children must be allowed to make choices about what they read. Finally, build in time each day to talk about books. This should include you talking about books, children talking about books, and any other person who loves to read. I do not mean to assign traditional book reports. Instead, the children should talk about books that they have chosen to read in their free time, as well as assigned books. Encourage a spontaneous dialogue and discussion of books. If teachers do not acknowledge the books students read outside of the school curriculum, we send a mixed message about the importance of lifelong reading. After all, when we read a good book, the first thing we want to do is share it with someone. Children want this opportunity, too. If we do not give pleasure reading the attention it deserves, "there will be consequences." If you want to reinforce this point with some books, read *Aunt Chip and the Great Cripple Creek Dam Affair* by Patricia Polacco, *Library Lil* by Suzanne Williams, and *The Library Dragon* by Carmen Agra Deedy. **All Subjects**

---

Sometimes the roadblocks to literacy have to do with pride and intimidation. Struggling readers are intimidated by books that have a lot of words and few or no pictures. These readers still need the comfort of picture books to help make the transition to chapter books. There are things you can do to make picture books a valuable resource in your classroom. First, have them available. Second, read picture books to your students. Talk about them. Make references to picture books. Set up reading buddies with your struggling readers and younger students in the school. These children may shy away from picture books at first because of the stigma attached to being seen with a "baby book," but when you let them know they are going to read to some first-graders or kindergarten students, they usually won't have any problems using a picture book. The best part is that they will practice the story, which helps their reading skills and confidence. I alert primary teachers to the situation, and they choose a small group of young students who would dote on an older student. This reading relationship spilled out of the classroom and onto the playground as well. The older students from my class often walked hand in hand with their young reading buddies. In my 15 years as an elementary teacher, this strategy was by far the most successful for turning reluctant readers into avid readers. A word of caution when using this strategy is to keep this reading to younger students a privilege for the reluctant readers and not as a whole class project. When your whole class does this, the students who need practice the most are lost in the activity. **All Subjects**

---

For educators in junior or senior high school settings, picture books still have a place. They can be used to demonstrate a point, start a lesson, or help students to better understand certain content. They can release student anxiety, launch a discussion, and hook students' curiosity and interest. Using a picture book gets students reading something more than an album cover, Web site, or video label. Another nice thing about picture books is that they can be read in a short time, leaving the rest of the period to finish the lesson.

When teachers take the time to read to their students, they send a strong message: Reading is enjoyable and an important part of learning in a person's life. They become a reading role model, demonstrating one of the necessary links to becoming a lifelong reader.

Let me share a few examples that have been used by secondary teachers with whom I have worked over the years. One social studies teacher starts his American Civil War unit with Patricia Polacco's *Pink and Say*. He said, "When I use this book, I get their attention immediately. *Pink and Say* sets a tone for wanting to learn the facts surrounding the war." This teacher uses many other picture books as well. A junior high math teacher I know has set up a literature library in her room in response to her students' desire to share books. She began with *Math Curse* by John Scieszka and Lane Smith, and that led to more books (e.g., *Counting on Frank* and *Sold! A Mothematics Adventure*). Starting her day by reading a story or chapter from a book has opened up a pathway for communicating with her students about reading and math. Besides the constant book sharing that occurs before class and after school, this teacher said the communication resulting from the books has reduced the math anxiety among students who normally might despise math.

A biology teacher in a neighboring high school provides each student with a recommended list of novels at the beginning of each semester. All the novels have science content interwoven into the stories. The students must choose one from the list or bring one for her to approve. Then they read it by a certain point in the semester. Then the students create visual displays for the books, along with a brief book talk. Another science teacher, who was working with the daughter of one of my colleagues, discovered the power of picture books. I had shared Gary Larson's book *Hey, There's a Hair in My Dirt!* with my colleague. He took it home for his daughter to read, who in turn took it to her teacher. The science teacher read it to the class and wanted to know if I had any other books like this one. Of course, I always have a suggestion or two, but I also referred her to Bette Ammon and Gale Sherman's book *Worth A Thousand Words: An Annotated Guide to Picture Books for Older Readers* for more possibilities. Encourage teachers at the secondary level to collaborate with colleagues across content areas. I have included a bibliography of resources full of ideas on how to connect literature with content areas and people collaborating across content at the end of this book. **All Subjects**

---

Educators are all well aware of the effect television viewing has had on children; reading time competes with viewing time. One of the best ways to address this issue is to arm students and parents with statistics on television viewing trends and the exposure to violence, and then offer alternatives on how to spend their free time. To raise parent awareness, send home the statistics and literature available through the International Reading Association, www.reading.org; American Library Association, www.ala.org; National Council of Teachers of English, www.ncte.org; local and state affiliates of IRA, NCTE, and ALA; National Network against TV Violence; Kaiser Family Foundation Study on Television, www.kff.org; National Center for Educational Statistics; TV-Free America (1-800-939-6737), www.tvfa.ofg; National Parent Teacher Association (1-202-775-3629), www.pta.org; and the Rethinking Schools Group, www.rethinkingschools.org. These are some of the organizations that offer information on television viewing to the public.

Another thing teachers can do in the classroom is to raise students' awareness by conducting some action research with the students. Have them graph the amount of time they watch television over a period of time, and then engage them in discussions about viewing and television violence. Have students define violence, then have them watch their favorite programs over the same aforementioned period of time and tally the acts of violence. Share with students the following national statistical projections on violence: By the time they reach eighth grade, they will have viewed between 40,000 and 140,000 acts of violence, depending on whether one refers to the most conservative or the greatest estimate. Either way, it is a great deal of violence. Have your students extrapolate the numbers they found over time and compare them with the national statistics (*In The Next Three Seconds . . .*, a picture book by Rowland Morgan, can help with the math formulas if needed). In one Oregon classroom, and another in Milwaukee, the students were so outraged when they realized how much violence they had witnessed on television (and how much time they spent watching it) that it prompted them to write letters to community and state leaders. At *Time Magazine*'s Web site, www.time.com/personal, teachers can obtain regular updates on violence in videos. Arm kids with the tools to be critically literate about television viewing; otherwise, the problem will remain undetected. **All Subjects**

---

Becoming a reader involves time, time spent learning to read and then time spent doing it. Time is an issue for all of us. We must make reading part of our daily routine, just as we make time to eat and sleep. Teachers, librarians, and parents must be role models. Give children access to a wide variety of books across genres, including multicultural and gender-conscious literature. Pay attention to children's interests and allow them the freedom to choose their own books. Equally important is providing students time to read and discuss books. I view the components for creating a lifelong reader as a triangle. The sides of the triangle represent the presence of role models, access to many books, and having someone to talk with about books. All sides of this triangle are equal and support each other. **All Subjects**

---

Some of my favorite Web sites connected to children's literature, reading, and promoting literacy are the following:

http://education.boisestate.edu/ssteine
www.lib.muohio.edu/pictbks/
www.ucalgary.ca/~dkbrown/index.html
www.ala.org/BookLinks/
www.ala.org/alsc/
www.ala.org/booklist/55yat5.html
www.cbcbooks.org
www.beyondbasals.com

www.mhhe.com/childlit
www.carolhurst.com/
www.childrenlit.com
www.4kids.org
www.historychannel.org
www.poetry4kids.com
www.soemadison.wisc.edu/ccbc/
www.aig.org
www.reading.org
www.ncte.org
www.idahoreads.com
www.lili.org/isl/readtome. **All Subjects**

---

Many authors have Web pages. Access them directly through a search engine, the first three Web sites listed above, or through the publisher (publisher Web pages are listed at the end of the book). Contacting authors via e-mail or contact through their Web pages increases the chance of receiving a response compared with "snail mail." Authors often are overwhelmed with mail and do not always have time to answer every letter. This is not true of all authors, of course, but many active authors have Web pages that give students information and answers to commonly asked questions. Others have interesting items for children and teachers to download. If you contact the publishers listed at the end of this book, ask them for a list of author Web sites. In some cases, they print a list in their catalog. **Language Arts, with Potential for All Subjects**

---

Paul Fleischman's book, *Weslandia,* is an amazing work of imagination and brilliance. Despite all the external forces, Wesley, the main character, creates a world of his own that is completely self-sustaining. He wears clothes that he produces from the plants he grows. He eats the food he grows. He creates his own alphabet and vocabulary to describe his world, Weslandia. He wins friends through his imagination and wit. This book has many things to think about and discuss with children and adults.

I was struck by Wesley's determination and imagination, his natural curiosity, his ability to stick up for what he believed, and his ability to create and live in a self-sustaining world. I also admired his willingness to share his knowledge with others. It was apparent to my children as they listened to the story that the author was encouraging them to use their imaginations, to believe in their convictions, not to give in to outside pressures, and to create a world they could share with others. My children loved this book. It offers meaningful discussion topics about friends, imagination, and determination in a world that may seem to be moving away from these values. A good companion book is *Out of Sight* by Claude Lapointe. **All Subjects**

# Part IV

# Part IV

## Books That Bring People Together

Multicultural literature is a literature of inclusion: Stories from and stories about all our children.

> —Harriet Rohmer, founder of Children's Book Press

As our world becomes increasingly interdependent, the use of multicultural literature as a tool to help children understand each other is more important than ever before. Promoting the concept of a "global village" is vital to our understanding and tolerance of all peoples. Considering this notion, I began to look at the choices of literature available to our children. I found most multicultural books promoted one particular ethnic group but did not necessarily reflect a global view. Although I recognize that books of this nature are important to our understanding of people, they do not necessarily have an underlying theme of bringing ethnic groups together. For this chapter, I sought books that portrayed people of various ethnic backgrounds interacting in positive ways. I also searched for books that promoted the concept of a global village through universal similarities.

In support of my criteria for promoting an interdependent global village, books such as *Smokey Night* by Eve Bunting and *Who Belongs Here* by Margy Burns-Knight start with an underlying theme of violence or hate but end with the implications for a nonviolent resolution as the result of people working together. I also found *Jamaica's Blue Marker* by Juanita Havill, *Mending Peter's Heart* by Maureen Wittbold, and *Pink and Say* by Patricia Polacco to be realistic examples of people from differing backgrounds coming together, initially under conflict, and then reaching a positive resolution, developing a friendship, or both.

Other books selected, such as *Welcoming Babies* by Margy Burns-Knight, *Play* by Ann Morris, *Children Just Like Me* by Sue Copsey, and *This Is the Way We Eat Our Lunch* by Edith Baer, provide a view of universal similarities. I felt these books promote the concept of a global village because readers see that people can have individual differences but also have much in common. In a world where survival demands cooperation, it is imperative to provide children with books reflecting role models of interconnectedness in ways to which they can relate.

95

Children hold the answers to the social problems of the world, but they shall never arrive at solutions unless they are given an opportunity to think through solutions to social problems. What is the likelihood that students will have a chance to discuss topics such as world peace, war, violence, homelessness, illiteracy, gender equity, racism, changing family structure, aging population, and diversity in the classroom? Is there a controlling effect from a middle-of-the-road, status quo curriculum that limits teachers and students from confronting world realities? Through carefully selected children's literature, educators can provide theoretical rationale and strategies to confront social issues and bring balance to the curriculum.

Why do we need to infuse literature into the curriculum? One reason might be evident from a closer look at the social studies curriculum. Do social studies texts alone provide us with information about *all* people? Do they offer an emotional "hook" to capture students' attention? Books such as *Pink and Say* by Patricia Polacco, *Countdown* by Ben Mikaelsen, *Peace Crane* by Sheila Hamanaka, or *Dragon's Gate* by Laurence Yep can help readers become more interested in the curriculum. For additional reasons to use multicultural literature see page xix.

Should teachers depend on textbooks as their only source of knowledge? Should we only use texts that limit the coverage of the minority population and working-class contributions toward making this nation? Children have a right to know historical truths. They have a right to see and read literature that is a reflection of themselves and their cultural heritage. Take the time to enable your students to become critically literate about the world through children's literature. Use generative themes, cross book talks, critical thinking, and higher-order questioning that evolves from literature and raises social consciousness. Become proactive toward building a world community. Bringing good books into the curriculum provides meaningful, humanizing depth that can bridge ethnic, cultural, and religious differences. I offer some thoughts from William Fulbright (founder of the Fulbright Scholarships for Educators) to ponder: "We must dare to think unthinkable thoughts. We must learn to explore all the options and possibilities that confront us in a complex and rapidly changing world. We must learn to welcome and not to fear the voices of dissent. We must dare to think about unthinkable things because when things become unthinkable, thinking stops and action becomes mindless."

# Picture Books

**Altman, Linda Jacobs.** *The Legend of Freedom Hill.* Illustrated by **Cornelius Van Wright and Ying-Hwa Hu.** Lee & Low Books, 2000. 32p. Grades 1 and up.
Rosabel and Sophie, girls from culturally different backgrounds, are best friends in a new setting. Their families moved to California during the Gold Rush. Rosabel's mother, Miz Violet, is a runaway slave. In California, slavery is against the law, but the Fugitive Slave Act allows bounty hunters to capture and return them to their owners. When Miz Violet is captured, Rosabel and Sophie must find a way to free her.

**Anzaldúa, Gloria.** *Friends from the Other Side/Amigos Del Otro Lado.* Illustrated by **Consuelo Méndez.** Children's Book Press, 1993. 24p. Grades 1–5.

This story takes place along the Rio Grande River between Mexico and Texas. A young girl befriends an illegal alien boy, who is trying to find work to help his family survive. A good story about empathy and compassion for others.

**Ashley, Bernard.** *Cleversticks.* Illustrated by **Derek Brazell.** Crown, 1991. 32p. Pre K–2.

Ling Sung has a difficult time fitting in with his classmates because they can do things he cannot. Tying shoes, buttoning his clothes, and putting on a paint apron are all things he finds difficult because he has never done them before. Then he shows his classmates how to use chopsticks, and he finds a special place in his class.

**Bercaw, Edna Coe.** *Halmoni's Day.* Illustrated by **Robert Hunt.** Dial, 2000. 32p. All ages.

Jennifer's grandmother Halmoni visits her. She arrives from Korea right before Grandparents Day at her American school. Jennifer's concern over Halmoni's language barrier becomes a heartfelt lesson for the whole classroom of guests.

**Bowie, C. W.** *Busy Toes.* Illustrated by **Fred Willingham.** Whispering Coyote, 1998. 32p. All ages.

Toes are the theme in this concept book, viewed through a multicultural lens. The playful text and illustrations warm the spirit. The format appeals to all ages, especially adults who enjoy reading to little children.

**Brandenberg, Aliki.** *Marianthe's Stories: Painted Words/Spoken Memories.* Greenwillow Books, 1998. 64p. Grades K–3.

This book contains two stories in one. The first is about Marianthe's arrival at her new school in the United States. She cannot speak the language and uses pictures to communicate her feelings. The second is about how she uses her artistic ability to tell her family's story. This book has an insightful teacher, who works through children's feelings of discomfort about immigrant children. Ultimately, the young people help build a classroom community.

**Bunting, Eve.** *The Blue and the Gray.* Illustrated by **Ned Bittinger.** Harcourt Brace, 1996. 32p. Grades 1–5.

Two boys from different backgrounds become neighbors in a new housing development. Their homes overlook an unmarked American Civil War battlefield. Historical truths about the war contrast with the boys' friendship. Symbolically, their homes and continued friendship become a monument to the historical fight.

**Bunting, Eve.** *Smokey Night.* Illustrated by **David Diaz.** Harcourt Brace, 1994. 32p. Pre K–5.

A crisis forces people from the same neighborhood, but differing ethnic backgrounds, to seek shelter. The rescue of two cats, once rivals, becomes a catalyst for friendship between neighbors who never communicated before, partly due to their differing ethnic backgrounds.

**Carlson, Margaret.** *The Canning Season.* Illustrated by **Kimanne Smith.** Carolrhoda Books, 1999. 40p. Grades 3–6.

This biographical story is set in 1959. Peggy's longtime best friend shares the same name. One day, they are both faced with the learned behavior of racism that had been masked up to that time. They were going to spend the night together, which they often did, but suddenly her friend was not allowed to spend the night at "a Negro's" house due to the racial tension of the time. This is a good tool to initiate discussions about the subtleties of racist behavior.

**Cohen, Miriam.** *Down in the Subway.* Illustrated by **Melanie Hope Greenberg.** DK, 1998. 32p. Grades Pre K–2.

Young Oscar is riding the subway when he meets the island lady. She tells him about her island by using the props in her bag. Imagery and delight abound in her stories.

**Cowen-Fletcher, Jane.** *It Takes a Village.* Scholastic, 1994. 30p. Pre K–3.

The African proverb, it takes a village to raise a child, is exemplified in this book. On market day, Yemi's family gives her the responsibility of watching her younger brother, Kokou, but he slips from her sight. Searching for Kokou, Yemi learns that everyone looks out for and helps raise the children.

**DiSalvo-Ryan, DyAnne.** *City Green.* William Morrow, 1994. 32p. Grades K–5.

This book shows what a neighborhood, regardless of its differences, can do when residents work together toward a common goal. Included is an address and tips for starting a community garden. For older readers, *Seedfolks* by Paul Fleischman offers another view of a community garden.

**DiSalvo-Ryan, DyAnne.** *Grandpa's Corner Store.* HarperCollins, 2000. 32p. Grades K–4.

The neighborhood stores are closing because the big chains are taking their business away. Soon Lucy's grandpa's grocery store is facing possible closure until Lucy rallies the neighborhood to save it. DiSalvo-Ryan once again shows her strong sense of community.

**Dooley, Norah.** *Everybody Bakes Bread.* Illustrated by **Peter J. Thornton.** Carolrhoda Books, 1996. 40p. Grades K–3.

Carrie and her brother Anthony learn about bread making across cultures. Carrie's mother sends her to the neighbors to borrow a "three-handled" rolling pin. Just like Carrie, readers will wonder what a three-handled rolling pin looks like. This is a companion book to *Everybody Cooks Rice,* discussed below.

**Dooley, Norah.** *Everybody Cooks Rice.* Illustrated by **Peter J. Thornton.** Carolrhoda Books, 1991. 32p. Grades K–3.

We all eat, and rice is a staple in many cultures. Young Carrie searches her multi-ethnic neighborhood for her brother and learns everyone is having rice for dinner, but everyone prepares it with a unique ethnic flavor.

**Friedman, Ina R.** *How My Parents Learned to Eat.* Illustrated by **Allen Say.** Houghton Mifflin, 1984. 32p. Grades K–5.

When people from different cultures come together, they should learn about each other's customs. This heartwarming story shares an interracial courtship as told by the couple's daughter.

**Gray, Libba Moore.** *Miss Tizzy.* Illustrated by **Jada Rowland.** Simon & Schuster, 1993. 29p. All ages.

Miss Tizzy is the matriarch of her multicultural neighborhood. All the children come to her for adventures with cooking, gardening, and play. When she gets sick, the roles are reversed, and all the children come to her house to lift her spirits.

**Gross, Ruth Belov.** *You Don't Need Words! A Book about Ways People Talk without Words.* Illustrated by **Susannah Ryan.** Scholastic, 1991. 48p. All ages.

This book does a remarkable job of explaining how people communicate across language and physical barriers. Also included is historical information showing ways people communicated in the past. Readers learn about historical communicative practices that still exist today.

**Hamanaka, Sheila.** *Peace Crane.* William Morrow, 1995. 40p. Grades 3 and up.

This story is about a young girl who is emotionally moved by the story of Sadako, the girl from Hiroshima who folded 1,000 cranes in hopes of a peaceful world. The girl in this story extrapolates the concept of a peaceful world to her own inner-city neighborhood. She wishes for harmony so that all people may no longer live in fear of violence or in poverty.

**Havill, Juanita.** *Jamaica's Blue Marker.* Illustrated by **Anne Sibley O'Brien.** Houghton Mifflin, 1995. 32p. Pre K–2.

Jamaica becomes a problem solver when Russel scribbles on her artwork. Her initial anger evolves into understanding when she realizes the reason for Russel's actions. His frustration is the result of an anticipated family move. Jamaica acknowledges his feelings by saying she will miss him, then she gives him a special going-away gift. Look for other stories about Jamaica that show her resolving realistic conflicts (e.g., *Jamaica's Find, Jamaica Tag-Along, Jamaica and Brianna, Jamaica and the Substitute Teacher,* all published by Houghton Mifflin).

**Hearne, Betsy.** *Who's in the Hall:* A *Mystery in Four Chapters.* Illustrated by **Christy Hale.** Greenwillow Books, 2000. 32p. Grades 1–3.

This beginning chapter book brings together in friendship children who live on different floors in a high-rise apartment. They discover that they have pets with personalities and similar interests. Some subtle lessons in the story for teachers to capitalize on are that children should never let strangers into their homes, job stereotypes, and cross-age interaction.

**Hesse, Karen.** *Come on, Rain!* Illustrated by **Jon J. Muth.** Scholastic, 1999. 32p. Pre K–3.

In this award-winning book, Hesse's words capture the hot days of summer, when people yearn for rain to offer a reprieve from the heat. When the rain comes, so does the celebration of neighborhood mothers and daughters, dancing in the street.

**Hoffman, Mary.** *Amazing Grace.* Illustrated by **Caroline Binch.** Dial, 1991. 26p. Pre K–3.

This gloriously illustrated and thoughtful story finds Grace's self-esteem at stake because she is told girls can't play the character of Peter Pan, nor can someone who is Black. In the end, the students learn a lesson about picking the best person for the lead role, regardless of gender or skin color. Hoffman also wrote a sequel, *Boundless*

*Grace,* that offers powerful insight on family structure and why it is important to have books in the classroom that reflect the students. In another book, *An Angel Just Like Me,* Hoffman offers a thought-provoking portrayal of the traditional Christmas story.

**Howlett, Bud.** *I'm New Here.* Houghton Mifflin, 1993. 32p. Grades 1–4.

This is a realistic look at an immigrant student from El Salvador on her first day of school in the United States. As Jazmine and her classmates work through many misunderstandings because of her limited English, she wins friends who make her feel welcome.

**Jiménez, Francisco.** *La Mariposa.* Illustrated by **Simón Silva.** Houghton Mifflin, 1998. 32p. Grades K–4.

This is a personal story from Jiménez's life. He moved with his family from Mexico to California to work in the fields when he was young. Francisco went to an English-only school, even though his native language was Spanish. He became an easy target for the older boys because of his limited English, but Francisco used his peaceful manner and drawing skills to make friends.

**King Jr., Martin Luther.** *I Have a Dream.* Illustrated by 15 Coretta Scott King Award and Honor Book artists. Scholastic, 1997. 40p. Pre K–3.

Martin Luther King Jr.'s speech, delivered on August 28, 1963, has been recognized as one of the most moving and inspirational speeches of the 20th century. His courage and tenacious spirit continue to be an inspiration to all who strive for equality and justice. The artwork, coupled with the words from King's speech, is a moving tribute to the continuing struggle to achieve King's dream. This speech can be accessed, viewed, and heard on CD-ROM. Look for *Encarta Africana* coedited by noted historian, Henry Louis Gates, and others. www.africana.com.

**Knight, Margy Burns.** *Who Belongs Here? An American Story.* Illustrated by **Anne Sibley O'Brien.** Tilbury House, 1993. 40p. Grades 3–8.

This is a poignant and realistic view of a young Cambodian refugee who comes to the United States. Nary's limited English and cultural identity make him a target of harassment. Other students have no idea what it is like to be a refugee. He talks to his teacher about his feelings, and together they plan a lesson for his social studies class. As his classmates begin to think about their own past and present backgrounds, they realize an important lesson about the origin of all Americans. A portion of the proceeds from this book goes to educational programs that teach tolerance.

**Kroll, Virginia.** *Pink Paper Swans.* Illustrated by **Nancy L. Clouse.** William B. Eerdmans, 1994. 32p. Grades K–5.

Young Janetta lives in a multicultural apartment complex with her mother. She befriends a neighbor, Mrs. Tsujimoto, who makes beautiful origami animals. When Mrs. Tsujimoto's arthritis makes it difficult for her to continue doing origami to supplement her income, Janetta finds a way to help. Directions for folding a paper swan are included.

**Krupinski, Loretta.** *Best Friends.* Scholastic, 1998. 32p. Grades 1–5.

Krupinski envisioned this story after viewing artifacts from the late 1800s and reading about the plight of the Nez Perce during U.S. westward expansion. In this story, two young girls, Lily, of Nez Perce descent, and Charlotte, a young girl from Kansas, become friends. They teach each other important skills that stress the endurance of friendship.

**Kurtz, Jane.** *Faraway Home.* Illustrated by **E. B. Lewis.** Harcourt Brace, 2000. 32p. Pre K–3.

This is a wonderful story about a young girl named Desta who learns through family stories about her heritage. Her grandmother in Ethiopia, whom Desta has never met, is sick. Desta's father wants to see his ailing mother. As he plans to make the journey from their home in Portland, Oregon, to Ethiopia, stories about his childhood help Desta understand the differences between their present life and her African heritage.

**Lin, Grace.** *The Ugly Vegetables.* Charlesbridge, 1999. 32p. Grades K–3.

This story depicts a diverse neighborhood, where most of the people grow beautiful flower gardens. The daughter of one family who grows Chinese vegetables thinks her family's garden isn't very pretty. She learns from her mother, however, that a garden can provide much more than flowers and color. The vegetables they harvest bring all the neighbors together for "ugly vegetable soup" (recipe included).

**Lorbiecki, Marybeth.** *Sister Anne's Hands.* Illustrated by **K. Wendy Popp.** Dial, 1998. 36p. Grades 1–5.

This conscientious book is set in the early 1960s, when racial tensions were particularly high. Sister Anne, who is Black, comes to teach at an all-white school. Even though the school is part of a church community, its members—including the children—are not immune to racist feelings. Anna and her classmates learn a memorable lesson from Sister Anne: People of all skin colors can get along.

**Lundgren, Mary Beth.** *We Sing the City.* Illustrated by **Donna Perrone.** Clarion Books, 1997. 32p. Grades K–3.

An ethnically diverse group of children celebrates diversity in their city. The children celebrate every aspect of their city: names, transportation, ethnic foods, occupations, places of worship, communities, and schools. This book is especially unique in the way Lundgren expands the perspective of diversity as being associated with more than just skin color. This book could be used as a model to explore the rich qualities of diversity in other cities.

**McDonough, Yona Zeldis.** *Sisters in Strength: American Women Who Made a Difference.* Illustrated by **Malcah Zeldis.** Henry Holt, 2000. 48p. Grades 3 and up.

Strong women throughout history have helped make the United States what it is today. These 11 mini-biographies of women serve as a tantalizing beginning for further exploration and research. Included in the collection are Pocahontas, Harriet Tubman, Elizabeth Cady Stanton, Susan B. Anthony, Clara Barton, Emily Dickinson, Mary Cassatt, Helen Keller, Eleanor Roosevelt, Amelia Earhart, and Margaret Mead. Also included are a handy time line and a bibliography.

**McGill, Alice.** *Molly Bannaky.* Illustrated by **Chris K. Soentpiet.** Houghton Mifflin, 1999. 32p. Grades 3 and up.

This is the story of Benjamin Banneker's grandmother. She was exiled from England in 1683 and was sentenced to serve as an indentured servant in America. After seven years, she staked a claim on a parcel of land in what is now Maryland. After a short period of time, she bought and then befriended an African slave. Later they were married and had four daughters. The oldest had a son, Benjamin. His grandmother Molly taught him to read and write. Benjamin grew up to be one of the first African American scientists and wrote the first African American almanac.

**Miller, William.** *The Piano.* Illustrated by **Susan Keeter.** Lee & Low Books, 2000. 32p. Grades 1 and up.

Tia has an ear for music. One day, she wanders into the white section of town so she can be closer to beautiful piano music. She accepts a job as a maid from Mrs. Hartwell, who lives in the house where music can be heard. The caring relationship between them is a wonderful tribute to cross-age and cross-cultural friendships.

**Miller, William.** *Richard Wright and the Library Card.* Illustrated by **Gregory Christie.** Lee & Low Books, 1997. 34p. Grades 2 and up.

This biographical story is from Richard Wright's life. Miller tells of a time when Black people often could not have library cards. Wright shared his determination to read with an understanding white man, who allowed Wright to use his own card to check out books.

**Millman, Isaac.** *Moses Goes to School.* Farrar, Straus & Giroux, 2000. 32p. Grades K–3.

This is the story of a boy named Moses, who attends a special school for children with hearing impairment. The students there communicate enthusiastically with sign language. They come from diverse backgrounds, reflective of many cultures. This book is a great example of varied learning conditions, crossing cultures in a natural situation.

**Mitchell, Lori.** *Different Just Like Me.* Charlesbridge, 1999. 32p. Grades K–3.

While traveling and visiting her grandmother, April learns that everyone is different, but people also have many things in common. Readers get a natural sense of the diversity that surrounds them on a daily basis and how these differences are positive qualities.

**Mochizuki, Ken.** *Heroes.* Illustrated by **Dom Lee.** Lee & Low Books, 1995. 32p. Grades 2–6.

Donnie is constantly bullied because of his heritage until his war-veteran father and uncle come to school one day, dressed in their U.S. military uniforms. The result is a new understanding of Asian Americans. To help build friendships, they encourage the boys to play a friendly game of football instead of war games.

**Moore, Inga.** *Six Dinner Sid.* Simon & Schuster, 1991. 32p. Pre K–3.

This heartwarming story about a clever cat named Sid will bring a smile to readers as they watch him outsmart his former owners. Six different households claim ownership of Sid, but no one is aware of each other's stake. The absence of communication in Sid's first neighborhood contrasts with the community spirit between his new owners.

**Older, Effin.** *My Two Grandmothers.* Illustrated by **Nancy Hayashi.** Harcourt Brace, 2000. 32p. Pre K–3.

Lily celebrates Christmas with one grandmother and Hanukkah with the other. Each celebration is unique and special, but Lily wants a celebration that brings her two grandmothers to her house. A good example of naturally blending family traditions.

**Patrick, Denise Lewis.** *The Car Washing Street.* Illustrated by **John Ward.** Tambourine Books, 1993. 26p. Grades K and up.

Car washing can be a chore or a rollicking good time. Saturday-morning car washes in this multicultural neighborhood get everybody talking and laughing. A charming book!

*The People with Five Fingers: A Native California Creation Tale.* Retold by **John Bierhorst.** Illustrated by **Robert Andrew Parker.** Marshall Cavendish, 2000. 32p. All ages.

Before this world, there was another world, where only animals lived. Coyote made wishes and plans in his mind. He then shared them with the other animals. They asked many questions, but Coyote said, we shall have people in this world because the Earth cannot stay naked. They also agreed that part of the New World's beauty would be people speaking different languages and having different skin colors. The people will be able to talk and laugh, too. Since that time, the animals no longer talk. This is an incredible pourquoi story that embraces a harmonious world, retold by a renowned expert on Native American stories.

**Pfeffer, Wendy.** *Marta's Magnets.* Illustrated by **Gail Piazza.** Silver Burdett, 1995. 32p. Grades 1–5.

Marta, a new girl in the neighborhood, is challenged with making new friends. She discovers that her magnet collection is a way to attract friendship. This book is a natural for blending literature and scientific understanding. Another nice aspect of this book is that it features a female protagonist who is involved in science-related activities.

**Polacco, Patricia.** *Chicken Sunday.* Philomel, 1992. 32p. Grades K–5.

Mrs. Eula May Walker helps the neighborhood children see the good in people through her own actions. In this touching story, friends and family find something special to do for her that creates memories of friendship in the process.

**Polacco, Patricia.** *Mrs. Katz and Tush.* Bantam Books, 1992. 32p. Grades K–5.

In a neighborhood that reflects diversity on several levels, Larnel believes he has the perfect cure for his lonely neighbor, Mrs. Katz. He finds a kitten for her. As a result of his thoughtful and caring act, a bright friendship begins that crosses generations.

**Polacco, Patricia.** *Pink and Say.* Philomel, 1994. 48p. Grades 3 and up.

In this story handed down in the Polacco family, set in the American Civil War, two young boys from different worlds create a powerful tale of friendship. The content and story line of this book works well for reading aloud in a social studies class.

**Pomerantz, Charlotte.** *You're Not My Best Friend Anymore.* Illustrated by **David Soman.** Dial, 1998. 32p. Grades K–3.

Molly and Ben live in a two-family house. They do everything together, until one day when they have an argument—a big argument. A good book about people from different backgrounds working to solve disagreements.

**Raschka, Chris.** *Ring! Yo?* DK, 2000. 40p. Pre K–2.

Raschka has an uncanny ability to turn a few words into a meaningful text. His seemingly simple illustrations emit an expressive power that works well with his brief script. In this book he concludes with a possible scenario for readers to ponder. This book is a sequel to the cross-cultural friendship found in *Yo! Yes?*

**Raschka, Chris.** *Yo! Yes?* Orchard, 1993. 32p. Pre K–2.

This Caldecott Honor book contains a simple text offering a positive image of cross-cultural friendship. Raschka's expressive illustrations could stand alone, but the combination of words and pictures makes the book even more powerful.

**Rattigan, Jama Kim.** *Dumpling Soup.* Illustrated by **Lillian Hsu-Flanders.** Little, Brown, 1993. 32p. Grades K–5.

Every New Year's Eve, Marisa's family gathers at her grandmother's home to make a traditional dumpling soup. Cooking meals, playing games, watching fireworks, and lots of laughter make this a special time for a family her grandmother calls "chop suey" because they are from Korean, Chinese, Hawaiian, and *haole* (Hawaiian for Anglos) descent.

**Reiser, Lynn.** *Margaret and Margarita/Margarita y Margaret.* Greenwillow Books, 1993. 32p. Pre K–2.

Two girls from different cultures play at the same park and become friends, despite a language barrier. Their attempts to communicate become a catalyst for a friendship between their mothers, too.

**Rohmer, Harriet (editor).** *Honoring Our Ancestors: Stories and Pictures by Fourteen Artists.* Children's Book Press, 1999. 32p. All ages.

This book is a beautiful tribute to people who have been influential in the lives of the artists featured here. The artists come from diverse cultural backgrounds, and the book's format encourages similar class projects. None of these ancestors are likely to be mentioned in a history book, but they left an impression on individual lives. A wonderful book connection is *Seven Brave Women* by Betsy Hearne.

**Ryan, Pam Munoz.** *One Hundred Is a Family.* Illustrated by **Benrei Huang.** Hyperion, 1994. 32p. Pre K–3.

Ryan does a great job of capturing the essence of a global family. She moves from the concept of the immediate family to capture the notion of larger "families," such as a classroom of children, a group of singers, and 100 people all caring for the Earth. Math applications abound.

**Scott, Elaine.** *Friends.* Photos by **Margaret Miller.** Atheneum, 2000. 40p. Pre K–3.

Friendship is universal and crucial for all people—especially children. This book for young children is filled with joy, depicting choices that children must make as they make friends.

**Shelby, Anne.** *Potluck.* Illustrated by **Irene Trivas.** Orchard, 1991. 32p. Grades K–3.

Preparing and sharing ethnic foods with people from other cultures has become the most natural means of acculturation between people, but there is no meal quite like this potluck, where everyone brings a special food item to share. This is also a useful alphabet book.

**Shelf-Medearis, Angela.** *The Adventures of Sugar and Junior.* Illustrated by **Nancy Poydar.** Holiday House, 1995. 32p. Grades 2–5.

Sugar, a girl "near" Junior's age, moves in next door. They play together, bake together, go to scary movies, and share ice-cream cones in a cross-cultural friendship that will have readers smiling.

**Sis, Peter.** *Madlenka.* Farrar, Straus & Giroux, 2000. 44p. Grades K–2.

Madlenka has a loose tooth. Like most kids her age, she is obsessed with the fact that it's loose. She wants to tell the world and walks around her multicultural neighborhood to let all her friends know. They greet her in their native languages. When her mother finally finds Madlenka, she says she has been around the world and lost her tooth. A charming story!

**Steptoe, John.** *Creativity.* Illustrated by **E. B. Lewis.** Clarion Books, 1997. 32p. Grades 3–6.

Charles gets a new classmate, Hector, from Puerto Rico. He can't figure out how Hector can look like him but speak a different language. Through their friendship, Charles learns more about cultural misconceptions, as well as important lessons about his ancestry.

**Tabor, Nancy Mar'a Grande.** *We Are a Rainbow.* Charlesbridge, 1997. 32p. Pre K–1.

Tabor combines a simple but expressive text with paper cutout illustrations, providing a nice message about how people are different, but very much the same.

**Vigna, Judith.** *Black Like Kyra, White Like Me.* Albert Whitman, 1992. 32p. Grades K–3.

Christy and Kyra are friends at the youth center, but when Kyra's family moves into Christy's neighborhood, their friendship is challenged. Ethnic groups don't normally mix in this neighborhood. Christy's family helps her understand racism and sets an example of acceptance for all the neighbors.

**Vizurraga, Susan.** *Miss Opal's Auction.* Illustrated by **Mark Graham.** Henry Holt, 2000. 32p. Grades K–3.

A touching relationship between young Annie and her neighbor Miss Opal comes to a crossroads when Miss Opal decides to sell her house and possessions so she can move into a retirement home. Annie and Miss Opal did many things together, including baking. When Miss Opal gives Annie her favorite cookbook, Annie knows that her friendship will last for generations.

**Williams, Karen.** *When Africa Was Home.* Orchard, 1991. 32p. Pre K–2.

Peter's family lives in Africa. His African nanny influences him as much as his mother does. She has children with whom he plays. He considers them part of his family. When Peter's family moves to the United States, Peter is unsure whether Africa or America is truly his home.

**Williams, Sherley Anne.** *Girls Together.* Illustrated by **Synthia Saint James.** Harcourt Brace, 1999. 32p. Grades K–3.

This beautiful story about friendship between five girls who live in a housing project uses illustrations to portray rich diversity. Williams's realistic description of the characters will remind readers of friends from their communities. This is a nice companion book to *We Sing the City* by Mary Beth Lundgren.

**Wing, Natashia.** *Jalapeno Bagels.* Illustrated by **Robert Casilla.** Atheneum, 1996. 24p. Grades K–3.

Pablo wants to bring something to school for International Day. His parents, who own a bakery, are from two ethnic groups. They suggest some of their favorite pastries. Pablo decides to bring something that represents his combined Jewish and Mexican heritage.

**Wittbold, Maureen.** *Mending Peter's Heart.* Illustrated by **Larry Salk.** Portunus, 1995. 32p. Grades 1–4.

Young Peter has lost his beloved dog, and old Mr. MacIntyre knows through experience what it feels like to lose a loved one. The need for someone to feel and understand their hurt evolves into a wonderful friendship across culture and age.

**Wong, Janet S.** *This Next New Year.* Illustrated by **Yangsook Choi.** Farrar, Straus & Giroux, 2000. 32p. Grades K–2.

This is a delightfully unique story in which a young boy of Korean and Chinese ancestry observes the Chinese New Year celebration in his neighborhood. His family follows many of the Chinese traditions, but they also have modified them to honor their Korean side, too. His multicultural neighbors adopt some of the Chinese traditions into their own celebrations.

**Yee, Brenda Shannon.** *Sand Castle.* Illustrated by **Thea Kliros.** Greenwillow Books, 1999. 24p. Pre K–2.

Jen is building a castle on the beach, and children from different backgrounds join in the fun. Together they build a moat, towers, windows, and other details for the sandcastle. They work in harmony and decide to do it all over again the next day. In addition to depicting children across ethnic groups playing together, this book is a nice representation of children's innate desire to play and communicate with others. Another book that shows this same concept is *Margaret and Margarita* by Lynn Reiser.

# Poetry

**Benson, Laura Lee.** *This Is Our Earth.* Illustrated by **John Carrozza.** Charlesbridge, 1994. 32p. All ages.

The verse and pictures in this captivating book have a message for all to hear: "This is our Earth to cherish and love, to clean and protect from below and above." In addition to the verse is text including brief facts and thoughts to ponder. Included at the end of the book is music to accompany the complete verse.

**Feldman, Eve B.** *Birthdays: Celebrating Life around the World.* Illustrated by children from 24 different nations. Bridge Water, 1996. 32p. Pre K–2.

This book, describing birthday celebrations from around the world, is written in rhyming text with playful illustrations contributed by children from many nations. Part of the proceeds support Paintbrush Diplomacy, an organization that promotes international communication through the exchange of children's letters and artwork. Information about Paintbrush Diplomacy is included.

**Gold, Julia.** *From a Distance.* Illustrated by **Jane Ray.** Dutton, 1998/1999. 24p. All ages.

This song, originally written by Gold before her 30th birthday in 1986, has become a wonderful inspiration for peace and harmony across the land. Nanci Griffith was the first to record the song and has since recorded it in four languages. Gold's inspirational message has been heard throughout the world and was even played to wake up astronauts on the space shuttle.

**Grimes, Nikki.** *Aneesa Lee and the Weaver's Gift.* Illustrated by **Ashley Bryan.** Lothrop, Lee & Shepard, 1999. 32p. All ages.

On one hand, this is a collection of poems that describe the tools and the process of weaving. On the other hand, Grimes's words are a metaphor for the beautiful colors and multicultural peoples that are so intricately woven together to make this beautiful world.

**Guthrie, Woody.** *This Land Is Your Land.* Illustrated by **Kathy Jakobsen.** Little, Brown, 1998. 32p. All ages.

This is Woody Guthrie's song in picture-book form. One only has to listen to or read Woody Guthrie's words to know that he was sincere about bringing people together in this great land. Kathy Jakobsen's marvelous illustrations share the same sentiment.

**Hamanaka, Sheila.** *All the Colors of the Earth.* William Morrow, 1994. 32p. Pre K–2.

Illustrated in warm tones that are interwoven with poems, Hamanaka's poetry enlightens readers about all the colors on this Earth. She projects her message through the eyes of children.

**Hoberman, Mary Ann (editor).** *My Song Is Beautiful: Poems and Pictures in Many Voices.* Little, Brown, 1994. 32p. Grades 3 and up.

This collection of verse from many poets celebrates the vibrancy and beauty of this world through the eyes of children. The combination of illustration and verse captures the essence of our multicultural world.

**Hopkins, Lee Bennett.** *My America: A Poetry Atlas of the United States.* Illustrated by **Stephen Alcorn.** Simon & Schuster, 2000. 83p. Grades 3 and up.

Hopkins is a master at compiling poetry around a theme. This anthology covers the 50 states. The poets reflect our rich heritage. Each poem speaks to a specific state in the United States.

**Katz, Bobbi.** *We the People.* Illustrated by **Nina Crews.** Greenwillow Books, 2000. 100p. Grades 3 and up.

Katz has compiled a collection of her poetry, in a first-person voice, that marvelously traces the history of the United States through significant events and famous people. This book supports multicultural contributions in the making of the nation.

**Maguire, Arlene.** *We're All Special.* Illustrated by **Sheila Lucas.** Portunus, 1995. 32p. All ages.

A poetic description of how each of us is unique, yet has universal qualities. The splendid illustrations depict diversity in a broad sense.

**Mavor, Salley.** *You and Me: Poems about Friendship.* Orchard, 1997. 32p. All ages.

The focus on friendship in this book has a universal appeal. The characteristics of friendships are truly universal.

**Nicholls, Judith.** *Someone I Like: Poems about People.* Illustrated by **Giovanni Manna.** Barefoot Books, 2000. 40p. All ages.

This thematic collection of poetry from 23 multicultural poets focuses on friendship and admiration for special people. The beautiful watercolor illustrations support cross-cultural friendships.

**Nikola-Lisa, W.** *Bein' with You This Way.* Illustrated by **Michael Bryant.** Lee & Low Books, 1994. 32p. Pre K–3.

This book, written in a poetic street rhyme chant, reflects the physical characteristics that make us who we are. It is a rhythmically upbeat book full of happy children.

**Nye, Naomi Shihab.** *This Same Sky: A Collection of Poems from around the World.* Four Winds Press, 1992. 224p. Grades 5 and up.

This is a unique thematic collection of poetry from 68 countries around the world. It includes poems on topics such as families, loss, human mysteries, and places where people live.

**Osborne, Mary Pope.** *The Calico Book of Bedtime Rhymes from around the World.* Illustrated by **T. Lewis.** Contemporary Books, 1990. 64p. Pre K–2.

Throughout history, adults have sung, recited, read, and lulled children to sleep with bedtime rhymes. This book is a marvelous anthology of some of the best bedtime rhymes. Enjoy the universal delight of people from a variety of ethnic backgrounds when they recognize a rhyme from their childhood that was lost in their "memory bank."

**Paul, Ann Whitford.** *All by Herself.* Illustrated by **Michael Steirnagle.** Browndeer Press, 1999. 40p. Grades 3 and up.

These poems are a tribute to 14 women who made a difference. Beautiful illustrations parallel Whitford's eloquent tribute to Amelia Earhart, Mary Jane McLeod, Rachel Carson, Violet Sheeny, Sacajawea, Ida Lewis, Wilma Rudolph, Wanda Gag, Harriet Hanson, Kate Shelley, Pocahontas, Maria Mitchell, Golda Mabovitch, and Frances Ward.

**Philip, Neil.** *It's a Woman's World: A Century of Women's Voices in Poetry.* Dutton, 2000. 93p. Grades 3 and up.

This collection includes the work of more than 50 female poets from diverse backgrounds. The poems are grouped according to the following themes: Dear Female Heart, News of a Baby, A Freedom Song, Domestic Economy, Power, I Live with a Bullet, and The Old Women Gathered.

**Rosen, Michael J. (editor).** *The Greatest Table.* Illustrated by various artists. Harcourt Brace, 1994. 16p. All ages.

This 12-foot accordion book has a message about world hunger. The illustrations of food are exceptional. Part of the proceeds go to support Share Our Strength's projects. More interesting information on this organization and the author and illustrators is included in the book extensions in Part II.

**Ryder, Joanne.** *Earth Dance.* Illustrated by **Norman Garbaty.** Henry Holt, 1996. 32p. Pre K–3.

No matter where or who we are, human beings share the same precious Earth. Verse and illustrations dance across the pages in tribute to the planet.

**Weiss, David, and Bob Thiele.** *What a Wonderful World.* Illustrated by **Ashley Bryan.** Atheneum, 1995 (original song, 1967). 28p. All ages.

"What a Wonderful World," originally recorded by Louis Armstrong, says many things to many people and emanates a spirit of togetherness. Armstrong's recording of this song would be a nice addition to a lesson using this book.

**Yolen, Jane (editor).** *Street Rhymes around the World.* Illustrated by 17 international artists. Boyds Mills Press, 1992. 40p. Pre K–5.

Children everywhere engage in play, and Yolen has edited a multicultural masterpiece with artists from around the world. This book features songs, rhymes, and chants in native languages and in English. Yolen uses this format in a great companion book, *Sleep Rhymes around the World,* featured in the first part of this book.

# Fiction and Nonfiction

**Adler, C. S.** *Youn Hee & Me.* Harcourt Brace, 1995. 183p. Grades 3–8.

Everything was fine with Caitlin, her mother, and adopted brother Simon (formerly Si Won) until Mrs. Lacy learns that Simon has an older sister living in a Korean orphanage. The story focuses on the struggles Caitlin and her new sister, Youn Hee, have as they learn about each other and reconcile their differences.

**Bat-Ami, Miriam.** *Two Suns in the Sky.* Front Street/Cricket Books, 1999. 220p. Grades 6 and up.

Two worlds come together in this riveting first-love story between an American Jewish girl and a Yugoslavian refugee. The story is set at the end of World War II.

**Bloor, Michael.** *Tangerine.* Harcourt Brace, 1997. 294p. Grades 6 and up.

Overshadowed by an older brother who is a sports hero, 12-year-old Paul must find his place in a new community and school, on a new soccer team, and within his family. This page-turning novel unveils some cross-cultural tensions in the community, as well as some unspoken family secrets. Paul learns some powerful messages about family loyalty and friendships across ethnic groups.

**Coleman, Penny.** *Girls: A History of Growing Up Female in America.* Scholastic, 2000. 192p. Grades 4 and up.

This book offers a marvelous contribution to U.S. history studies. Coleman's theme of female contributions crosses many cultures. This book provides an overdue perspective on the making of America, drawn from diaries, memoirs, letters, household manuals, magazines, and advice books.

**Crew, Linda.** *Children of the River.* Bantam Doubleday, 1989. 213p. Grades 6 and up.

Cambodian refugees who came to work the land near the author's home inspired this captivating story. Through the eyes of a teenage girl, Crew describes the move to the United States and the conflict between Cambodian and American culture.

**Draper, Sharon M.** *Romiette and Julio.* Atheneum, 1999. 236p. Grades 7 and up.

What happens when a new kid from the South with Hispanic roots moves to a school in the North where Blacks rule? To add to the tension, Julio befriends Romiette, a Black girl. The Blacks from "the 'hood" don't want anybody outside their race messing with "their kind." This is a timely and thought-provoking story about gangs, resistance, coping, and friendship.

**Fleischman, Paul.** *Seedfolks.* HarperCollins, 1997. 69p. Grades 4 and up.

Each chapter in this book is about one of the colorful characters in Kim's neighborhood. Kim is trying to find a way to connect with her father, who died eight months before she was born. She knows he was a farmer in Vietnam, and she thinks that planting seeds in the vacant lot near her apartment in Cleveland might help her connect with him. Ana, the old lady who loves spying on people from her apartment window, thinks Kim is up to no good. Why was she sneaking around an empty lot? As more characters unfold, new thoughts and perceptions are revealed. What is it that connects these people? This is a fascinating and quick read for reluctant readers.

**Gaskins, Pearl Fuyo.** *What Are You? Voices of Mixed-Race Young People.* Henry Holt, 1999. 273p. Grades 6 and up.

Gaskins is the offspring of mixed-race parents, one Japanese American and the other European American. Over the years, she has received a variety of reactions, ranging from disapproval to acceptance. What do teens of mixed race face today? Gaskins offers readers 80 in-depth interviews with mixed-race teens. An excellent resource section for additional reading and viewing is included.

**Hamilton, Virginia.** *Bluish.* Blue Sky, 1999. 127p. Grades 4–8.

Bluish is a nickname given to a new sixth-grade classmate who is frail, strange, and wears knitted hats all the time. Dreenie and Tuli find Bluish enough of a curiosity to befriend her. When their class learns Bluish is in remission from acute lymphoblastic leukemia, they have many questions. They soon come to an understanding about having an ill classmate. Hamilton has a moving and realistic setting for readers to help understand friendship in difficult times.

**Hobbs, Will.** *Far North.* William Morrow, 1996. 226p. Grades 6 and up.

What happens if the only thing you have in common with your roommate at the boarding school is your birthday? This page-turning survival adventure and coming-of-age novel puts a Texan in a room with a Northwest Native American. Their survival forces them to depend on one another. Hobbs has a talent for blending life lessons with Native American traditions, cross-cultural friendships, survival, and adventure. Look for Hobbs's other books, including *Bearstone* and *Beardance*.

**Lee, Marie S.** *Necessary Roughness.* HarperCollins, 1996. 228p. Grades 6 and up.

Chan Yung Kim had no problems fitting in when he lived in Los Angeles, but moving to a small community in Minnesota challenges his popularity. Everything is different. Soccer was the most popular sport in his California school, but football is all students want to talk about in Minnesota. His father doesn't seem to appreciate what he does either. His sister just pretends to accept all the changes. Marie Lee emotionally captures the tensions between traditional and Western values. A Korean American teenager's need to belong and feel appreciated offers readers an emotional and insightful story that includes both agony and humor.

**Levine, Anna.** *Running on Eggs.* Front Street/Cricket Books, 1999. 128p. Grades 6 and up.

This powerful novel set in contemporary Israel is about two girls on the same track team. Karen is Jewish, and Yasmine is Arab, two cultures that have been at odds with one another for centuries. As their friendship grows, so does the tension of age-old prejudice from their families. This is a great story for discussing current tensions in the Middle East.

**Mikaelsen, Ben.** *Countdown.* Hyperion, 1996. 248p. Grades 4–8.

What if you were the first student in space? Elliot is a ranch kid from Montana who gets the one-in-a-million chance to be America's first student in space. Part of his duty while orbiting Earth is to communicate with ham radio operators around the world. Little does he know that a Maasai boy from Kenya, who is his own age, will challenge what Elliot thought to be central to the world's truths. Mikaelsen has readers spellbound from beginning to end in this thought-provoking story about life, friendships, and the uncertain future of our planet.

**Namioka, Lensey.** *Yang the Third and Her Impossible Family.* Little, Brown, 1995. 143p. Grades 3–6.

This book is a sequel to *Yang the Youngest and His Terrible Ear.* In this humorous and heartwarming contemporary story, the third sister Yingmei Yang wants to become "American" in every way. Unfortunately, the rest of her family doesn't seem to know the right things to do. One fiasco after another plagues Yingmei's futile attempts. More important, Yingmei learns about true friendship and the preservation of cultural traditions.

**Olson, Gretchen.** *Joyride.* Boyds Mills Press, 1998. 200p. Grades 7 and up.

This is an eye-opening story of an Anglo teenager who must make restitution for the damages he caused while driving in a farmer's newly planted strawberry field. Working alongside the *campesinos* and the owner's family causes Jeff to reevaluate all the racial slurs toward Hispanics that he has heard most of his life. An excellent book to use in communities with migrant workers.

**Salisbury, Graham.** *Under the Blood Red Sun.* Delacorte Press, 1994. 246p. Grades 5 and up.

Tomi was born in Hawaii, but his parents and grandparents were born in Japan. On the day that Japan attacks Pearl Harbor, his world—along with those of other Japanese descendants living in American territory—is turned upside down. His father is taken prisoner. His grandfather is loyal to Japan, and his friendships were being tested. How can you be friends one day and enemies the next, just because of one's heritage? Salisbury captures the tension of the time in this award-winning novel set at the beginning of U.S. involvement in World War II.

**Spinelli, Jerry.** *Maniac Magee.* Little, Brown, 1990. 184p. Grades 3–8.

Spinelli spent 10 years writing this story, and his careful crafting and patience paid off. He won the Newbery Award, and readers reap the benefits of his genius. This story touches on every social issue we encounter in the United States, including racism, gangs, homelessness, illiteracy, aging, and death. Maniac knows no boundaries and works to achieve a positive relationship with everyone he meets. He is a legend in the neighborhood. This book is in my top-10 list of the best children's books I have ever read.

**Staples, Suzanne Fisher.** *Dangerous Skies.* Farrar, Straus & Giroux, 1996. 232p. Grades 5 and up.

This is a compelling look at friendship and the hypocrisy of racism that continues to haunt this country. Buck Smith and his closest friend, Tunes, have shared their concept of the world since the day they were born. They are raised together, attend the same school, know all the good fishing spots and hiding places, and enjoy watching animals in the wild. They do everything together except live in the same house. Buck comes from a long line of farmers who settled the land. Tunes's ancestry goes back to the African people who were brought as slaves to work the Smith's farm. But that was back in the 1700s, and it's now 1991. All the negative feelings about African Americans are behind them—or are they? When Tunes is accused of killing their good friend, Jorge, the wounds of racism are opened, and Buck is confused about why the grown-ups won't believe him.

**Taylor, Theodore.** *The Cay.* Doubleday, 1969. 138p. Grades 5 and up.

This story has become a ritualistic read in many classrooms, and justifiably so. Master storyteller Theodore Taylor has ingeniously interwoven racial prejudice and human compassion into a gripping story of survival. Phillip's mother had always told him that Blacks were inferior to whites. Then the Germans bomb the freighter on which they are traveling. His mother dies, and Phillip is marooned on an island with an elderly Black man named Timothy. Phillip must depend on Timothy. To complicate matters, Phillip was blinded by a blow to his head. The friendship and understanding that grow with their struggle to survive will make an impression on readers. Taylor later wrote a "prequel," *Timothy of the Cay,* to accompany this book. More recently, he wrote a biographical novel, *The Bomb,* that is based on his experience evacuating the natives off the Atoll Islands during World War II.

**Testa, Maria.** *Dancing Pink Flamingos and Other Stories.* Lerner, 1995. 115p. Grades 5 and up.

This is a brilliant collection of Testa's short stories, written from the perspective of 10 diverse teenagers who are challenged with the struggles of surviving in a world that would like to take them down a path of self-defeat. This is a great collection for reluctant readers.

**Traylor, Betty.** *Buckaroo.* Delacorte Press, 1999. 196p. Grades 5–8.

This story is set in the late 1950s, a time of segregation. Preston Davis, a.k.a. "Buckaroo," is sent to live with his eccentric Aunt Eugenia, who had raised his mother. From Preston's perspective, his life centers around the following facts: His mother has died; his father has remarried a woman with two daughters, whom Preston despises; and the situation has forced him to move to Aunt Eugenia's. His hero is Western movie star, Roy Rogers. Someday, he plans to move to Arizona and become a real buckaroo. Life with Aunt Eugenia is different than what he has known. For one thing, she has "colored folks" for friends, something that was unheard of in Preston's hometown. In this coming-of-age novel, Preston learns that life doesn't always seem fair, but there are things that he can control in his life, such as his choice of friends and words and his feelings about others.

**Woodson, Jacqueline.** *I Hadn't Meant to Tell You This.* Delacorte Press, 1994. 117p. Grades 5–8.

This is a touching story about a friendship that never fully materializes. Marie, a popular Black girl, is befriended by a white girl, Lena Bright. As their friendship grows, Marie learns that Lena is a victim of abuse and is determined to help, but how can she do it without adults interfering? Your heart goes out to Lena and Marie in this emotional novel.

**Woodson, Jacqueline.** *If You Come Softly.* Putnam, 1998. 183p. Grades 7 and up.

Jeremiah is going to attend a new school away from the neighborhood, his "comfort zone." This school is not friendly to Blacks, but meeting Ellie makes any sacrifices all worthwhile. Even though she's Jewish and he's African American, they are sure they can work things out between them and with their parents. But what happens if an African American boy leaves his guard down in an all-white neighborhood? Woodson's novel raises some important questions about communities.

**Yep, Laurence.** *Dragon's Gate.* HarperCollins, 1993. 276p. Grades 7 and up.

Laurence Yep's interest and passion for writing about the Chinese and Chinese Americans benefit readers. He brings to light a part of U.S. history that is slighted all too often. In this story, which centered around the building of the railroads in California, Yep captures racial tensions, discrimination, and glimmers of hope among the

Chinese immigrants who have come to America in search of a better life. As in Yep's book *Dragon Wings,* a wonderful cross-cultural friendship leaves readers believing that surely there were people from the past who had a sense of justice and fairness toward people of all backgrounds.

**Yep, Laurence.** *Thief of Hearts.* HarperCollins, 1995. 197p. Grades 3–8.

In this contemporary story, Stacey, a Chinese American middle school student, faces realistic challenges. Her cultural ties connect her to a new Chinese immigrant but jeopardizes an existing relationship with her best friend, Karen.

# Universal Similarities

**Ajmera, Maya, and Anna Rhesa Versola.** *Children from Australia to Zimbabwe: A Photographic Journey around the World.* Charlesbridge, 1997. 64p. All ages.

For each of the countries featured, this alphabet book includes colorful photos, interesting facts, and a brief summary. Also included is a list of other countries beginning with the same letter of the alphabet.

**Ajmera, Maya, and John D. Ivanko.** *To Be a Kid.* Charlesbridge, 1999. 32p. All ages.

Ajmera and Ivanko capture the wonder of children from throughout the world. Photos feature children smiling, playing, going to school, eating, dancing, painting, helping, and hugging. A nice tribute to children the world over. A good series connection is the *Williamson Kids Can!* series (published by Gareth Stevens).

**Ajmera, Maya, Olateju Omolodun, and Sarah Strunk.** *Extraordinary Girls.* Charlesbridge, 1999. 48p. All ages.

Beautiful photos celebrate girls worldwide. The tone is exuberant and uplifting.

**Ancona, George.** *Let's Dance.* William Morrow, 1998. 32p. Pre K–3.

Master photographer George Ancona takes readers on a photo journey around the world, celebrating the many forms of dance.

**Anno, Mitsumasa.** *All in a Day.* Illustrated by artists from around the world. Philomel, 1986. 22p. Pre K–5.

Anno collaborated with nine other renowned artists in this multimedia worldview of the 24-hour period beginning at midnight on December 31. Each picture, reflecting the lives of children, represents a time zone on an inhabited continent. The Public Broadcasting System's *Millennium Celebration* provides a good video example of this phenomenon.

**Baer, Edith.** *This Is the Way We Eat Our Lunch.* Illustrated by **Steve Bjorkman.** Scholastic, 1995. 40p. Pre K–3.

Everybody eats, and Baer and Bjorkman provide us with a playful look at children around the world engaged in this universal activity. Look for their previous collaboration, *This Is the Way We Go to School,* for another example of universal similarities of children going to school around the world.

**Beeler, Selby B.** *Throw Your Tooth on the Roof: Tooth Traditions from around the World.* Illustrated by **G. Brian Karas.** Houghton Mifflin, 1998. 32p. Pre K–2.

Two universals among children are teeth and the certainty of losing them. How do cultures around the world acknowledge this rite of passage? Beeler has researched this question and presents what she learned to readers.

**Bernhard, Emery.** *Happy New Year.* Illustrated by **Durga Bernhard.** Lodestar, 1996. 32p. Pre K–4.

The mark of a New Year in any culture does not go unnoticed. This book provides the origins and celebrations of the New Year from around the world. Readers may recognize some of their family and community traditions as they peruse the lively illustrations.

**Bernhard, Emery, and Durga Bernhard.** *A Ride on Mother's Back: A Day of Baby Carrying around the World.* Gulliver, 1996. 32p. Pre K–2.

As the mothers go about their daily routines, infants snuggle while sleeping or observing their world. The informative text and simple, warm illustrations support the bonding of mother and child.

**Brandenberg, Aliki.** *Hello! Good-Bye!* Greenwillow Books, 1996. 32p. Pre K–2.

There are many ways to say hello and good-bye, and these greetings are universal. Aliki captures the emotions behind the greetings with her trademark illustrations and words. Check out some of her other books that promote friendship: *We Are Best Friends* and *Best Friends Together Again* (published by Greenwillow Books).

*A Children's Chorus.* **UNICEF.** Illustrated by 11 international artists. Dutton, 1989. 26p. All ages.

This book pays respect to the rights of children throughout the world, supported by illustrations from 11 international artists. Included are the 10 principles adopted by the United Nations in 1959 that are worth reading and discussing with your students.

**Copsey, Susan E.** *Children Just Like Me: A Unique Celebration of Children from around the World.* DK, 1995. 82p. All ages.

Lively photos of children from around the world, together with their families, homes, interests, and favorite foods, and informative text make this a book focusing on similarities. Photos showing children dressed in traditional clothing is juxtaposed with everyday dress. Included at the end of the book is information on making a cross-cultural friend by becoming a pen pal.

**Corwin, Judith Hoffman.** *Harvest Festivals around the World.* Silver Burdett, 1995. 48p. Grades 1–6.

All crop-producing peoples celebrate the harvest, the season of reward, and diverse cultural traditions make each celebration unique. Many activities and recipes are included.

**Curtis, Marci.** *Big Sister, Little Sister.* Dial, 2000. 32p. All ages.

Sisters can be found in every culture. The relationship between younger and older sisters is something special, and the photos in this book highlight this relationship.

**Feldman, Eve B.** *Birthdays! Celebrating Life around the World.* Illustrated by children from around the world through Paintbrush Diplomacy. Bridge Water, 1996. 32p. Pre K–2.

Feldman features 25 countries celebrating birthdays in their unique way. The similarities evolve around a joyous occasion with friends and family, specially prepared foods, and special dress. The children's illustrations clearly reflect the celebrations.

**Fox, Mem.** *Whoever You Are.* Illustrated by **Leslie Staub.** Harcourt Brace, 1997. 32p. All ages.

Fox promotes and celebrates the similarities of people all over the world. Emotions and smiles are the same wherever we go.

**Frasier, Debra.** *On the Day You Were Born.* Harcourt Brace, 1991. 32p. Pre K–1.

Regardless of where we were born, people on Earth all have the same sun, moon, and sky. Earth is our common home. Frazier also worked with the Minnesota Orchestra on a video adaptation of this award-winning book (available by calling toll-free 1-888-MN-NOTES).

**Gray, Nigel.** *A Country Far Away.* Illustrated by **Philippe Dupasquier.** Orchard, 1988. 32p. Pre K–3.

This book is a clever narrative coupled with playful illustrations of two young boys living a typical day in separate communities. Readers will experience similarities in two distant locations, North America and Africa.

**Kermit the Frog (Jim Henson).** *For Every Child a Better World.* Illustrated by **Bruce McNally.** Muppet Press/Golden Books, 1993. 40p. All ages.

Produced in cooperation with the United Nations, the text and illustrations in this book reflect universal agreement about children's rights. Included at the end of the book are additional organizations that support and aid children throughout the world.

**Kindersley, Anabel.** *Celebrations: Festivals, Carnivals, and Feast Days from around the World.* Photos by **Barnabas Kindersley.** DK, 1997. 62p. Grades 2–6.

In the tradition of this well-known publisher, hundreds of colorful photos and brief captions capture the spirit of celebrations worldwide. Readers can spend hours admiring, learning, and dreaming about faraway places. This book also includes a calendar of celebrations to help plan special activities.

**Kissinger, Katie.** *All the Colors We Are: The Story of How We Get Our Skin Color.* Photos by **Wernher Krutein.** Redleaf Press, 1994. 32p. Pre K–3.

There are three things that determine our skin color: our ancestors, the sun, and melanin. Skin color is one of the things that makes us special and different from one another. To support this idea, there are wonderful sets of multicultural markers available for children when drawing human figures.

**Knight, Margy Burns.** *Welcoming Babies.* Illustrated by **Anne Sibley O'Brien.** Tilbury House, 1994. 34p. Pre K–2.

In this beautiful book, we experience the celebration of birth in 14 different cultures.

**Kroll, Virginia.** *Hats Off to Hair!* Illustrated by **Kay Life.** Charlesbridge, 1995. 32p. Pre K–2.

This book is a tribute to hair, its many colors, and the various hairstyles people wear. Kay Life's illustrations add playfulness to Kroll's lively verse. It is a nice companion book to *All the Colors We Are* by Katie Kissinger.

**Lankford, Mary D.** *Dominoes around the World.* Illustrated by **Karen Dugan.** Morrow, 1998. 40p. Grades 1 and up.

This book features directions and graphics for playing eight different versions of dominoes. The countries included are Cuba, France, Malta, The Netherlands, Spain, Ukraine, the United States, and Vietnam. Excellent companions to this book are *Hopscotch around the World* and *Jacks around the World,* also by this writer-illustrator team. Combining the games in these three books with *International Playtime: Classroom Games and Dances from around the World* by Wayne Nelson and Henry "Buzz" Glass can provide students with many activities for recesses, festivals, physical education, and free time.

**Lewin, Ted.** *Market!* Lothrop, Lee & Shepard, 1996. 48p. Grades 3–6.

A wonderfully illustrated book that depicts the theme and essence of markets across the continents. This is a good book for discussing how markets have changed over time and across cultures.

**Markel, Michelle.** *Cornhusk, Silk, and Wishbones: A Book of Dolls from around the World.* Houghton Mifflin, 2000. 48p. Grades 1 and up.

Dolls have held their place in cultures the world over. This tribute reflects the folk art qualities and their enduring nature. A good companion book is *Elizabeti's Doll* by Stephanie Stuve-Bodeen.

**McDonald, Megan.** *My House Has Stars.* Illustrated by **Peter Catalanotto.** Orchard, 1996. 32p. Grades K–3.

Children from eight geographic locations describe their homes, with one similarity: Children throughout the world see stars in the sky. Do you suppose children everywhere are curious about stars? A book to pair with this one is Debra Frazier's *On the Day You Were Born.*

**Morris, Ann.** *The Daddy Book.* Photographs by **Ken Heyman.** Silver Burdett, 1996. 32p. Pre K–1.

This heartwarming look at fathers worldwide and their special qualities is one of the books in the World's Family series. Other books in the series are *The Mommy Book, The Baby Book, The Grandma Book,* and *The Grandpa Book.*

**Morris, Ann.** *Play.* Photos by **Ken Heyman.** Lothrop, Lee & Shepard, 1998. 32p. Pre K–5.

Ann Morris has created a wonderful series of books that trace common themes across a variety of cultures. In this book about play, readers will experience children, adults, and animals playing through photographs from across the globe. Look for other books in the series: *Houses and Homes; Bread, Bread, Bread; Shoes, Shoes, Shoes; Weddings; Hats, Hats, Hats; Loving; On the Go; Tools; Teamwork; Families;* and *Work.*

*Nursery Tales around the World.* Selected and retold by **Judy Sierra.** Illustrated by **Stefano Vitale.** Clarion Books, 1996. 114p. All ages.

Sierra researched and collected these tales from around the world. Her retellings are arranged within enticing themes, including Runaway Cookies, Incredible Appetites, Victory of the Smallest, Chain Tales, Slowpokes and Speedsters, and Fooling the Big Bad Wolf. The childlike characters take control of their situations using wit and charm rather than force.

**Patten, Brian.** *The Blue Green Ark.* Illustrated by 11 artists. Scholastic, 1999. 56p. Grades 1 and up.

This beautiful alphabet book embraces the Earth and its wonders. The subtle message is for all of us to look after the Earth so that future generations may experience its beauty, too. The artwork from the perspective of 11 illustrators makes this a unique book.

**Pooley, Sarah (compiler).** *Jump the World: Stories, Poems, and Things to Make and Do from around the World.* Dutton, 1997. 76p. All ages.

This book offers enough activities to keep readers and children entertained for hours. Illustrated instructions are clear and easy to follow. This is a handy book for international celebrations and promoting multiculturalism every day.

**Rotner, Shelley, and Sheila M. Kelly.** *Lots of Moms.* Dial, 1996. 24p. Pre K–1.

Mothers live all over the world. This collection of photographs depict many of the special things that mothers do, from playing with their young to comforting them. Look for other books by the authors, including *Lots of Dads* (Dial), *Faces* (Macmillan), and *About Twins* (DK).

**Scott, Elaine.** *Friends.* Photos by **Margaret Miller.** Atheneum, 2000. 40p. Pre K–3.

Friendship is universal and crucial for all people, especially children. This book for young children is filled with joys, depicting the choices children must make as they make friends.

**Siegen-Smith, Nikki.** *Songs for Survival: Songs and Chants from the Tribal Peoples around the World.* Illustrated by **Bernard Lodge.** Dutton, 1996. 80p. Grades 5 and up.

Siegen-Smith compiled these songs and chants with themes that include genesis, animals, the elements, and survival. Also included is a brief summary of the indigenous peoples from six regions across the globe.

**Singer, Marilyn.** *Nine O'Clock Lullaby.* Illustrated by **Frané Lessac.** HarperCollins, 1991. 32p. Pre K–3.

It's 9:00 o'clock in Brooklyn, New York, and Mama is singing a lullaby. What is the rest of the world doing? Singer's book tracks a 24-hour period around the world and back again. See also the author and illustrator's latest book, *On the Same Day in March: A Tour of the World's Weather* (page 10). This interesting book looks at weather changes across the Earth's lines of latitude, from the North Pole to the South Pole.

**Steele, Philip.** *The World of Festivals.* Rand McNally, 1996. 46p. Grades 3 and up.

This book compares festivals throughout the year from many nations. Festival themes found in this book focus on religious celebrations, death, seasons, independence, family, rites of passage, and more.

**Wild, Margaret.** *Our Granny.* Illustrated by **Julie Vivas.** Ticknor & Fields, 1994. 32p. All ages.

Grannies have always been special, but after reading this book, they may seem even more so. Julie Vivas's lively watercolors and Wild's vibrant text show that grandmothers can do anything, but none is as special as one's own.

# Book Extensions

One of the challenges we face in classrooms today is making a new student feel welcome. When language barriers compound this dilemma, a teacher can feel frustrated. Learning simple phrases such as "hello" and "how do you say" in the new child's native language can make a world of difference for you and for the other students. Some books that can help students and teachers learn native phrases are *Hello! Good-Bye* by Aliki Brandenberg, *This Is My House* by Arthur Dorros, and the *Count Your Way Through . . .* series, published by Carolrhoda Books. Partnering the new student with a vocal and empathetic child also is important, as is acknowledging strengths and helping a child to succeed. There is a nice series called *Williamson Kids Can!*, published by Gareth Stevens, that can help you discover a new child's strengths through the arts and sciences. For some excellent insights, look for the following books: *I'm New Here* by Bud Howlett, *Marianthe's Stories: Painted Words/Spoken Memories* by Aliki Brandenberg, *La Mariposa* by Francisco Jiménez, *My Name Is Jorge: On Both Sides of the River* by Jane Medina, *Who Belongs Here?* by Margy Burns Knight, *My Name Is Maria Isabel* by Alma Flor Ada, *The Magic Shell* by Nicholasa Mohr, and *Creativity* by John Steptoe. **Language Arts, Social Studies**

Children can make a difference in this world through social activism. If you are looking for some examples, consider these sources: *Acting for Nature: What Young People around the World Have Done to Protect the Environment* by Sneed B. Collard, *It's Our World Too: Stories of Young People Who Make a Difference* by Phillip Hoose, *No Kidding Around! America's Youngest Activists Are Changing Our World and You Can Too* by Wendy Lesko, *Kids with Courage: True Stories about Young People Making a Difference* by Barbara Lewis, *The Kid's Guide to Social Action: How to Solve the Social Problems You Choose— and Turn Creative Thinking into Positive Action* by Barbara Lewis, *Kids Who Have Made a Difference* by Teddy Milne, *Kids Who Make a Difference* by Gary Chandler and Kevin Graham, and the *Earth Day 2000 Special Edition* of *Time Magazine,* www.time.com. Another Web site worth checking out is www.makeadifferenceday.com. **Social Studies, Political Science, Geography**

Using the books listed in the heading "Universal Similarities," schools can establish year-round multicultural events featuring international games, foods, stories, music, poetry, art, and cultural activities. Anabel Kindersley and Barnabas Kindersley's book *Celebration! Festivals, Carnivals, and Feast Days from around the World* offers a monthly calendar of celebrations. Check the festivals around the world section in the first chapter for more ideas. **All Subjects**

Many of the books that reflect universal similarities show people from all corners of the Earth. To enhance a geography lesson, use a world map to find the location of the settings mentioned in books your students read. Check out the new geography series, *Mapping Our World*, published by Benchmark. A computer software connection that enhances geography skills is *Where in the World Is Carmen Sandiego?* **Social Studies, Geography**

Bring the idea of universal similarities closer to home by creating a classroom map of all the places your students have lived or traveled. To build geography skills, create a map that pinpoints all the continents, nations, countries, states, provinces, cities, and towns where members of your class have friends and family. This could be done individually or as a group. I have had interesting discussions with children about the places they would or would not like to travel. Their rationale for choosing these locations is enlightening. There are many fascinating series that provide a lot of enticing information about each country. The *Cultures of the World* series, published by Marshall Cavendish, features 120 different countries in the set to get you started. Lerner has a 100-book series, called *Visual Geography*, and Gareth Stevens has two 64-book series, *Countries of the World* and *Welcome to My Country*. The latter two include suggested books for further reading, video suggestions, and Web sites. **Social Studies, Geography, Language Arts**

As you move from country to country studying universal similarities, determine the air miles from place to place. At the end of your calculations, compare this to the circumference in miles and kilometers of the Earth. You can also make extrapolations and comparisons of distances. An example might be the number of times one would have to walk to school matched with a trip around the circumference of the globe. A great book to help with the mathematical extrapolations is *In the Next Three Seconds. . .,* compiled by Rowland Morgan. Another unique connection involves asking an airline pilot or airline representative for old air-travel maps. Navigators use these maps of the sky, which are unusual in appearance and offer a view quite different from one-dimensional road maps. Children and adults are always fascinated to learn that many pilots often use routes that cross one of the poles in order to travel the shortest distance. Use a globe to help demonstrate these air routes. **Social Studies, Geography, Math, Language Arts**

Teachers can demonstrate global interdependence in their classrooms. Have students check clothing and product labels in the classroom and graph the results by country. This activity could be extended to individual homes and collectively shared and graphed on a subsequent day at school. Set up displays of the items people have in their homes that were made in another country different from yours. Which items were collected firsthand and others through local economies? If you take time to listen to the stories that accompany the artifacts acquired from abroad you extend the learning possibilities and benefits of this activity for children and adults. One book series that connects to this activity is the *Look What Came From. . .* series, published by Franklin Watts. **Social Studies, Geography, Economics, Language Arts, Art, Math**

Books such as Shelby and Trivas's *Potluck,* Morris's *Bread, Bread, Bread,* and Dooley and Thornton's *Everybody Cooks Rice* can be used to discuss and show the acculturation of food that has taken place. The last two books include recipes. Check the "Food around the World" section in Part I for more cooking possibilities. The school or classroom might integrate a food festival or potluck into their celebration of a global community. **Social Studies, Culinary Arts, and More**

Using Maya Ajmera and Anna Rhesa Versola's alphabet book, *Children from Australia to Zimbabwe: A Photographic Journey around the World,* students can research the countries listed under various letters of the alphabet. Students also can replicate the format the authors use to describe other countries. Another fun challenge is to have students go on a picture "scavenger hunt" of the continents. Ask each team to find pictures and then show them to the class. Discarded magazines, such as *National Geographic,* are good sources. Perhaps have them try to find pictures that represent each country from a single continent. **Social Studies, Geography, Language Arts, Art**

In today's world, we literally have at our fingertips access to information about another country. While exploring some of the new book series available on the market, I was impressed with their suggestions for further reading, video suggestions, and Web sites. Two broad series (published by Gareth Stevens) are *Countries of the World* and *Welcome to My Country.* Check out the Odyssey Web site for some world adventures at www.worldtrek.org. **Social Studies, Geography, Political Science, Economics, History, Anthropology, Art, Physical Education**

Use Mitsumasa Anno's *All in a Day* and Marilyn Singer's *Nine O'Clock Lullaby* to help explore and study time zones across the Earth. You can also chart time zone changes as students travel through the countries in the books listed in this section. For historical background on time, see Betsy Maestro and Giulio Maestro's *The Story of Clocks and Calendars: Marking a Millennium* or Larry Dane Brimmer's *The Official M&M's Book of the Millennium.* Perhaps one of the most visual and recent demonstrations of the international time zones was the Public Broadcasting System's *Millennium Celebration.* An interesting resource that marked the millennium that offers extending possibilities into the future is *Dorling Kindersley's Millennium Pack 2000.* **Social Studies, Geography, History, Math, Art, Language Arts**

*Children Just Like Me* by Sue Copsey includes information on establishing international pen pals. Set up pen pals in your location with children across the world. Under the right conditions this writing relationship may occur through electronic mail. There may be no greater force for impacting future peace efforts than children across nations establishing friendships. **Language Arts, Social Studies, Geography**

Write to the countries students read about in these books and ask for free materials such as maps and highlights about their country. Don't forget Internet searches for additional information. The *World Celebrations and Ceremonies* series (published by Blackbirch Press) includes Web sites of the featured country's tourism bureau. Another writing connection is the "Great Mail Race," in which kids send an open letter asking for information to any school at a certain zip code. I was involved in a project like this in the late 1980s. Take the same idea and go global. Zip codes are not going to work in every case, but embassies, city and town governments, education ministers, and other sources may help you. **Social Studies, Language Arts**

Poetry is a form of expression that has very unique qualities. Capturing your emotions and feelings through carefully selected words provides the poet freedom. To read and listen to these crafted words is truly a wonderful experience. Students can also listen, read, and write beautiful poetry with the right encouragement. There are many selections in the poetry sections throughout this book to help launch their creativity. **Language Arts, Social Studies**

———

Books such as *Extraordinary Girls* (by Ajmera, Omolodun, and Strunk) include additional resources for further information. Contact these valuable resources to extend knowledge and understanding of the humanitarian projects taking place throughout the world. Maya Ajmera, one of the authors of *Extraordinary Girls,* is the founder and executive director of SHAKTI for children. This project is a Global Fund for Children; visit the following Web sites for more information: www.shakti.org and www.globalfundforchildren.org. Charlesbridge also produces a useful resource, *Raising Children to Become Caring Contributors to the World,* by Lisa Daughtry and Maya Ajmera. **Social Studies, Language Arts**

———

There are so many great authors who write multicultural literature. One of my favorites is Patricia Polacco. She has a way of writing and sharing stories from her family that have become favorites of many readers. Some of her stories were passed down through ancestors, and others are reflections of her childhood. She lived in a multicultural neighborhood, and some of her best friends are from other backgrounds. You can meet many of these people in her stories, such as *Mrs. Katz and Tush, Pink and Say,* and *Chicken Sunday.* Patricia Polacco is also a strong teachers' advocate, which is evident in *Thank You, Mr. Falker.* In 2000, she gave the plenary address at the Reading Renaissance Conference held in Nashville, Tennessee, holding thousands of teachers and administrators spellbound for more than an hour. Reading Renaissance has made that speech available on videotape to the public. If you are looking for an inspirational talk for a staff meeting, in-service, or discussion, I highly recommend this recording. Not only does she revere teachers, she has a powerful message about the importance of embracing all humanity, regardless of race or religion. **All Subjects**

———

Compare and contrast toys, instruments, and clothing from various countries. Which ones use natural resources? Which require special equipment or tools to manufacture? What is the origin and history behind some toys? Are toys universal? Where did Legos or Pokemon toys originate (for some clues, see DK's *The Ultimate Lego Book,* published in 1999)? This type of exploration can lead to a discussion of international trade, one of the ways the world is connected. Perhaps businesses in your community specialize in selling or importing international products, such as toys, clothing, games, and instruments. Invite these people to your schools or take a field trip to their workplace. One of my favorite local stores is 10,000 Villages, a cooperative that markets hand-made products from indigenous people around the world. The profits go directly to the artisans. **Social Studies, Economics, History, Geography, Art**

---

One of the most unique book series I found that has a built-in integration theme across the curriculum is the *Williamson Kids Can!* series, published by Gareth Stevens. This six-book series (featured in Part V of this text) promotes children's creativity and imagination through a wide range of activities. Instructions are easy to understand, and the text includes information from a multitude of cultures throughout the world. Titles include *Hands around the World, Kids Create!, The Kid's Multicultural Art Book, The Kid's Nature Book, The Kid's Science Book,* and *The Kid's Wildlife Book. Hands around the World* alone includes 365 creative ways to build cultural awareness and global respect. **Social Studies, Geography, Science, Language Arts, Art**

---

International celebrations are popular ways to encourage understanding of many cultures. If you want to hold a festival, try some of the activities found in *International Playtime: Classroom Games and Dances from around the World* by Wayne E. Nelson and Henry "Buzz" Glass; the *Worldwide Crafts* series and *Williamson Kids Can!* series (both published by Gareth Stevens); *Travel the Globe: Multicultural Story Times* by Desiree Webber et al. or *Celebrations!: Festivals, Carnivals, and Feast Days from around the World* by Anabel Kindersley. Try some of the songs from *Round the World Songbook* by Emma Danes. Bring in storytellers who can share multicultural stories. Learn stories from the numerous resources listed in this text. One example is Margaret Read MacDonald's book, *Celebrate the World: Twenty Telltale Folktales for Multicultural Festivals.* Serving food, potluck style or otherwise, is an attractive feature of festivals. Try some of the recipes from Caroline Young's *Round the World Cookbook,* Mark Zanger's *The American Ethnic Cookbook for Students,* or Diane Vezza's *Passport on a Plate: Around the World Cookbook for Children.* Don't overlook the opportunities for students to make displays featuring a country of their choice. Display books, pictures, artifacts, and students' expository writing for guests to read and peruse. **All Subjects**

---

Three of the books in this part have unique characteristics. *What a Wonderful World* by David Weiss and Bob Thiele and *This Land Is Your Land* by Woody Guthrie are lyrics put to music. *I Have a Dream* by Martin Luther King Jr. is a speech. All three are beautifully illustrated, and each book has a message that promotes harmony, caring for humanity, and peace. These songs and the speech also can be found as audio or visual recordings in various forms. Taking the time to listen and analyze the words of the music and speech bring an important dimension to understanding. All too often, we passively hear, recite, or sing words without discussing what they mean, yet it is worth the effort to study them. Woody Guthrie and others have recorded *This Land Is Your Land.* Louis Armstrong's recording of *What a Wonderful World* is a classic. A new resource, the CD-ROM *Encarta Africana* by Henry Louis Gates et al., was released in the fall of 1999. It includes recorded live footage of Martin Luther King Jr. giving his famous speech. This CD-ROM recording is a phenomenal encyclopedia of Black history, www.africana.com. **Social Studies, Music, Art, and Other Subjects**

---

The theme of families is one of universal similarity. We now live in an age where the makeup of families is as diverse as the religions of the world. The way we define the term *family* must include many possibilities. One out of nine grandparents are care providers. Single mothers by choice are raising children. Divorce or death have also created single parents. Blended families abound, both through marriage and across ethnic groups. Other parenting situations include gay and lesbian couples, adoptive families, older parents who wait until later life to have children, foster care, and people raising relatives' children. The last statistic I read on traditional families that directly impacts the United States pointed out that less than 6 percent of the children in schools today come from a family setting in which the father works and the mother cares for children at home. Add to this statistic the number of homeless children in or out of school, and we can begin to visualize the complex nature associated with defining family. Recognizing this diversity among family structures is another way of becoming more inclusive. Some book series that take a universal look at family are *Children of the World* (Gareth Stevens); *Families the World Over* (Lerner); *Our American Family* (Blackbirch Press); the *Let's Talk Library on Families* (PowerKids Press); and *World's Family* (Silver Burdett). One book that reflects courageous people and a natural blending of families across ethnic groups is *Molly Bannaky* by Alice McGill. **Social Studies**

# Part V

# Part V

## Multicultural Books in a Series

Through literature, students learn to explore possibilities and consider options for themselves and humankind. They come to find themselves, imagine others, value difference, and search for justice. They gain connectedness and seek vision. They become the literate thinkers we need to shape the decisions of tomorrow.

—Judith Langer, author of *Envisioning Literature: Literary Understanding and Literature Instruction*

As I gathered books with multicultural themes, I ran across a number of wonderful series. Although it often took a complete series of books to capture my goal of a multicultural point of view, I found many items that were too good to overlook. Nonfiction can have a more universal appeal than any other genre. Therefore, I felt compelled to create a separate space to feature nonfiction. The formats of the series described below are impressive and captivating. I was delighted to find a multitude of universal themes. Some offered a multicultural view within one book; others did so in the many titles within the series. These books would make excellent additions to a school or public library.

Series provide a way to connect with many ethnic groups. One way to make new people feel welcome in a community is to have books on hand about their homeland or ancestry. The series featured here provide a view of people and their environments from around the world.

I include a brief description of the books, as well as the number of titles in a set. The format of each series varies, but some common elements surfaced among the different publishers. Most series included beautiful, full-color photographs or illustrations, a contemporary view of people, a discussion of the geography and features of a given country, and maps featuring location highlights. Some of the sets had a specific focus, such as refugee stories or food crops, whereas others highlight a city. There is yet another group of series books listed that offers a global perspective by focusing on unique features such as ecosystems, record breakers, inventions, costumes, traditions, or other tempting subjects for exploration. These books can help educators integrate more content into their curriculums. The series should complement a community's specific needs.

As another possible selection criteria, I was interested in whether the books could be purchased individually or as a complete set. Most were available individually, but I did note in a few instances where set purchase was the only option. The number of books available reflects the timing of my research; publishers may expand books in the set each year. I felt the individual or set purchase option was a great way of allowing schools and libraries to recognize international children in their community as they obtain copies of the books that feature an individual's homeland. Many of the series have teacher guides and activity books available. I have suggested many connections for the book sets in the extension ideas found in the previous parts. At the end of this book is a complete list of publishers to help readers obtain catalogs and updated information.

The following are among the topics covered: individual countries, cities, geographical features, government, tourist attractions, landmarks, maps, economics, commerce, history, past civilizations and rulers, traditions, the arts, recreation, living styles, schools, plants, and human stories. Additional attractive themes included a global view of cartoons, comics, musical instruments, stamps, superstitions, horses, Santas, greetings, costumes, and much more. Many application possibilities are available for the inquisitive minds. As author Mark Twain once said, "I never let schoolin' interfere with my education." Let imagination—along with books and life adventures—guide your students' knowledge.

**Bears of the World.** PowerKids Press. Grades K–4.

Bears fascinate children and adults. Find out why as students learn that these animals have a universal connection. In this six-book series, the titles include *Polar Bears, Brown Bears, Black Bears, Panda Bears, The Koala: The Bear That's Not a Bear,* and *Famous Bears.*

**Biomes.** Charlesbridge. Grades K–5.

This is an attractive set of books that offers a worldview of biomes. The illustrations are breathtaking, and the text has a lyrical quality to complement the beautiful pictures. There are nine books in this set. Titles include *Our Wet World, The Forest in the Clouds, Our Natural Homes, At Home in the Rain Forest, Desert Discoveries, Tundra Discoveries, At Home in the Coral Reef, This Is Our Earth,* and *At Home in the Tide Pool.*

**Biomes of the World.** Benchmark Books. Grades 3 and up.

The Biomes of the World series provides another way to discover universal similarities: by studying ecosystems. The eight titles are *Rainforest, Tundra, Temperate Forest, Ocean, Desert, Taiga, Grassland,* and *Chaparral.* This series examines the human impact on the environment through colorful photos, ecological perspectives, and expository text.

**Birthdays around the World.** Children's Press. Grades K–3.

This four-book set highlights the celebration of birthdays around the world. The books have full-color pictures featuring young children at a happy time in their lives.

**Building Block Books.** Carolrhoda Books. Pre K–3.

This nine-book set includes universal themes such as bridges, canals, dams, farms, libraries, parks, roads, schools, and towers. The photos supporting the brief text take readers on excursions to many locations. Also included is a section identifying the location in each photo.

### Celebrating the Peoples and Civilizations of . . . . PowerKids Press. Grades K–4.

This is a unique approach to geographical regions and continents. For example, one set of six books on Southeast Asia features people from many countries (Laos, Vietnam, Thailand, Philippines, and Cambodia), as well as a title about the Hmong. The focus is on children and promoting diversity as a strength. Another set of six books in this series features Africa. Titles include *The Asante of West Africa, The Benin Kingdom of West Africa, The Dogon of West Africa, The Maasai of East Africa, The Yoruba of West Africa,* and *The Zulu of Southern Africa.* We likely will see more books added to this series.

### Children in Crisis. Blackbirch Press. Grades 3–5.

This four-book set features Bosnia, Rwanda, Vietnam, and the Middle East through a multitude of photos and first-person narratives. The series provides eyewitness accounts of people struggling for their lives as their homelands face turmoil.

### Children of the World. Gareth Stevens. Grades 2–6.

This series offers a view of children from around the world, depicting their routines, neighborhoods, schools, social events, and families. Also included are brief descriptions of the history, economy, government, population, climate, maps, education, arts, sports, and recreation activities. There are 15 books in this series.

### Christmas around the World. Children's Press. Grades K–3.

There are eight full-color books in this set at present. Given the attention Christmas receives in America, comparing and contrasting celebrations from around the world can be a fascinating learning experience.

### Cities of the World. Children's Press. Grades 3–8.

This highly informative series features major cities around the world through full-color photos, facts, historical points, landmarks, and the people. If your class has the opportunity to take a field trip to one of these cities, the books can serve as reference tools. There are 26 books in the series, and Children's Press is currently adding four new titles each year.

### Costume Reference. Chelsea House. All ages.

This seven-book set would be a natural for theater departments and for any other students interested in costuming, fashion, or period clothing. The set is fully illustrated in black and white, with some color highlights. Also included are a glossary, bibliography, and index. Titles in the set include: *Costume of Ancient Egypt, Costume of Ancient Rome, Costume of the Classical World, Everyday Dress 1650–1900, History of Children's Costume, History of Men's Costume,* and *History of Women's Costume.* The children's costume book is laid out by century and sectioned by gender. It includes a section on babies that could be handy for doll collectors.

### Costume, Tradition, and Culture: Reflecting on the Past. Chelsea House. Grades 4 and up.

This is a unique 12-book set filled with illustrations that were originally printed as collector's cards in the early 20th century. Each 64-page book is fully indexed. A one-page brief describes each picture, and the books also include suggestions for further reading. Some of the interesting titles that fit with the multicultural theme are *Musical*

*Instruments from around the World, Rare and Interesting Stamps, Inventors and Their Discoveries, Popular Superstitions,* and *Infamous Pirates.* These tantalizing titles provide many options for multicultural exploration and understanding.

### Count Your Way Through . . . . Carolrhoda Books. Grades K–3.

The enticing format in this series helps students learn to count from 1 to 10 in a featured country's native language. Each book includes a pronunciation guide, a brief preview of products, some identifying features, cultural events, and highlighted customs from the country. There are more than 15 books in this set, with additional titles added each year.

### Countries of the World. Gareth Stevens. Grades 3 and up.

This series offers a complete look at the geography, history, government, economy, language, the arts, literature, festivals, foods, landmarks, famous people, and events from each country featured. I found the format enticing, attractive, and informative. This series also includes suggested books, videos, and Web sites to explore for more information. Readers will enjoy the wonderful color photos in these 18 books, and there are plans to expand the series to 64 books.

### Crafts of the World. PowerKids Press. Grades K–4.

This six-book set provides insights about achieving acculturation through artisan crafts. Crafts have maintained their ethnic roots, and this series provides a nice overview of each craft, its history, and its present use in the world. Titles to date include *American Quilt Making: Stories in Cloth, The Art of Native American: Turquoise Jewelry, Japanese Origami: Paper Magic, Mayan Weaving: A Living Tradition, Ndebele Beadwork: African Artistry,* and *Ukrainian Egg Decoration: A Holiday Tradition.*

### Cultures of the Past. Benchmark Books. Grades 5 and up.

The *Cultures of the Past* series will expand to 18 books in the future. I was impressed with the unique way the authors focus on the historical importance of past cultures. A look at the cultures' histories, belief systems, societal effects, and ongoing legacies provide readers with some good insights on how these cultures have influenced modern-day civilizations through the past artisans, methods of recording information, governing systems, people, and lifestyles.

### Cultures of the World. Marshall Cavendish. Grades 3 and up.

The *Cultures of the World* series includes the geography, history, government, economy, people, lifestyles, religion, language, the arts, festivals, food, and recreation found in featured countries. Hundreds of photos complement the informative text, and the series covers a broad range of cultures. There are 120 books in the series, and Marshall Cavendish plans to revise and update the information.

### Earth at Risk. Chelsea House. Grades 4 and up.

This 19-book set is the most comprehensive multicultural and environmental look at the Earth that I have found. After looking at this series, students will have no problem finding global connections in the Earth's environment. Included are addresses for environmental organizations in North America. Titles include *Acid Rain, The Automobile and the Environment, Clean Air, Clean Water, Degradation of the Land, Economics and the Environment, Environmental Action Groups, Environmental Disasters, Extinction, Global Warming, The Living Ocean, Nuclear Energy/Nuclear Waste, Overpopulation, The Ozone Layer, The Rainforest, Recycling, Solar Energy, Toxic Materials,* and *Wilderness Preservation.*

*Enchantment of the World.* Children's Press. Grades 3–8.

This highly informative series features the history, geography, lifestyles, economy, spirituality, landmarks, and people of each country. At the end of the books are time lines, fast facts, additional sources for information (including Web sites), and an index. There are 80 books in the original series and 30 books in the second series. Children's Press is replacing the older series with the *Enchantment of the World Second* series, with updated and revised versions, at the rate of six books per year. At the time of my inquiry, they had 30 updated titles available.

*Endangered!* Gareth Stevens. Grades 4 and up.

This four-book series takes a closer look at the endangered natural world. It includes books on mammals, birds, sea life, and a book about endangered lands. Much of the information for this series was gathered from the World Conservation Monitoring Center (WCMC) in Cambridge, England.

*The Eventful 20th Century.* Penguin Putnam. Grades 3 and up.

This six-book set offers a host of possibilities for looking at the world through a multicultural lens. Titles include: *Wonders of the Modern World, The Fragile Peace, 1919–1939, Great Mysteries of the 20th Century, Inventions That Changed the World, The Way We Lived,* and *The World at War, 1939–1945.*

*Exploring Cultures of the World.* Benchmark Books. Grades 3–8.

This 25-book series features geography, history, arts, education, festivals, food, recreation, and people from each country. This set provides a smaller version (with less text and fewer photographs) of the information found in Marshall Cavendish's *Cultures of the World* series.

*Exploring the Science of Nature.* Gareth Stevens. Grades 3–7.

Another great way to look at the world is through themes in nature. Consider topics such as bubbles, seeds, shells, eggs, wings, waste, flowers, rocks, and more. At present, there are 16 books in this series with plans for 36 titles. The pictures of nature are exquisite. Gareth Stevens publishes another science-related series of six books—called *Look Once, Look Again*—that works well with this one.

*Extreme Weather.* PowerKids Press. Grades K–4.

Combine science and social studies to look at the world in this six-book set. Titles include *Blizzards, Electrical Storms, Hail, Heat Waves and Droughts, Tornadoes,* and *Tropical Storms and Hurricanes.* A nice companion series, also by this publisher, is *Natural Disasters.*

*Families the World Over.* Lerner. Grades 3–6.

Each book features an in-depth description of a family from one country. Rich color photos support informative text on the lives of the families. Included are a section of facts, background on the predominant religion practiced, and a location map. There are 35 books in this series, with no plans to add titles.

*Festivals of the World.* Gareth Stevens. Grades 3–7.

This was the largest set of books on festivals that I found, and it features different aspects of celebrations, including traditional dress, customs, recipes, and products. I was impressed by the presentation of each festival using clear text, maps, and colorful photographs on every page. Another feature is the detailed directions for making some of the crafts. There are 48 books in this series.

*Folk Tales and Fables of* . . . . Chelsea House. Grades 4 and up.

This is a great four-book set by award-winning illustrator Robert Ingpen and Barbara Hayes. Each book has 92 pages of entertainment that will provide several hours of listening, viewing, and reading pleasure. Stories range from the familiar to lesser-known tales. The set covers the continents with the following titles: *The Americas & the Pacific, Asia & Australia, Europe,* and *The Middle East & Africa.*

*Geography Detective.* Carolrhoda Books. Grades 3–8.

This environment series highlights similar geographical features found throughout the world. There are eight books in the series, including *Deserts, Islands, Rivers and Valleys, Mountains, Rain Forests, Oceans, Tundra,* and *Grasslands.*

*Globe-Trotters Club.* Carolrhoda Books. Grades 3–5.

This series features each country in full-color photos. An attractive format includes one- to two-page highlights and facts on high-interest topics about each country. A pronunciation guide, glossary, and suggestions for further reading also are included. There are 20 books in this series, and the publisher plans to produce more. This series works well with Carolrhoda's *A Ticket to . . .* series.

*Great Cities Library.* Blackbirch Press. Grades 3–8.

This older but unique series features a chronology of historical events associated with cities. Each book features people of all ages. A fun addition is a section offering a bus tour through the city. At present, this series is out of print.

*Great Rivers.* Benchmark Books. Grades 4 and up.

This six-book set features the world's largest rivers. Captivating photos, together with facts, historical information, and informative text, give students an opportunity to compare rivers around the world. Titles include *The Nile, The Ganges, The Rhine, The Mississippi, The Yangtze,* and *The Amazon.*

*Ideas That Changed the World.* Chelsea House. Grades 4 and up.

This four-volume set spans the globe, assimilating ideas and discoveries across cultures. These titles have many possibilities for the classroom. Titles include *The Early Inventions, Art and Technology through the Ages, The Industrial Revolution,* and *Transportation.*

*The Incredible World of Plants.* Chelsea House. Grades 3 and up.

This six-book set is fully illustrated. Each book has 32 pages of high-interest material, presented with brief descriptions and adjoining magnified images. The titles include *The Great Plains, The Mysterious Jungles, Plants of the Desert, Plants of the Forest, Plants Under the Sea,* and *Vegetation of Rivers, Lakes, and Swamps.*

*Journey between Two Worlds.* Lerner. Grades 3–8.

This series discusses the plight of refugees as they journey from their homeland to the United States. Each book focuses on one family's story, interwoven with historical facts and events that occurred during the time of their journey to freedom. There are more than 12 books in the set.

*Kids in the Kitchen: The Library of Multicultural Cooking.* PowerKids Press. Grades K–4.

Yum! This six-book set is about cooking and preparing ethnic foods from around the world. Each book features an overview from each ethnic group, discussing its meals, its utensils, and its traditions associated with eating. Clear recipe directions with children's safety in mind, as well as readily available ingredients, make this volume useful for the classroom or home. This set includes recipes for African, Caribbean, Chinese, Greek, Japanese, and Mexican cuisine, and the publisher plans to expand the series. This company also publishes the *Cooking throughout American History* series.

*Kids throughout History.* PowerKids Press. Grades K–4.

This is a fascinating series that looks at history in the context of children. Readers get a glimpse at the everyday lives of children from the past and learn what their responsibilities were. It includes information about period clothing for young people, their concerns, their dreams, and more. A combination of photos, art, and illustrations support the text. Vocabulary associated with the historical setting is highlighted in context and listed in the glossary. There are 12 titles with plans for expansion. At present, the settings include Ancient Egypt, Age of Exploration, Great Depression, Industrial Revolution, Ancient Rome, Maya, Colonial Times, Pioneer Times, Middle Ages, Renaissance Period, Ancient Greece, and the American Civil War Era.

*Letters Home From . . . .* Blackbirch Press. Grades 3–5.

This new series takes readers on a journey through the eyes of a young traveler. Features include geography, culture, history, wildlife, cities, food, daily life, and maps, as well as many photos. The unique format is presented in letters written to the reader as the author travels through the country. There are 12 books at present in the series and plans to add additional titles.

*Life Times.* Benchmark Books. Grades 3 and up.

A fascinating view of the human life cycle in the context of six major religions is the focus of this series. Titles include *New Beginnings, Growing Up, Wedding Days,* and *Journey's End.* Enticing color photos and complementary text make this a nice four-book set.

*Look What Came From . . . .* Franklin Watts. Grades 2–5.

This unique series highlights products and inventions from countries around the world. Readers are sure to find some wonderful discoveries about the origin of some familiar—and not-so-familiar—products. This series celebrates customs, pets, children's stories, food, and language and provides sources for further reading, including Web sites. These books serve as a nice connection for demonstrating products in the global market, both imports and exports. At present, there are 13 books in the series with plans to add more. Featured countries are Australia, China, Egypt, England, France, Germany, Greece, India, Italy, Japan, Mexico, Russia, and the United States.

*Looking into the Past: People, Places, and Customs.* Chelsea House. Grades 4 and up.

This is a great 12-book set filled with color reproductions of 19th-century trading-card illustrations. A one-page text summary describes each illustration. The traditions, customs, and people featured come from cultures around the world. This series lends itself to some historical research and wonderful comparisons of past and present cultural practices. Titles include *Children of the World, Ancient and Annual Customs, Customs of the World, Good Luck Symbols and Talismans, Greetings of the World,* and *Santas of the World.*

*Magnificent Horses of the World.* Gareth Stevens. Grades 3 and up.

As stated in the title, this series takes readers on a world tour to study horses. Beautiful photos will make this set highly appealing to horse lovers. Included are suggestions for further information, including books and videos, as well as information about where to write for more information. There are six titles in the set: *Andalusian, Arabian, Friesian, Icelandic, Lipizzaner,* and *Palomino.*

*Major World Nations.* Chelsea House. Grades 3 and up.

There are more than 80 countries featured in this set, and Chelsea House plans to add new countries to the collection. The books provide a comprehensive overview of each nation's geography, history, economy, government, culture, and people. Each title is filled with both black-and-white and color photos, maps, a glossary, and an index. The handy, novel-sized books range from 94 to 144 pages.

*Mapping Our World.* Benchmark Books. Grades 4 and up.

This atlaslike series takes an in-depth look at cartography, including climate, vegetation, ocean, and continent maps. At present, there are eight books in this series: *Europe and the Middle East, North America, Asia, Africa, South America, Australia and the South Pacific, Maps and Mapmaking,* and *Oceans and Skies.*

*Natural Disasters.* PowerKids Press. Grades K–4.

Experiencing a natural disaster can devastate a community. Lives are lost, and people are left homeless. These terrifying events can happen in locations around the globe. Graphic photos in this series hold readers' attention from cover to cover. This six-book set includes the following titles: *Avalanches, Earthquakes, Floods, Forest Fires, Tsunamis: Killer Waves,* and *Volcanoes.* A nice companion series by the same publisher is *Extreme Weather.*

*Our American Family.* PowerKids Press. Grades K–4.

This inspiring and timely set of books celebrates our nation's strength through diversity. Each book recognizes a different ethnic group. The title format is *I Am _____ American.* At present, the following 12 books are available (more titles are in the works): African, Chinese, Irish, Italian, Japanese, Mexican, Jewish, Native, Polish, Indian, Vietnamese, and Korean.

*Our Human Family.* Blackbirch Press. Grades 5 and up.

This is a marvelous, four-book set centered on the themes of *Lessons for Life, Ties That Bind, Taking Time Out,* and *Worlds of Belief.* The series offers an in-depth and thought-provoking look at hundreds of ethnic groups as they share ceremonies, traditions, and customs. The incredible photos in each book capture the celebratory moods of the people.

*Peoples and Customs of the World.* Chelsea House. Grades 4 and up.

This is an attractive, four-book set illustrated by award-winning artist Robert Ingpen. Each book has more than 90 pages of intriguing drawings and information. Historical overviews interspersed throughout each book provide additional information. Titles include *Feasts and Festivals; Hunting, Harvesting, and Home; Living with the Gods;* and *Rites of Passage.*

*Peoples and Their Environments.* PowerKids Press. Grades K–4.

This interesting series looks at people of the world within their ecosystems. Bright pictures and reader-friendly text make this an attractive format for many students. Vocabulary associated with the setting is in bold print with a glossary at the end of the book. There are six books at present, with the potential for more titles. Featured in this set are children of the Arctic, River Valley, Desert, Rain Forest, Mountains, and Savanna.

### Picture a Country. Franklin Watts. Grades K–4.

This series offers an enthralling photo exhibit of countries and their citizens. The text is brief and meshes well with the attractive photographs. There are 12 books, and the publisher plans to produce more. Countries available at this time are Australia, China, the Czech Republic, Egypt, France, Germany, India, Italy, Jamaica, Japan, Russia, and Spain.

### Places of Worship. Gareth Stevens. Grades 2 and up.

There are six books in this series, with titles that cover six of the major religions of the world. The format includes many colorful photos of places of worship, icons, customs, dress, and founding principles from each religion. I was impressed with how the format wove children's religious roles into the text, highlighted with a variety of photographs. Titles included are *Sikh Gurdwara, Christian Church, Hindu Mandir, Buddhist Temple, Jewish Synagogue,* and *Muslim Mosque.*

### Plants We Eat. Lerner. Grades 3 and up.

There are several books in this series about food, and the publisher plans to add more. The book format takes readers on location to experience the planting, harvesting, and processing of plants. Interwoven in the text are health facts and tips, along with recipes. The authors include the history of plants whenever possible. Titles available are *Buried Treasure: Roots and Tubers; Cool as a Cucumber, Hot as a Pepper: Fruit Vegetables; Flavor Foods: Spices and Herbs; Glorious Grasses: The Grains; Green Power: Leaf & Flower Vegetables; Hard to Crack: Nut Trees; Spill the Beans and Pass the Peanuts: Legumes; Stinky and Stringy: Stem & Bulb Vegetables; Tall and Tasty: Fruit Trees;* and *Yes, We Have Bananas: Fruits from Shrubs and Vines.*

### Postcards From . . . . Steck-Vaughn. Grades 3–6.

The format for this series catches the eye. Each paperback book features one country with attractive, full-color, postcardlike photos accompanied by a brief, postcard-length description. There are 13 informative facts given for each country featured in this unique format, with an added index and glossary. At present, there are 20 books in this set, and the publisher plans to add to the series.

### Record Breakers. Gareth Stevens. Grades 4 and up.

Studying record breakers, such as the world's longest river or the planet's hottest desert, is an interesting concept, offering students the chance to learn about places all over the globe. There are four books in this set, including *Earth and Universe, The Living World, Machines and Inventions,* and *People and Places.* A nice feature of this series is the beautiful pictures and descriptions, which make it different from the list format found in the *Guinness Book of World Records.*

### Religions of the World. PowerKids Press. Grades K–4.

This series takes a look at religion through a child's perspective. Each of 14 books describes the beliefs and ceremonies of individual religions. The first set of six books is subtitled *In a Child's Voice;* the second set is subtitled *Through a Child's Eyes.* To date, there are books on the following religions: Bahá'í, Baptist, Mormon, Lutheran,

Quaker, Rastafarian, Jewish, Muslim, Roman Catholic, Eastern Orthodox, Protestant, Buddhist, Shinto, and Hindu.

### Rulers and Their Times. Benchmark Books. Grades 5 and up.

This unique new series focuses on world leaders from the past. Individual leaders act as a starting point for readers to study everyday life in a given period. The format includes first-person accounts from diaries, photos of period artwork, and poetry. At present, there are four books, and there is potential for more to follow. Titles available are *Alexander the Great and Ancient Greece, Augustus and Imperial Rome, Peter the Great and Tsarist Russia,* and *Hatshepsut and Ancient Egypt.*

### Season Festivals. Bookwright Press. Grades 3–6.

There are four books in this set. Features of the series include multicultural festivals, food, and people celebrating around the world.

### Small World. Carolrhoda Books. Pre K–2.

This series includes four titles: *Smiling, Eating, Carrying,* and *Celebrating.* Each theme reflects a universal activity. Text is simple and highly positive with wonderful photos to match. The theme of this series lends itself to an expansion of titles.

### A Ticket To . . . . Carolrhoda Books. Grades 3–5.

Each book in this series features one country. I was impressed with the wide coverage of topics, which would appeal to children. A combination of photos and illustrations enhances the text. The books offer three enticing ways to learn new vocabulary, along with suggestions for additional reading. This attractive series is the only one I discovered with a large-print format. There are more than 20 books in this series, and there are plans to add more. This is a nice companion series to Carolrhoda Books's *Globe-Trotters Club* series.

### Turning Points in History. Chelsea House. Grades 4 and up.

There are four books in this unique set. The focus in this fully illustrated and highly attractive series is on people throughout the world who have had an impact on history. I found this set to be a welcome addition, embracing the multicultural contributions of our world. A natural fit for science and social study lessons. Titles include *Generals Who Changed the World, People Who Changed the World, Scientists Who Changed the World,* and *Statesmen Who Changed the World.*

### Visual Geography. Lerner. Grades 3–8.

This remarkable series features the land, history, government, economy, maps, and people of each featured country. Attractive photos, both in full color and black and white, make this an attractive series. There are more than 100 books in the series, with room to add more.

### Voices from around the World: Voices from Distant Lands. Steck-Vaughn. Grades 4–8.

This older series features the people, highlights, historical development, natural resources, and geography from each country featured. This series is now out of print.

### We All Share. Blackbirch Press. Grades 2–5.

This four-book series focuses on universal themes: grandparents, food, family, and play. Each book covers 14 different countries, featuring cultural similarities and differences. The photographs are exquisite reflections of each theme, and the simple text is inviting and informative.

**Welcome to My Country.** Gareth Stevens. Grades 2 and up.

There are 12 books in this series, and Gareth Stevens plans to publish 64 titles. Readers will find colorful photographs of smiling people, plant and animal life, and art. There is plenty of information about education, lifestyle, history, and more in this exciting series. The overall format is a great introduction that may stimulate students to further explore a country. Included are suggestions for further information, including books, videos, and Web sites.

**What Do We Know About?** Benchmark Books. Grades 3 and up.

This is the largest series on world religions that I found. Included in this 16-volume set are facts about food, clothing, languages, and religious customs. The depth of coverage offers a useful introduction to the cultures behind the world's major religions.

**Williamson Kids Can!** Gareth Stevens. Grades 3 and up.

This six-book series promotes kids and their amazing ability to use their imaginations to do just about anything, given resources and opportunities. With this series, educators will have enough activities to integrate across your entire curriculum. The impressive text includes clear directions. Among the titles are *Hands around the World, Kids Create!, The Kid's Multicultural Art Book, The Kid's Nature Book, The Kid's Science Book,* and *The Kid's Wildlife Book.*

**Wonderworks of Nature.** Gareth Stevens. Grades 3 and up.

There are similar features in nature that can be found in several locations. In this beautiful seven-book set, readers can explore the following titles: *Cave: An Underground Wonderland, Icebergs: Titans of the Oceans, Storms: Nature's Fury, Volcanoes: Fire from Below, Coral Reefs: Hidden Colonies of the Sea, Deserts: An Arid Wilderness,* and *Rain Forests: Lush Tropical Paradise.*

**World Celebrations and Ceremonies.** Blackbirch Press. Grades 3–5.

This four-book set discusses universal themes, including birth, coming of age, harvest, and New Year celebrations from many countries. The format is much like other mini-series from Blackbirch Press, with colorful and enticing text that includes a glossary and index. It also includes tourism Web sites for each country. I was particularly intrigued by *Coming of Age* because of the ever-present struggle of adolescents to belong in the United States.

**The World Encyclopedia of Cartoons.** Chelsea House. Grades 6 and up.

This seven-book set will impress anyone who has enjoyed reading cartoons. The set has been updated with more than 1,100 entries and 1,000 illustrations, a glossary, and bibliography. Many research possibilities arise from cartoons, especially those on political issues. The books must be purchased as a complete set.

**The World Encyclopedia of Comics.** Chelsea House. Grades 6 and up.

This series is the ultimate volume set about the history of graphic comics from around the world. Each volume has 144 pages, plenty of detail, glossary, bibliography, and descriptions. This updated seven-volume series must be purchased as a complete set.

*World Explorers.* Chelsea House. Grades 4 and up.

This comprehensive 23-book set covers explorers throughout history, beginning with early adventures. The set covers land, waterways, undersea exploration, space, polar regions, and every expedition in between. Maps, paintings, drawings, and photographs fill each book. A comprehensive bibliography for further reading and chronology make this a nice set for social studies.

*The World in Focus.* Blackbirch Press. Grades 4–6.

This is a new series that includes books featuring the people and characteristics of each continent. The completed set of eight books includes teacher guides and activity books. Another unique addition is a literature-based guide for additional reading.

*World Leaders Past and Present.* Chelsea House. Grades 4 and up.

There are 44 hardcover and 10 paperback titles in this set. The biographical content focuses on each leader's life in the context of their political reign, featuring both female and male leaders. Each book is more than 100 pages in length and includes illustrations, photographs, maps, and an index.

*A World of Communities.* Blackbirch Press. Grades 3–5.

This series presents the history, geography, and economics of the countries in a format that integrates a number of social studies and language arts skills. Many bright, full-color photos of people of all ages bring world cultures to the reader. There are eight books in this series with no further titles planned.

*The World's Children.* Carolrhoda Books. Grades 2–6.

This set of 22 books featuring children of the world is attractive. Multiple enlarged photos with descriptions adorn each full-page spread. The focus is on children and all of the events they might encounter throughout the seasons. The format of this series will likely lead to additional titles in the future.

*World's Family.* Silver Burdett. Pre K–3.

There are five full-color books in this series. The text is simple, yet the universality of moms, dads, grandpas, grandmas, and babies will always have appeal to readers of all ages.

*Worldwide Crafts.* Gareth Stevens. Grades 3 and up.

This four-book set is filled with ideas. Clear directions, supported by photos and additional information, are bursting with possibilities for a multicultural celebration. Many ideas and spin-offs across the curriculum are possible. Titles include *Animal Crafts, Food Crafts, Costume Crafts,* and *Festival Crafts.*

*Young Artists of the World.* PowerKids Press. Grades K–4.

What a great concept! This series is a showcase of children's artwork from around the world. Their illustrations are juxtaposed with photographs of the countries. This set of six books combines imagination, creativity, art, social studies, literacy, and also provides possible connections to English as a second language classes. At present, the countries featured are Argentina, Finland, Gabon, Nepal, Taiwan, and Ukraine.

# Resources for Multicultural Literature: Publishers of Books and Materials

This section includes a list of publishers that I have found useful in my search for multicultural books. Having this information in one place can be very helpful when doing research. There may be some publishers I have overlooked or have yet to discover. I tried to include toll-free telephone numbers and Internet addresses whenever possible. Also note that most of the publishers listed in the nonfiction section also publish a line of picture or fiction books. In my search, I consistently encountered cordial and helpful staff members at each publisher. When educators have a question about any book or about ordering information, they should not hesitate to call publishers directly.

## Publishers Specializing in Multicultural Literature

Arte Público Press
University of Houston
4800 Calhoun
Houston, TX 77204-2090
1-800-633-ARTE

Asia for Kids
Master Communications, Inc.
4480 Lake Forest Drive, Suite 302
Cincinnati, OH 45242-3726
1-800-888-9681
www.asiaforkids.com

Children's Book Press
246 First Street, Suite 101
San Francisco, CA 94105
1-800-788-3123
cbookpress@cbookpress.org

Cinco Puntos Press
2709 Louisville
El Paso, TX 79930
1-915-566-9072
www.cincopuntos.com

Del Sol Books
29257 Bassett Rd.
Westlake, OH 44145
1-888-335-7651

Elm Group Early Learning Materials
6322 Sovereign Drive, Suite 110
San Antonio, TX 78229
1-800-367-5166

Lectorium Publications, Inc.
111 Eighth Avenue, Suite 804
New York, NY 10011
1-800-288-9756

Lee & Low Books
95 Madison Avenue
New York, NY 10016
1-800-320-3395
www.leeandlow.com

Multicultural Books & Videos, Inc.
28880 Southfield Road, Suite 183
Lathrup Village, MI 48076
1-800-567-2220

Santillana Publishing, Inc.
1-800-245-8584
www.santillana.com

The Shoe String Press, Inc.
P.O. Box 657
2 Linsley Street
North Haven, CT 06473-2517
1-203-239-2702

# Additional Publishers That Produce
# Some Multicultural Titles

Abbeville Press, Inc.
22 Cortlandt Street
New York, NY 10007
1-212-577-5555
www.abbeville.com

Albert Whitman & Company
6340 Oakton Street
Morton Grove, IL 60053-2723
1-800-255-7675

Atheneum Books
1230 Avenue of the Americas
New York, NY 10020
1-212-698-7200

August House
P.O. Box 3223
Little Rock, AR 72203
1-800-284-8784
www.augusthouse.com

Avon Books, Inc.
1350 Avenue of the Americas
New York, NY 10019
1-800-223-0690

Bantam Doubleday Dell
1540 Broadway
New York, NY 10036
1-800-323-9872
www.bdd.com/teachers/

Barefoot Books
37 West 17th Street
4th Floor East
New York, NY 10010
1-212-604-0505
www.barefoot-books.com

Beyond Words Publishing, Inc.
20827 NW Cornell Road, Suite 500
Hillsboro, OR 97124-9808
1-503-531-8700
www.beyondwords.com

Boyds Mills Press
815 Church Street
Honesdale, PA 18431
1-877-512-8366
www.boydsmillspress.com

Candlewick Press
2067 Massachusetts Avenue
Cambridge, MA 02140
1-617-661-3330
bigbear@candlewick.com

Charlesbridge Publishing
85 Main Street
Watertown, MA 02472-4411
1-800-225-3214
www.charlesbridge.com

Chronicle Books
85 Second Street, 6th Floor
San Francisco, CA 94105
1-800-722-6657
www.chroniclebooks.com/kids

Clarion Books
215 Park Avenue South
New York, NY 10003
1-212-420-5883

Conari Press
2550 Ninth Street, Suite 101
Berkeley, CA 94710
1-800-685-9595
www.conari.com

Dawn Publications
14618 Tyler Foote Road
Nevada City, CA 95959
1-800-545-7475
www.dawnpub.com

EDC Publishing
Usborne Books
10302 East 55th Place
Tulsa, OK 74146
1-800-475-4522
www.edcpub.com

Farrar, Straus & Giroux
19 Union Square West
New York, NY 10003
1-800-631-8571

Firefly Books
P.O. Box 1338
Ellicott Station
Buffalo, New York 14205
1-800-221-1274
www.fireflybooks.com

Front Street/Cricket Books
Carus Publishing
332 South Michigan Avenue
Suite 1100
Chicago, IL 60604
1-800-967-2085
www.cricketbooks.net

Graphic Arts Center Publishing
Company
P.O. Box 10306
Portland, OR 97296-0306
1-800-452-3032
www.gacpc.com

Grolier Publishing Company
90 Sherman Turnpike
Danbury, CT 06813
1-800-243-7256
http://publishing.grolier.com

Groundwood Books
720 Bathurst Street, Suite 500
Toronto, Ontario,
M5S 2R4 Canada
1-800-667-6902 (within Canada)
1-800-788-3123 (USA)
susanm@groundwood-dm.com

Harcourt Brace
525 B Street
San Diego, CA 92101
1-800-831-7799
www.harcourtbrace.com

HarperCollins
10 East 53rd Street
New York, NY 10022-5299
1-800-242-7737
www.harpercollins.com/kids/

Harry N. Abrams, Inc.
100 Fifth Avenue
New York, NY 10011
www.abramsbooks.com

Henry Holt & Company
115 West 18th Street
New York, NY 10011
1-212-886-9398
www.henryholt.com

Holiday House
425 Madison Avenue
New York, NY 10017
1-212-688-0085

Houghton Mifflin Company
222 Berkeley Street
Boston, MA 02116-3764
1-800-733-1717
Www.hmco.com/hmcom/trade
/childrens/index.html

Hyperion Books
114 Fifth Avenue
New York, NY 10011-5690
1-212-633-4400
1-800-759-0190
www.disneybooks.com

Kane/Miller Book Publishers
P.O. Box 8515
La Jolla, CA 92038-8515

Kids Can Press
4500 Witmar Estates
Niagara Falls, NY 14305-1386
1-800-265-0884
info@kidscan.com

Kingfisher
95 Madison Avenue
New York, NY 10016
1-800-497-1657

Knopf Publishing Group
201 East 50th Street
New York, NY 10022
1-800-726-0600

Little, Brown and Company
200 West Street
Waltham, MA 02254
1-800-343-9204
www.littlebrown.com

Marshall Cavendish Corporation
P.O. Box 2001
99 White Plains Road
Tarrytown, NY 10591
1-800-821-9881
www.marshallcavendish.com

McClelland & Stewart
c/o Tundra Books
P.O. Box 1030
Plattsburg, NY 12901
1-800-788-1074

Millbrook Press
2 Old New Milford Road
Brookfield, CT 06804-0335
1-800-462-4703
www.neca.com/mall/millbrook

Mondo Publishing
One Plaza Road
Greenvale, NY 11548
1-888-88-MONDO

North-South Books
1123 Broadway, Suite 800
New York, NY 10010
1-800-282-8257
www.northsouth.com

Orca Book Publishers
P.O. Box 468
Custer, WA 98240-0468
1-800-210-5277
www.orcabook.com

Orchard Books
95 Madison Avenue
New York, NY 10016
1-212-951-2600

Oxford University Press
198 Madison Avenue
New York, NY 10016
1-212-726-6002
1-800-451-9714
www.oup-usa.org/childrens

Oyate Publishers
2702 Mathews Street
Berkeley, CA 94702
1-415-848-6700
www.oyate.com

Peachtree Publishers
494 Armour Circle, NE
Atlanta, GA
1-404-876-8761

Penguin/Putnam Group
345 Hudson Street
New York, NY 10014-3657
1-212-366-2374
www.penguinputnam.com

Portunus
27875 Berwick Drive, Suite A
Carmel, CA 93923
1-888-450-5021
www.portunus.net

Random House, Inc.
1540 Broadway
New York, NY 10036
1-800-726-0600
www.randomhouse.com

Rising Moon/Northland Publishing
P.O. Box 1389
Flagstaff, AZ 86002-1389
1-800-346-3257
www.northlandpub.com

Scholastic, Inc.
555 Broadway
New York, NY 10012-3999
1-800-SCHOLASTIC
www.scholastic.com

Shoe String Press, Inc.
P.O. Box 657
2 Linsley Street
North Haven, CT 06473-2517
1-203-239-2702
SSPBooks@aol.com

Sierra Club Books for Children
85 Second Street
San Francisco, CA 94105
1-800-935-1056
www.sierraclub.org/books

Simon & Schuster
1230 Avenue of the Americas
New York, NY 10020
1-800-223-2348
www.SimonSaysKids.com

Stoddart Kids
85 River Rock Drive, Suite 202
Buffalo, NY 14207-2170
1-800-805-1083
gdsinc@genpub.com
info@kidscan.com

Ten Speed Press/Tricycle Press
P.O. Box 7123
Berkeley, CA 94707
1-800-841-2665
www.tenspeed.com

Theytus Books Ltd.
Green Mountain Road, Lot 45
R.R. #2, Site 50, Comp. 8
Penticton, BC
V2A 6J7 Canada
1-250-493-5302
theytusbooks@vip.net

Tilbury House Publishers
2 Mechanic Street, #3
Gardiner, ME 04345
1-800-582-1899
www.tilburyhouse.com

Time Warner Trade Publishers
3 Center Plaza
Boston, MA 02108-2003
1-800-759-0190

Tundra Books
481 University Avenue, Suite 802
Toronto, Ontario
M5G 2E9 Canada
1-416-598-4786
1-800-363-2665
www.tundrabooks.com

Walker and Company
435 Hudson Street
New York, NY 10014
1-800-289-2553
orders@walkerbooks.com

W. H. Freeman and Company
41 Madison Avenue
New York, NY 10010
1-800-877-5351
www.whfreeman.com

Whispering Coyote Press, Inc.
300 Crescent Court, Suite 860
Dallas, TX 75201
1-800-929-6104

William B. Eerdmans Publishing Co.
255 Jefferson Avenue, SE
Grand Rapids, MI 49503
1-800-253-7521
wbesales@eerdmans.com

William Morrow & Company
1350 Avenue of the Americas
New York, NY 10019
1-800-223-0690
www.williammorrow.com

Winslow Press
115 East 23rd Street
10th Floor
New York, NY 10010
1-212-254-2025
www.winslowpress.com

Workman Publishing
708 Broadway
New York, NY 10003-9555
1-800-722-7202
www.workmanweb.com

# Publishers Specializing in Nonfiction

Benchmark Books
Marshall Cavendish Corporation
P.O. Box 2001
99 White Plains Road
Tarrytown, NY 10591
1-800-821-9881
www.marshallcavendish.com

Blackbirch Press, Inc.
P.O. Box 3573
260 Amity Road
Woodbridge, CT 06525
1-800-831-9183
www.blackbirch.com

Chelsea House Publishers
1974 Sproul Road, Suite 400
Broomall, PA 19008
1-800-848-BOOK
www.chelseahouse.com

Crabtree Publishing
Dept. 2SCR9F, PMB 16A
350 Fifth Avenue, Suite 3308
New York, NY 10118
1-800-387-7650

Dorling Kindersley (DK) Publishing
95 Madison Avenue
New York, NY 10016
1-888-DIAL DKP
www.dk.com

Gareth Stevens Publishers
155 North River Center Drive
Suite 201
Milwaukee, WI 53212-3952
1-800-542-2595
info@gsinc.com

Grolier Publishing Company
Franklin Watts/Children's Press
90 Sherman Turnpike
Danbury, CT 06813
1-800-621-1115
http://publishing.grolier.com

Lerner/Carolrhoda Publications Company
241 First Avenue North
Minneapolis, MN 55401
1-800-328-4929
www.lernerbooks.com

Newbridge Educational Publishing
P.O. Box 1270
Littleton, MA 01460
1-800-867-0307
www.newbridgeonline.com

PowerKids Press
Rosen Publishing Group
29 East 21st Street
New York, NY 10010
1-800-237-9932

Raintree/Steck-Vaughn
P.O. Box 26015
Austin, TX 78755
1-800-877-5351
www.steck-vaughn.com

Shortland Publications, Inc.
50 South Steele Street, Suite 755
Denver, CO 80209
1-800-775-9597
www.shortland.com

Silver Burdett Press
299 Jefferson Road
Parsippany, NJ 07054
1-973-739-8354

Sundance Publishers
P.O. Box 1326
Littleton, MA 01460
1-508-486-9201

W. H. Freeman and Company
41 Madison Avenue
New York, NY 10010
1-212-561-8221
www.whfreeman.com

# Additional Support Materials for Libraries and Classrooms

American Library Association
50 East Huron
Chicago, IL 60611
1-800-545-2433
www.ala.org

Asia for Kids
Master Communications, Inc.
4480 Lake Forest Drive, Suite 302
Cincinnati, OH 45242-3726
1-513-563-3100
www.AsiaforKids.com

The Booksource
1230 Macklind Avenue
St. Louis, MO 63110
1-800-444-0435
www.booksource.com

Children's Book Council
568 Broadway, Suite 404
New York, NY 10012
1-800-999-2160
www.cbcbooks.org

Christopher-Gordon Publishers, Inc.
1502 Providence Highway, Suite 12
Norwood, MA 02062
1-800-934-8322

Colorful World
5765-F Burke Centre Parkway
Burke, VA 22015
1-800-934-FUNN

Cooperative Children's Book Center
4290 Helen C. White Hall
600 North Park Street
Madison, WI 53706-1403
www.soemadison.wisc.edu/ccbc/

Econo-Clad Books
P.O. Box 1777
2101 North Topeka Boulevard
Topeka, KS 66608
1-913-233-4252

Fabulous Records
P.O. Box 8980
Minneapolis, MN 55408
fabrecords@aol.com

Fulcrum Publishing
16100 Table Mountain Parkway
Suite 300
Golden, CO 80403
1-800-992-2908
www.fulcrum-resources.com

GPN Reading Rainbow
P.O. Box 80669
Lincoln, NE 68501-0669
1-800-306-2330

Gryphon House
P.O. Box 207
Beltsville, MD 20704-0207
1-800-992-2908
www.ghbooks.com

Highsmith Press
P.O. Box 800
Fort Atkinson, WI 53538-0800
1-800-558-2110
www.highsmith.com

Hunter House Inc., Publishers
P.O. Box 2914
Alameda, CA 94501-0914
1-510-865-5282

Libraries Unlimited
P.O. Box 6633
Englewood, CO 80155-6633
1-800-237-6124
www.lu.com

Linworth Publishing, Inc.
480 East Wilson Bridge Road, Suite L
Worthington, OH 43085-2372
1-800-786-5017
www.linworth.com

Nana's Book Warehouse, Inc.
El Almacén de Libros de Nana
848 Herber Avenue
Calexico, CA 92231
1-800-737-NANA
www.nanasbooks.com

Oryx Press
P.O. Box 33889
Phoenix, AZ  85067-3889
1-800-279-6799
www.oryxpress.com

Pacific Educational Press
6365 Biological Sciences Road
Faculty of Education
University of British Columbia
Vancouver, BC V6T 1Z4
1-604-822-5385
cedwards@interchange.ubc.ca

Perma Bound Books
Vandalia Road
Jacksonville, IL 62650
1-800-637-6581

R. R. Bowker
121 Chanlon Road
New Providence, NJ 07974
1-888-269-5372
www.booksinprint.com

Rethinking Schools
1001 East Keefe Avenue
Milwaukee, WI 53212
1-414-964-9646
www.rethinkingschools.org

Scarecrow Press
4720 Boston Way
Lanham, MD 20706
1-800-462-6420
www.scarecrowpress.com

Social Studies School Service
P.O. Box 802
10200 Jefferson Boulevard, Room R6
Culver City, CA 90232-0802
1-800-421-4246
www.socialstudies.com

# Resources for Promoting Children's and Young Adult Literature

I have added this section to offer further reading about the many applications of literature—including multicultural literature—in schools and libraries. Reading these professional references, together with youth books, has influenced the way I think about reading and literature. I have referenced some of my writing, which has helped solidify my thinking about the importance of literature. By no means is this list meant to be exhaustive, but rather a place to go for more reading.

Ada, A. F. 1990. *A Magical Encounter: Spanish-Language Children's Literature in the Classroom*. Compton, CA: Santillana Publishing.

Ada, A. F., V. J. Harris, V. J. Hopkins, and L. B. Hopkins. 1993. *A Chorus of Cultures: Developing Literacy through Multicultural Poetry*. Carmel, CA: Hampton-Brown.

Allen, A. A. 1993. "Diversity Education." In *Facts and Fiction: Literature across the Curriculum,* pp. 14–30. Edited by B. E. Cullinan. Newark, DE: International Reading Association.

Ammon, B. D., and G. W. Sherman. 1996. *Worth a Thousand Words: An Annotated Guide to Picture Books for Older Readers*. Englewood, CO: Libraries Unlimited.

Atwell, N. 1998. *In the Middle: New Understandings about Reading, Writing, and Learning*. 2nd ed. Portsmouth, NH: Boynton/Cook.

Au, K. 1993. *Literacy Instruction in Multicultural Settings*. Fort Worth, TX: Harcourt Brace Jovanovich.

Bair, L., M. Holley, S. F. Steiner, and R. Stewart. 1997. "Librarian or Media Specialist." *Portals* 4, no. 2: 20–23.

Barrera, R. B., V. D. Thompson, and M. Dressman, eds. 1997. *Kaleidoscope: A Multicultural Booklist for Grades K–8*. 2nd ed. Urbana: National Council of Teachers of English.

Bieger, E. M. 1996. "Promoting Multicultural Education through a Literature-Based Approach." *The Reading Teacher* 49, no. 4:308–12.

Bishop, R. S., ed. 1994. *Kaleidoscope: A Multicultural Booklist for Grades K–8*. Urbana: National Council of Teachers of English.

Bowker, R. R. 1998. *From Biography to History: Best Books for Children's Entertainment and Education.* New Providence, NJ: R. R. Bowker.

————. 1999. *Reading in Series: A Selection Guide to Books for Children.* New Providence, NJ: R. R. Bowker.

Burke, E. M. 1990. *Literature for the Young Child.* 2nd ed. Boston: Allyn & Bacon.

Burke, J. 1999. *I Hear America Reading: Why We Read What We Read.* Westport, CT: Heinemann.

Buss, K., and L. Karnowski. 2000. *Reading and Writing Literary Genres.* Newark, DE: International Reading Association.

Corliss, J. C. 1998. *Crossing Borders with Literature of Diversity.* Norwood, MA: Christopher-Gordon Publishers.

Cramer, E. H., and M. Castle, eds. 1994. *Fostering the Love of Reading: The Affective Domain in Reading Education.* Newark, DE: International Reading Association.

Cullinan, B. E. 2000. *Read to Me: Raising Kids Who Love to Read.* New York: Scholastic.

Cullinan, B. E., ed. 1987. *Children's Literature in the Reading Program.* Newark, DE: International Reading Association.

————, ed. 1992. *Invitation to Read: More Children's Literature in the Reading Program.* Newark, DE: International Reading Association.

Cullinan, B. E., and L. Galda. 1994. *Literature and the Child.* 3rd ed. Fort Worth, TX: Harcourt, Brace College Publishers.

Daniels, H. 1994. *Literature Circles: Voice and Choice in the Student Centered Classroom.* York, ME: Stenhouse Publishers.

Davidson, J., and D. Koppenhaver. 1993. *Adolescent Literacy: What Works and Why.* 2nd ed. New York: Garland Publishing.

Day, F. A. 1994. *Multicultural Voices in Contemporary Literature.* Portsmouth, NH: Heinemann.

Donovan, D. P. 1992. *The Best of the Best for Children.* Chicago: American Library Association.

Finazzo, D. A. 1997. *All for the Children: Multicultural Essentials of Literature.* Albany, NY: Delmar Publishers.

Fox, M. 1993. *Radical Reflections.* San Diego, CA: Harcourt Brace.

Freeman, E., and B. Lehman. 2001. *Global Perspectives in Children's Literature.* Boston: Allyn & Bacon.

Gillespie, J. T. 1998. *Best Books for Children: Preschool through Grade 6.* 6th ed. New Providence, NJ: R. R. Bowker.

———. 2000. *Best Books for Young Teen Readers: Grades 7–10.* New Providence, NJ: R. R. Bowker.

Glazer, J. I. 2000. *Literature for Young Children.* 4th ed. Upper Saddle River, NJ: Merrill.

Gunning, T. G. 1998. *Best Books for Beginning Readers.* Boston: Allyn & Bacon.

———. 2000. *Best Books for Building Literacy for Elementary School Children.* Boston: Allyn & Bacon.

Hancock, M. R. 2000. *A Celebration of Literature and Response: Children, Books and Teachers in K–8 Classrooms.* Upper Saddle River, NJ: Merrill.

Hansen, J. 1987. *When Writers Read.* Portsmouth, NH: Heinemann.

Harris, V. J., ed. 1992. *Teaching Multicultural Literature in Grades K–8.* Norwood, MA: Christopher Gordon Publishers.

———. 1997. *Using Multicultural Literature in the K–8 Classroom.* Norwood, MA: Christopher Gordon Publishers.

Hart-Hewins, L., and J. Wells. 1999. *Better Books! Better Readers! How to Choose, Use and Level Books for Children in Primary Grades.* York, ME: Stenhouse Publishers.

Hayes, C. W., R. Bahruth, and C. Kessler. 1998. *Literacy Con Carino: A Story of Migrant Children's Success.* 2nd ed. Portsmouth, NH: Heinemann.

Hearne, B., with D. Stevenson. 1999. *Choosing Books for Children: A Commonsense Guide.* 3rd ed. Urbana: University of Illinois Press.

Hillman, J. 1995. *Discovering Children's Literature.* Englewood Cliffs, NJ: Merrill.

Hopkins, L. B. 1998. *Please Pass the Poetry.* 3rd ed. New York: Harper-Collins.

Huck, C. S., S. Hepler, and J. Hickman. 2001. *Children's Literature in the Elementary School.* 7th ed. Madison, WI: Brown & Benchmark.

Hurst, C.O. 1999. *Open Books: Literature in the Curriculum, Kindergarten through Grade 2.* Worthington, OH: Linworth Publishing.

Hynds, S.1997. *On the Brink: Negotiating Literature and Life with Adolescents.* New York: Teachers College Press; Newark, DE: International Reading Association.

International Reading Association. 1992. *Teen's Favorite Books.* Newark, DE: International Reading Association.

———. 1993. *Teacher's Favorite Books for Kids.* Newark, DE: International Reading Association.

Jensen, J. M., and N. L. Roser, eds. 1993. *Adventuring with Books: A Booklist for Pre-K–Grade 6.* 10th ed. Urbana: National Council of Teachers of English.

Jobe, R., and M. Dayton-Sakari. 1999. *Reluctant Readers: Connecting Students and Books for Successful Reading Experiences.* Markham, Ontario: Pembroke Publishers.

Kaywell, J. F., ed. 2000. *Adolescent Literature as a Complement to the Classics.* Norwood, MA: Christopher Gordon Publishers.

Kiefer, B. Z. 1995. *The Potential of Picture Books: From Visual Literacy to Aesthetic Understanding.* Columbus, OH: Prentice-Hall.

Killingsworth-Roberts, S. 1998. "Using Literature Study Groups to Construct Meaning in an Undergraduate Reading Course." *Journal of Teacher Education* 49, no. 5:366–71.

Kobrin, B. 1988. *Eyeopeners! How to Choose and Use Children's Books about Real People, Places, and Things.* New York: Penguin.

Lamme, L. L. 1985. *Growing Up Reading.* Washington, DC: Acropolis Books.

Langer, J. A. 1995. *Envisioning Literature: Literary Understanding and Literature Instruction.* New York: Teachers College Press; Newark, DE: International Reading Association.

Larrick, N. 1965. "The All-White World of Children's Books." *Saturday Review*, September 11, 63–65.

Lehr, S., ed. 1995. *Battling Dragons: Issues and Controversy in Children's Literature.* Portsmouth, NH: Heinemann.

Lima, C. W., and J. A. Lima. 1998. *A to Zoo: Subject Access to Children's Picture Books.* 5th ed. New Providence, NJ: R. R. Bowker.

Littlejohn, C. 1999. *Talk That Book! Booktalks to Promote Reading.* Worthington, OH: Linworth Publishing.

———. 2000. *Keep Talking That Book! Booktalks to Promote Reading, Volume 2.* Worthington, OH: Linworth Publishing.

Lukens, R. J., and R. K. Cline. 1995. *A Critical Handbook of Literature for Young Adults.* New York: HarperCollins.

Lynch-Brown, C., and C. M. Tomlinson. 1999. *Essentials of Children's Literature.* 3rd ed. Boston: Allyn & Bacon.

Madigan, D. 1993. "The Politics of Multicultural Literature for Children and Adolescents: Combining Perspectives and Conversations." *Language Arts* 70, no. 3:168–76.

Marant, S., and K. Marantz. 1997. *Multicultural Picture Books: Art for Understanding Others, Vol. II.* Worthington: OH: Linworth Publishing.

May, J. P. 1995. *Children's Literature and Critical Theory.* New York: Oxford University Press.

McElmeel, S. L. 1997. *Literature Frameworks: From Apples to Zoos.* Worthington, OH: Linworth Publishers.

McGovern, E. M., and H. D. Muller. 1994. *They're Never Too Young for Books.* Buffalo, NY: Prometheus Books.

Mikkelsen, N. 2000. *Words and Pictures: Lessons in Children's Literature and Literacies.* Boston: McGraw-Hill.

Monroe, S. S. 1996. "Multicultural Children's Literature: Canon of the Future." *Language Arts Journal of Michigan* 12, no. 1:84–89.

Nodelman, P. 1995. *The Pleasures of Children's Literature.* 2nd ed. White Plains, NY: Longman.

Noe, K. S., and N. J. Johnson. 1999. *Getting Started with Literature Circles.* Norwood, MA: Christopher Gordon Publishers.

Norton, D. E. 1995. *Through the Eyes of a Child.* 4th ed. Columbus, OH: Prentice-Hall.

———. 2001. *Multicultural Children's Literature: Through the Eyes of Many Children.* Upper Saddle River, NJ: Merrill/Prentice-Hall.

Paterson, K. 1999. "Noteworthy Authors: Connecting Past and Present to Ourselves." *Signal Journal* 23, no. 2:11–15.

Pennac, D. 1999. *Better Than Life.* York, ME: Stenhouse Publishers.

Pierce, K. M. 2000. *Adventuring with Books: A Booklist for Pre-K–Grade 6.* 12th ed. Urbana: National Council of Teachers of English.

Post, A. D., M. Scott, and M. Theberge. 2000. *Celebrating Children's Choices: 25 Years of Children's Favorite Books.* Newark, DE: International Reading Association.

Pratt, L., and J. J. Beaty. 1999. *Transcultural Children's Literature.* Upper Saddle River, NJ: Prentice-Hall.

Ramirez, G., and J. L. Ramirez. 1994. *Multiethnic Children's Literature.* Albany, NY: Delmar Publishers.

Reed, A. J. S. 1988. *Comics to Classics: A Parents Guide to Books for Teens and Preteens.* Newark, DE: International Reading Association.

Reimer, K. M. 1992. "Multiethnic Literature: Holding Fast to Dreams." *Language Arts* 69:14–21.

Rochman, H. 1993. *Against Borders: Promoting Books for a Multicultural World.* Chicago: American Library Association.

Rosenblatt, L. 1991. "The Reading Transaction: What For?" In *Literacy in Process.* Edited by B. Power and R. Hubbard. Portsmouth, NH: Heinemann.

Rudman, M. K. 1989. *Children's Literature Resource for the Classroom.* Norwood, MA: Christopher Gordon Publishers.

———. 1995. *Children's Literature: An Issues Approach.* 3rd ed. Toronto: Longman.

Saltman, J. 1985. *The Riverside Anthology of Children's Literature.* 6th ed. Boston: Houghton Mifflin.

Savage, J. F. 2000. *For the Love of Literature: Children and Books in the Elementary Years.* Boston: McGraw-Hill.

Schwartz, E. G. 1995. "Crossing Borders/Shifting Paradigms: Multiculturalism and Children's Literature." *Harvard Educational Review* 65, no. 4:634–50.

Short, K. G., and K. M. Pierce, eds. 1990. *Talking about Books: Creating Literature Communities.* Portsmouth, NH: Heinemann.

Simmons, J. S., ed. 1994. *Censorship: A Threat to Reading, Learning, Thinking.* Newark, DE: International Reading Association.

Steiner, S. 1995. "Coming Home: The Power of Discourse about Literature." *The Reading Teacher* 48, no. 7:612–13.

————. 1998. "Who Belongs Here? Portraying American Identity in Children's Picture Books." *Multicultural Review* 7, no. 2:20–27.

Steiner, S., and L. Cobiskey. 1997. "Books That Bring People Together." *Book Links* 7, no. 3:27–31.

————. 1998. "Refugees and Homeless: Nomads of the World." *Book Links* 8, no. 3:55–62.

Steiner, S., and J. Steiner. 1999. "Navigating the Road to Literacy." *Book Links* 8, no. 4:19–24.

Stewig, J. W. 1988. *Children and Literature.* 2nd ed. Boston: Houghton Mifflin.

————. 1995. *Looking at Picture Books.* Fort Atkinson, WI: Highsmith Press.

Stoodt, B. D., L. B. Amspaugh, and J. Hunt. 1996. *Children's Literature: Discovery for a Lifetime.* Scottsdale, AZ: Gorsuch Scarisbrick Publishers.

Stubbs, E., and A. Sutton. 1996. *Only Connect: Readings on Children's Literature.* 3rd ed. New York: Oxford University Press.

Sutherland, Z. 1997. *Children and Books.* 9th ed. New York: Longman.

Sutherland, Z., and M. H. Arbuthnot. 1986. *Children and Books.* 7th ed. Glenview, IL: Scott, Foresman.

Sutherland, Z., and M. C. Livingston. 1991. *The Scott, Foresman Anthology of Children's Literature.* New York: HarperCollins.

Temple, C., M. Martinez, J. Yokota, and A. Naylor. 1998. *Children's Books in Children's Hands: An Introduction to Their Literature.* Boston: Allyn & Bacon.

Tiedt, I. M. 2000. *Teaching with Picture Books in the Middle School.* Newark, DE: International Reading Association.

Tomlinson, C. M., ed. 1998. *Children's Books from Other Countries.* Lanham, MD: Scarecrow Press.

Trelease, J. 1995. *The Read-Aloud Handbook.* 4th ed. New York: Penguin Books.

Tunnel, M. O., and J. S. Jacobs. 2000. *Children's Literature, Briefly.* 2nd ed. Upper Saddle River, NJ: Prentice-Hall.

Wadham, T., and R. L. Wadham. 1999. *Bringing Fantasy Alive for Children and Young Adults.* Worthington, OH: Linworth Publishing.

Watson, D. 1996. *Making a Difference: Selected Writings of Dorothy Watson.* Portsmouth, NH: Heinemann.

Webb, C. A., ed. 1993. *Your Reading: A Booklist for Junior High and High School.* 9th ed. Urbana: National Council of Teachers of English.

Wells, G. 1986. *The Meaning Makers: Children Learning Language and Using Language to Learn.* Portsmouth, NH: Heinemann.

Wilhelm, J. D. 1997. *You Gotta Be the Book: Teaching Engaged and Reflective Reading with Adolescents.* Urbana: National Council of Teachers of English; New York: Teachers College Press.

Williams, N. S. 2000. *Children's Literature Selections and Strategies for Students with Reading Difficulties: A Resource for Teachers.* Norwood, MA: Christopher Gordon Publishers.

Yokota, J. 1993. "Issues in Selecting Multicultural Children's Literature." *Language Arts* 70, no. 3:156–67.

# Resources for Infusing Literature into Content Areas

I have added this section because educators today seek literature applications across the curriculum more than ever before. Literature across the curriculum is taking hold around the nation. Teachers recognize that using trade books in conjunction with a textbook can add power to a lesson, and this has increased the demand for nonfiction and literature in the publishing marketplace.

Children's literature is the third largest publishing market, preceded by adult novels and paperbacks (including children's paperbacks). The integration of literature into curricula will continue to grow. The downside of the book explosion is that finding a good starting point can be difficult. A good approach is to start with one subject and proceed from there. Students will lead their teachers to the next level.

Many teachers have already applied this literature to their curricula, and they can provide excellent suggestions. Finding new sources will always be a challenge, but collaborative efforts can make a difference. I offer the following resources, which I have used as both a classroom teacher and workshop leader. This is not an exhaustive list, but a resource for further reading. I have included items on which I have collaborated that discuss literature applications I have used in the content areas.

Ammon, B. D., and G. W. Sherman. 1996. *Worth a Thousand Words: An Annotated Guide to Picture Books for Older Readers.* Englewood, CO: Libraries Unlimited.

Bamford, R. A., and J. V. Kristo. 1998. *Making Facts Come Alive: Choosing Quality Nonfiction Literature K–8.* Norwood, MA: Christopher Gordon Publishers.

———. 2000. *Checking Out Nonfiction K–8: Good Choices for Best Learning.* Norwood, MA: Christopher Gordon Publishers.

Barchers, Suzanne I., and Patricia C. Marden. 1999. *Cooking Up U.S. History: Recipes and Research to Share with Children.* 2nd ed. Englewood, CO: Libraries Unlimited.

Butzow, Carol M., and John W. Butzow. 1998. *More Science through Children's Literature: An Integrated Approach.* Englewood, CO: Libraries Unlimited.

———. 1999. *Exploring the Environment through Children's Literature: An Integrated Approach.* Englewood, CO: Libraries Unlimited.

————. 2000. *Science through Children's Literature: An Integrated Approach.* 2nd ed. Englewood, CO: Libraries Unlimited.

Cornett, C. E. 1999. *The Arts as Meaning Makers: Integrating Literature and the Arts throughout the Curriculum.* Upper Saddle River, NJ: Merrill.

Cullinan, B. E., ed. 1993. *Fact and Fiction: Literature across the Curriculum.* Newark, DE: International Reading Association.

Cullinan, B. E., M. C. Scala, and V. C. Shroder. 1995. *Three Voices: An Invitation to Poetry across the Curriculum.* York, ME: Stenhouse Publishers.

Donovan, D. P. 1992. *The Best of the Best for Children.* Chicago: American Library Association.

Fredericks, A. 1998. *The Integrated Curriculum: Books for Reluctant Readers, Grades 2–5.* Englewood, CO: Libraries Unlimited.

————. 2000. *More Social Studies through Children's Literature: An Integrated Approach.* Englewood, CO: Libraries Unlimited.

Freeman, E. B., and D. G. Person. 1992. *Using Nonfiction Trade Books in the Elementary Classroom: From Ants to Zeppelins.* Urbana: National Council of Teachers of English.

————. 1998. *Connecting Informational Children's Books with Content Area Learning.* Boston: Allyn & Bacon.

Hansen, J. 1987. *When Writers Read.* Portsmouth, NH: Heinemann.

Harvey, S. 1998. *Nonfiction Matters: Reading, Writing, and Research in Grades 3–8.* York, ME: Stenhouse Publishers.

Hurst, C. O., and R. Otis. 1999. *Using Literature in the Middle School Curriculum.* Worthington, OH: Linworth Publishing.

Hurst, C. O., L. O. Palmer, V. Churchill, M. S. Ahearn, and B. G. McMahon. 1999. *Curriculum Connections: Picture Books in Grade 3 and Up.* Worthington, OH: Linworth Publishing.

International Reading Association. 1992. *Teen's Favorite Books.* Newark, DE: International Reading Association.

————. 1993. *Teacher's Favorite Books for Kids.* Newark, DE: International Reading Association.

Jensen, J. M., and N. L. Roser, eds. 1993. *Adventuring with Books: A Booklist for Pre-K–Grade 6.* 10th ed. Urbana: National Council of Teachers of English.

Johnson, N. M., and M. J. Ebert. 1992. "Time Travel Is Possible: Historical Fiction and Biography—Passport to the Past." *The Reading Teacher* 45:488–95.

Kiefer, B. Z. 1995. *The Potential of Picture Books: From Visual Literacy to Aesthetic Understanding.* Columbus, OH: Prentice-Hall.

Kite, T., T. Smucker, S. Steiner, and M. Bayne. 1994. "Using Program Music for Interdisciplinary Study." *Music Educators Journal* 80, no. 5:33–36, 53.

Kobrin, B. 1988. *Eyeopeners! How to Choose and Use Children's Books about Real People, Places, and Things.* New York: Penguin Books.

Miller, K. W., S. F. Steiner, and C. D. Larson. 1996. "Strategies for Science Learning." *Science and Children* 33, no. 6:24–27, 61.

Miller, W. J. 1997. *U.S. History through Children's Literature: From the Colonial Period to World War II.* Englewood, CO: Libraries Unlimited.

———. 1998. *Teaching U.S. History through Children's Literature: Post-World War II.* Englewood, CO: Libraries Unlimited.

Odean, K. 1997. *Great Books for Girls.* New York: Ballantine Books.

———. 1998. *Great Books for Boys.* New York: Ballantine Books.

Phelan, C. 1996. *Science Books for Young People.* Chicago: American Library Association.

Richardson, J. K. 2000. *Read It Aloud! Using Literature in the Secondary Content Classroom.* Newark, DE: International Reading Association.

Roberts, P. L. 1998. *Literature-Based History Activities for Children Grades 1–3.* Needham Heights, MA: Allyn & Bacon.

Rogers, L. K. 1997. *Geographic Literacy through Children's Literature.* Englewood, CO: Libraries Unlimited.

Rudman, M. K. 1989. *Children's Literature Resource for the Classroom.* Norwood, MA: Christopher Gordon Publishers.

———. 1995. *Children's Literature: An Issues Approach.* 3rd ed. Toronto: Longman.

Steiner, S. 1993. "Preparing Prospective Elementary Teachers to Teach Geographical Features with an Integrated Approach." *Journal of Geography* 92, no. 5:231–33.

———. 1996. "Ordinary People on an Extraordinary Adventure: Reliving the Oregon Trail." *Social Studies and the Young Learner* 8, no. 3:7–10, 14, 17.

Steiner, S., and R. Stewart. 1999. "Crossing Boundaries, Crossing Tradition: Rethinking Our Role as Teachers of Literature." *Signal Journal* 23, no. 2:7–10.

Steiner, S., and P. Ware. 1993. "Literature That Stirs the Dust and Stirs the Soul." *Portals* 1, no. 1:12–17.

Stephens, C. G. 2000. *Coretta Scott King Award Books: Using Great Literature with Children and Adults.* Englewood, CO: Libraries Unlimited.

Sutton, W. K., ed. 1997. *Adventuring with Books: A Booklist for Pre-K–Grade 6.* 11th ed. Urbana: National Council of Teachers of English.

Thiessen, D., and M. Matthias, eds. 1992. *The Wonderful World of Mathematics: A Critically Annotated List of Children's Books in Mathematics.* Reston, VA: National Council of Teachers of Mathematics.

Tomlinson, C. M., ed. 1998. *Children's Books from Other Countries.* Lanham, MD: Scarecrow Press.

Tunnell, M. O., and R. Ammon. 1993. *The Story of Ourselves: Teaching History through Children's Literature.* Portsmouth, NH: Heinemann.

Webb, C. A., ed. 1993. *Your Reading: A Booklist for Junior High and High School.* 9th ed. Urbana: National Council of Teachers of English.

# Author Index

# Literature Index

# About the Author and Illustrator

Professor **Stan Steiner** has been dubbed "The Bookman" by his students because of his vast knowledge of children's literature. He has written or coauthored a number of articles connecting literature and content areas for such journals as *Book Links* and *MultiCultural Review.* Prior to his present position teaching children's and young adult literature at Boise State University, he taught elementary school for fifteen years. Stan and his storytelling wife Joy present across America, combining their love of literature and story.

**Peggy Hokom**, illustrator and freelance artist, resides in Caldwell, Idaho. Peggy has completed her Masters in Reading from Boise State University. She teaches first grade in a multicultural elementary school as well as "Written and Illustrated by Kids" classes for children in the Caldwell School District. Her favorite media are pen and ink and Prismacolor, as used in the illustrations for this book.